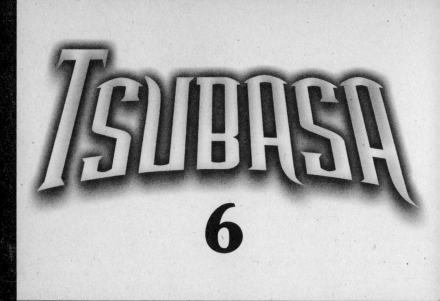

6

CLAMP

TRANSLATED AND ADAPTED BY
William Flanagan

LETTERED BY
Dana Hayward

BALLANTINE BOOKS · NEW YORK

Tsubasa, Volume 6 is a work of fiction. Names, characters, places, and incidents are the products of the author's imagination or are used fictitiously. Any resemblance to actual events, locales, or persons, living or dead, is entirely coincidental.

A Del Rey Books Trade Paperback Original

Copyright © 2005 CLAMP. All rights reserved.

Published in the United States by Del Rey Books, an imprint of The Random House Publishing Group, a division of Random House, Inc., New York.

Del Rey is a registered trademark and the Del Rey colophon is a trademark of Random House, Inc.

First published in serialization and subsequently published in book form by Kodansha Ltd. Tokyo in 2004.

ISBN 0-345-47793-6

Printed in the United States of America

www.delreymanga.com

9 8 7 6 5 4

Lettered by Dana Hayward

Contents

Honorifics Explained   iv

Chapitre 36   1

Chapitre 37   43

Chapitre 38   63

Chapitre 39   83

Chapitre 40   103

Chapitre 41   123

Chapitre 42   165

About the Creators   188

Translation Notes   189

Preview of *Tsubasa* Volume 7   194

Honorifics Explained

Throughout the Del Rey Manga books, you will find Japanese honorifics left intact in the translations. For those not familiar with how the Japanese use honorifics and, more important, how they differ from American honorifics, we present this brief overview.

Politeness has always been a critical facet of Japanese culture. Ever since the feudal era, when Japan was a highly stratified society, use of honorifics — which can be defined as polite speech that indicates relationship or status — has played an essential role in the Japanese language. When addressing someone in Japanese, an honorific usually takes the form of a suffix attached to one's name (example: "Asuna-san"), or as a title at the end of one's name or in place of the name itself (example: "Negi-sensei," or simply "Sensei!").

Honorifics can be expressions of respect or endearment. In the context of manga and anime, honorifics give insight into the nature of the relationship between characters. Many translations into English leave out these important honorifics, and therefore distort the "feel" of the original Japanese. Because Japanese honorifics contain nuances that English honorifics lack, it is our policy at Del Rey not to translate them. Here, instead, is a guide to some of the honorifics you may encounter in Del Rey Manga.

-san: This is the most common honorific, and is equivalent to Mr., Miss, Ms., Mrs., etc. It is the all-purpose honorific and can be used in any situation where politeness is required.

-sama: This is one level higher than "-san." It is used to confer great respect.

-dono: This comes from the word "tono," which means "lord." It is an even higher level than "-sama" and confers utmost respect.

-kun: This suffix is used at the end of boys' names to express familiarity or endearment. It is also sometimes used by men among friends, or when addressing someone younger or of a lower station.

-chan: This is used to express endearment, mostly toward girls. It is also used for little boys, pets, and even among lovers. It gives a sense of childish cuteness.

Bozu: This is an informal way to refer to a boy, similar to the English term "kid" or "squirt."

Sempai/Senpai: This title suggests that the addressee is one's senior in a group or organization. It is most often used in a school setting, where underclassmen refer to their upperclassmen as "sempai." It can also be used in the workplace, such as when a newer employee addresses an employee who has seniority in the company.

Kohai: This is the opposite of "sempai," and is used toward underclassmen in school or newcomers in the workplace. It connotes that the addressee is of lower station.

Sensei: Literally meaning "one who has come before," this title is used for teachers, doctors, or masters of any profession or art.

-[blank]: Usually forgotten in these lists, but perhaps the most significant difference between Japanese and English. The lack of honorific means that the speaker has permission to address the person in a very intimate way. Usually, only family, spouses, or very close friends have this kind of permission. Known as *yobisute*, it can be gratifying when someone who has earned the intimacy starts to call one by one's name without an honorific. But when that intimacy hasn't been earned, it can also be very insulting.

Tsubasa crosses over with *xxxHOLiC*. Although it isn't necessary to read *xxxHOLiC* to understand the events in *Tsubasa*, you'll get to see the same events from different perspectives if you read both!

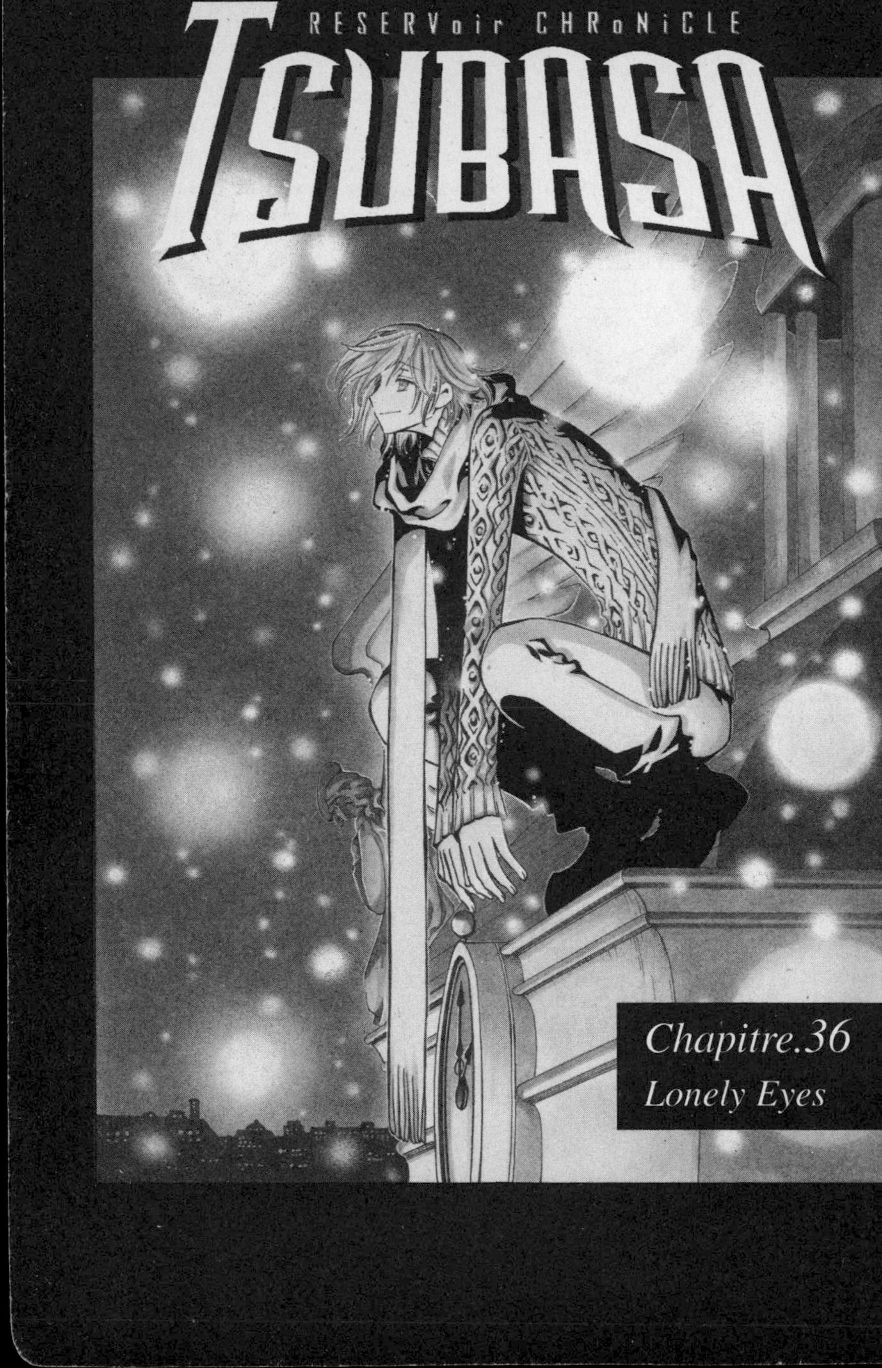
RESERVoir CHRoNiCLE
TSUBASA
Chapitre.36
Lonely Eyes

ツバサ

RESERVoir CHRoNiCLE

WHERE ARE MOKONA, SYAORAN-KUN, AND KUROGANE-SAN?

THEY WENT TO CITY HALL.

THERE WAS ANOTHER ONI ATTACK LAST NIGHT.

THEY WENT TO GET THE BOUNTY FOR TAKING THE THINGS OUT OF ACTION.

LAST NIGHT?!

DOES THAT WORRY YOU?

HMMM...

SYAORAN-KUN... JUST A LITTLE, THOUGH.

SOME-BODY GOT WOUNDED AGAIN... ?

YOU CAN SLEEP VERY SOUNDLY, SAKURA-CHAN.

YEP.

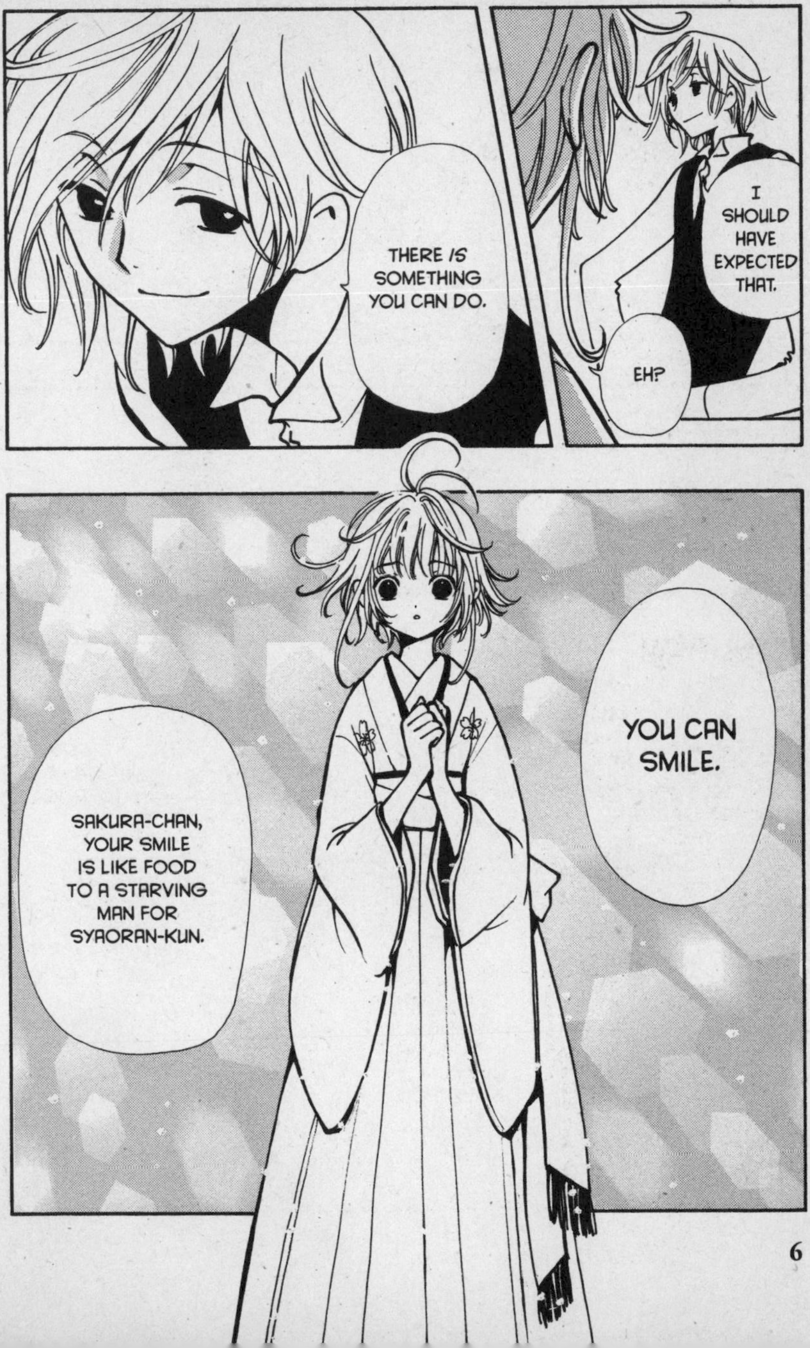
I SHOULD HAVE EXPECTED THAT.
EH?
THERE IS SOMETHING YOU CAN DO.
YOU CAN SMILE.
SAKURA-CHAN, YOUR SMILE IS LIKE FOOD TO A STARVING MAN FOR SYAORAN-KUN.

7

THE "BIG PUPPY" ON THE OTHER HAND...

EVEN THOUGH SYAORAN-KUN AND MOKONA WERE HAPPY WITH WHAT I COOKED...

BUT...

Country of Ōto
CENTRAL CITY HALL

AHH-CHOO!!

MOKONA THINKS SO TOO!!

BUT IT WAS DELICIOUS!
A NICE BREAKFAST!

SOME-BODY'S TALKING ABOUT YOU!!

PHWEE! ♥ PHWEE! ♥

PROBABLY THAT MAGICIAN! HE CAN NEVER SHUT UP!

TSK!

KUROGANE-SAN, HAVE YOU CAUGHT COLD?

ZNIFF

YOU'RE HERE BECAUSE OF YOUR WORK LAST NIGHT, RIGHT?

AFTER FORCING ME TO EAT THAT AWFUL, SWEET JUNK!
IN THE MORNING!!

NO!

8

KYUUUUUN

BEEP BEEP BEEP

KACHIK

YOU ONLY HID!

MOKONA HELPED OUT TOO!

AND YOU'D LIKE THE BOUNTY?

YES.

NOW THAT YOU TWO ARE OFFICIALLY ENTERED AS ONI HUNTERS, ANY REWARD MONEY WILL AUTOMATICALLY BE ADDED TO THE AMOUNT RECORDED ON THIS PIECE.

THIS IS WHAT THE COUNTRY OF ÔTO USES FOR A WALLET.

YOU MUST BE VERY CAREFUL NOT TO LOSE IT.

THE BOUNTY FOR DEFEATING THE ONI LAST NIGHT IS NOW ENTERED INTO THIS.

KYAA!

BUT IF YOU HAVE ANY QUESTIONS, YOU CAN ALWAYS COME TO ONE OF OUR "EXPRESS ASSESSMENT" BOOTHS LIKE THIS ONE TO GET SOME ANSWERS.

ALL RIGHT, THEN...

I UNDER-STAND.

KUROGANE IS JEALOUS BECAUSE EVERYBODY JUST LOVES MOKONA!!

THERE IS NO NEED FOR YOU TO COME TO CITY HALL EVERY TIME YOU ELIMINATE ONI.

10

SHE SAID THAT'S ANOTHER THING THAT'S JUST THE WAY IT IS.

THE LADY AT THE BOOTH.

GRR

SHOULDN'T THEY HAVE GIVEN IT TO US THE *FIRST* TIME WE WENT TO THAT CITY HALL?

WE GOT SHORT-CHANGED!

YEAH, ABOUT THAT!

HERE IT IS.

12

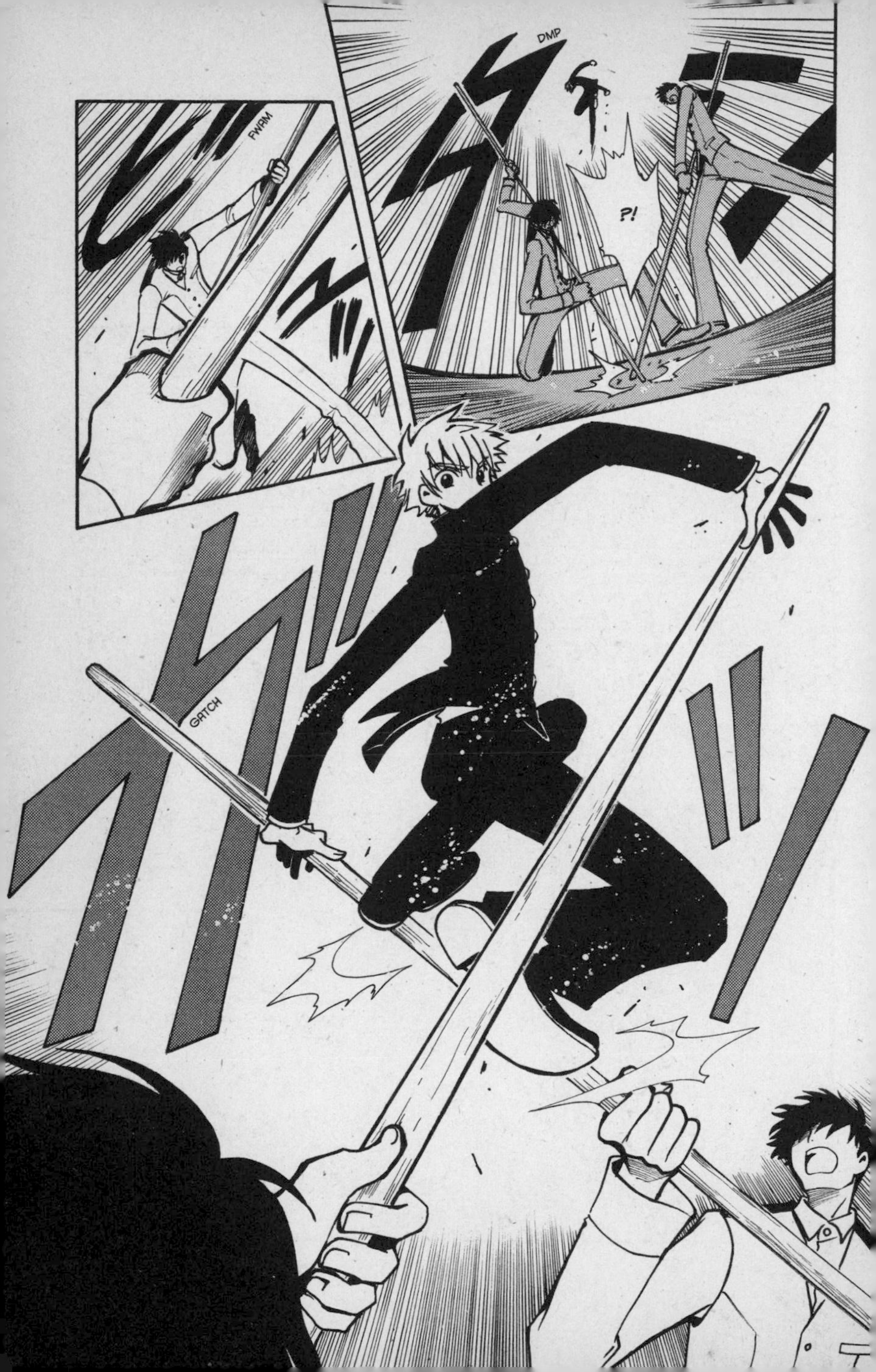
DMP
?!
FWAM
GRTCH

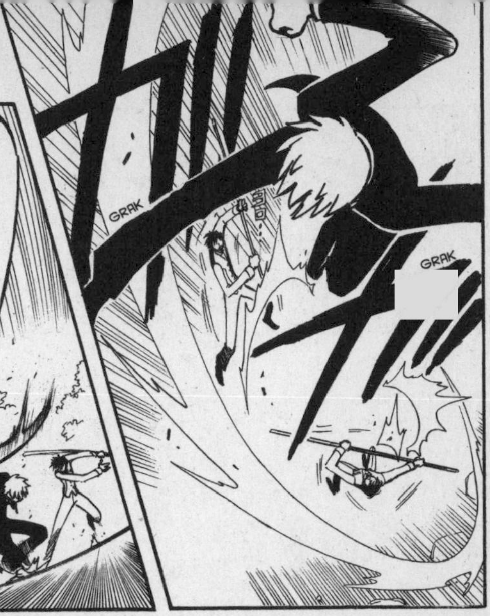
GRAK
GRAK
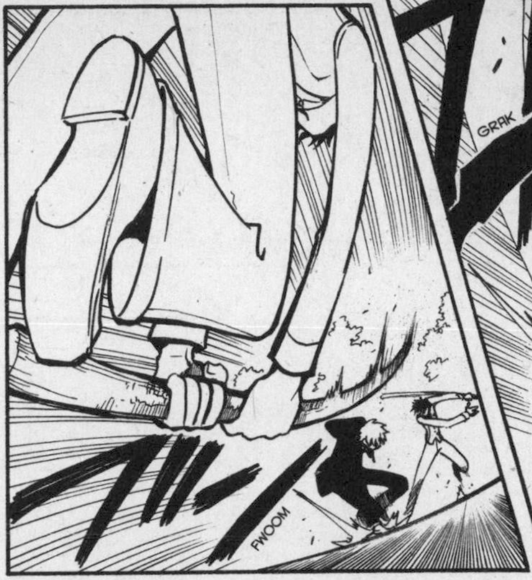
FWOOM
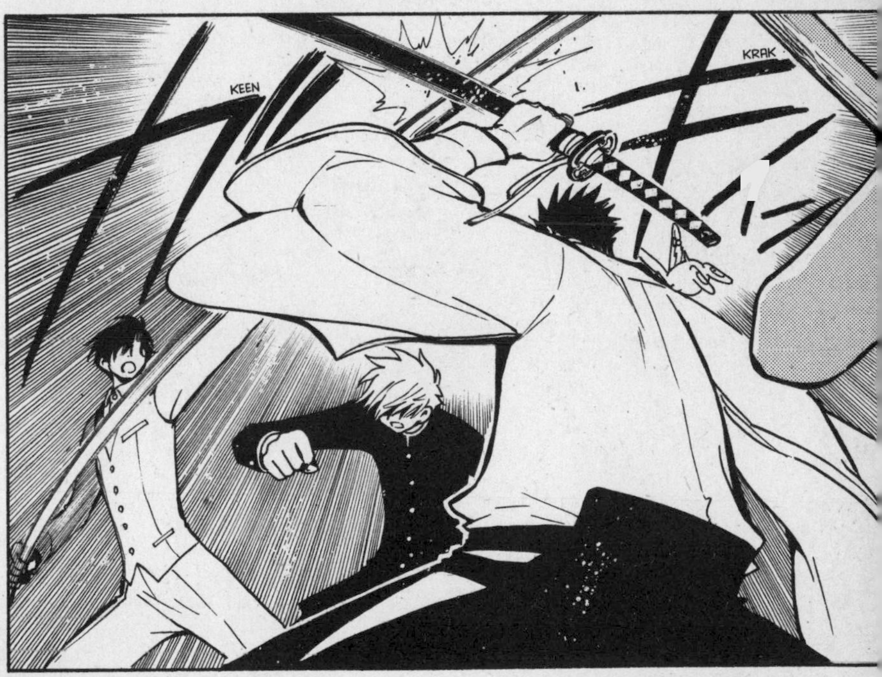
KRAK
KEEN

...AND AFTERWARD THEY BAGGED NINETEEN HA-2 ONI, SO I IMAGINE THEY HAVE SOME TALENT.

WELL... THEY *DID* HUNT DOWN ONE HA-5...

.....

HOW DID YOU KNOW THAT?

きゅう @WISH

AMAZING!

SMILE

YOU SAID YOU HAD QUESTIONS?

MY BUSINESS IS INFORMATION.

POP

SHUT UP, IDIOT!

IF YOU *KNEW*, THEN DON'T HIT US!!

HAVE THERE BEEN ANY ODD OCCURRENCES OR ACCIDENTS RECENTLY?

OR IT MAY BE A STRANGE LEGEND...

BUT LET'S SEE...

ODD OCCURRENCES AND ACCIDENTS HAPPEN ALL THE TIME...

DO YOU HAVE A MAP?

WOULD YOU LIKE TO TALK TO SOMEONE WHO *HAS* SEEN IT?

SHFFL

AT THIS SPOT.

THEY OPEN EVERY NIGHT AT SIX.

ZLOOP

YES.

DO YOU HAVE ANY OTHER QUESTIONS?

THANK YOU VERY MUCH.

THE REST WILL HAPPEN AUTO-MATICALLY.

TELL THE BARTENDER THAT ERII THE INFORMANT WANTS YOU ALL TO BE INTRODUCED.

1000 EN, PLEASE!

AND SINCE THIS IS YOUR FIRST TIME, I'LL GIVE YOU A DISCOUNT!

OF COURSE IF YOU COME UP WITH ANY NEW QUESTIONS, YOU CAN ALWAYS ASK ME.

NO, NOT FOR NOW...

...BUT...

20

WE'RE INFORMANTS!

MOKONA IS MOKO-PI!

I'M KEN-PO!

HE'S TAKE-PO!

YOU TAKE *MONEY* FOR THIS?

RECENTLY THE COUNTRY HAS BEEN A LITTLE ON EDGE.

OH! I REMEMBERED ONE MORE THING!

1000 EN TRANSFERRED!

PE-PEEP

YOU SHOULD RETURN TO CITY HALL OFTEN!

ぎゅ ぎゅ

RIGHT.

KNEAD IT THAT WAY.

GYUN GYUN

22

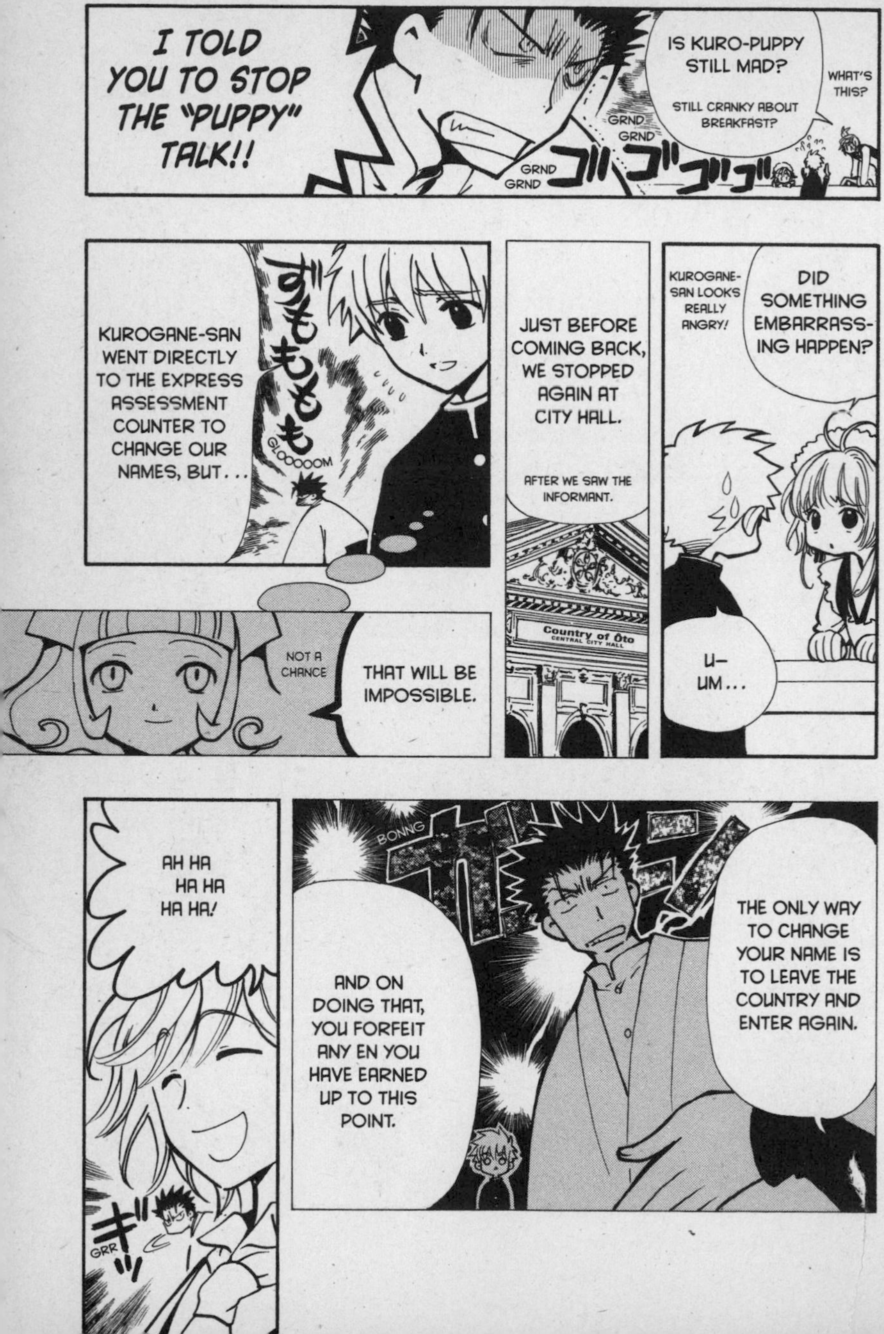
WHAT'S THIS?
IS KURO-PUPPY STILL MAD?
STILL CRANKY ABOUT BREAKFAST?
GRND GRND
ゴゴゴゴ
GRND GRND
I TOLD YOU TO STOP THE "PUPPY" TALK!!
KUROGANE-SAN LOOKS REALLY ANGRY!
DID SOMETHING EMBARRASS-ING HAPPEN?
U-UM...
JUST BEFORE COMING BACK, WE STOPPED AGAIN AT CITY HALL.
AFTER WE SAW THE INFORMANT.
Country of Ôto
CENTRAL CITY HALL
KUROGANE-SAN WENT DIRECTLY TO THE EXPRESS ASSESSMENT COUNTER TO CHANGE OUR NAMES, BUT...
ずもももも
GLOOOOOM
THAT WILL BE IMPOSSIBLE.
NOT A CHANCE
BONNG
THE ONLY WAY TO CHANGE YOUR NAME IS TO LEAVE THE COUNTRY AND ENTER AGAIN.
AND ON DOING THAT, YOU FORFEIT ANY EN YOU HAVE EARNED UP TO THIS POINT.
AH HA HA HA HA HA!
GRR

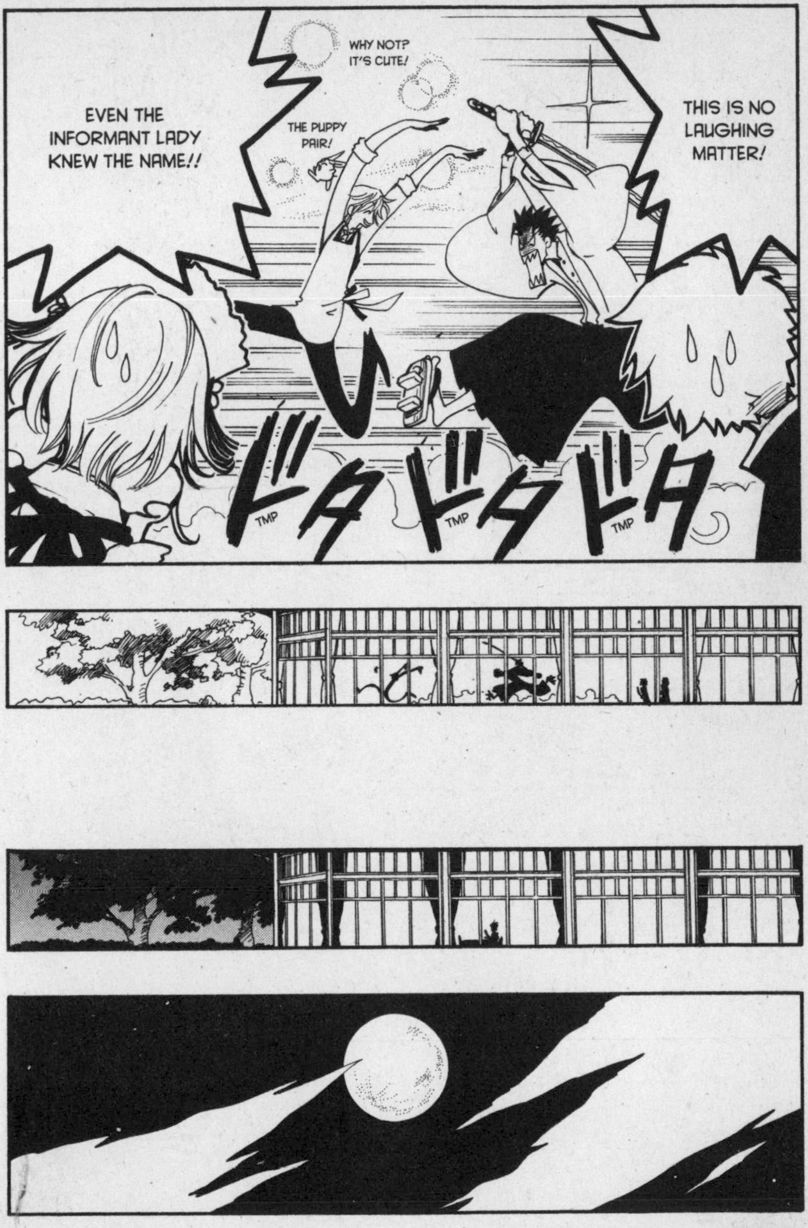
THIS IS NO LAUGHING MATTER!
WHY NOT? IT'S CUTE!
THE PUPPY PAIR!
EVEN THE INFORMANT LADY KNEW THE NAME!!
ドタドタドタ
TMP
TMP
TMP

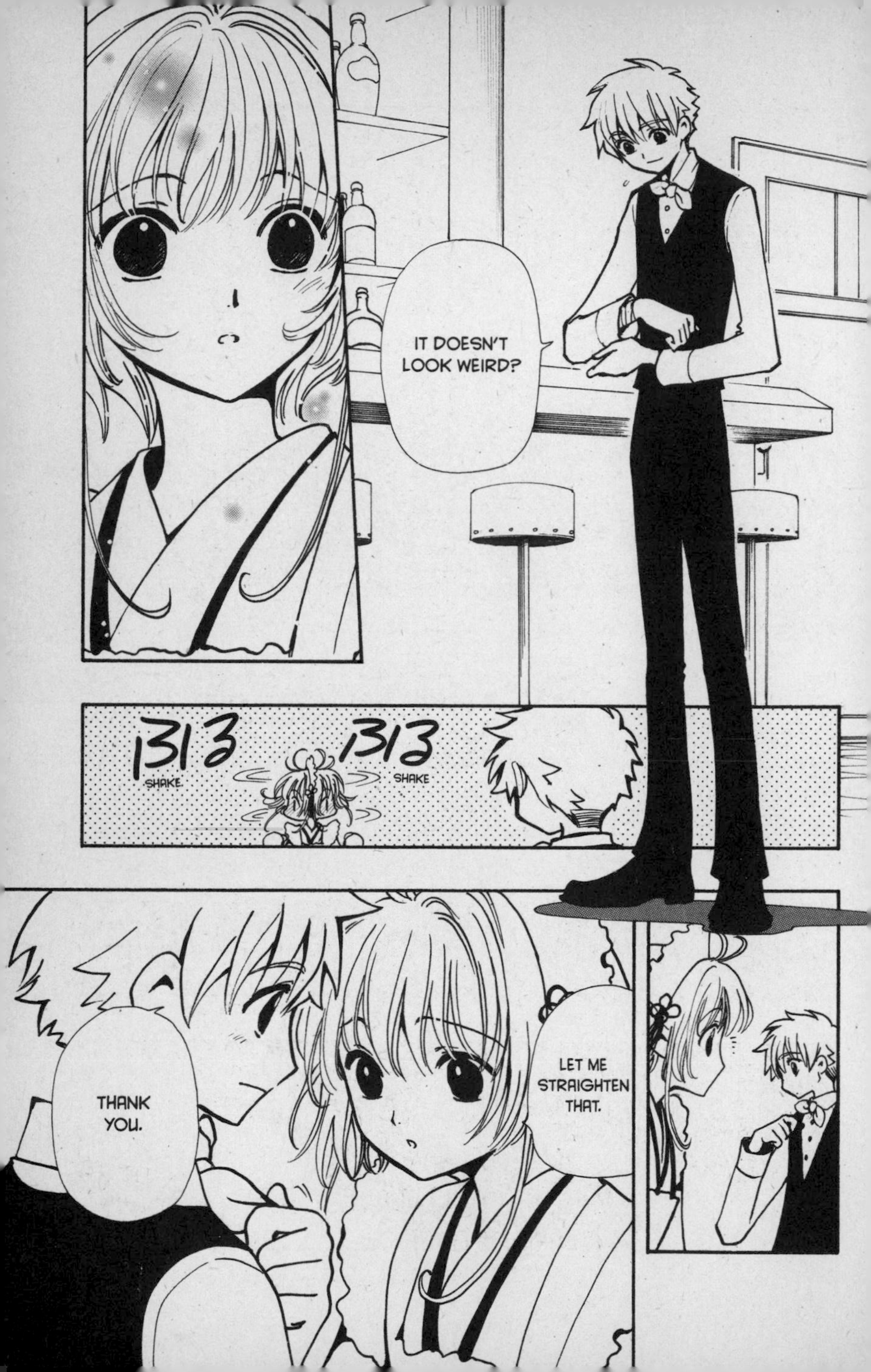
IT DOESN'T LOOK WEIRD?
SHAKE
SHAKE.
LET ME STRAIGHTEN THAT.
THANK YOU.

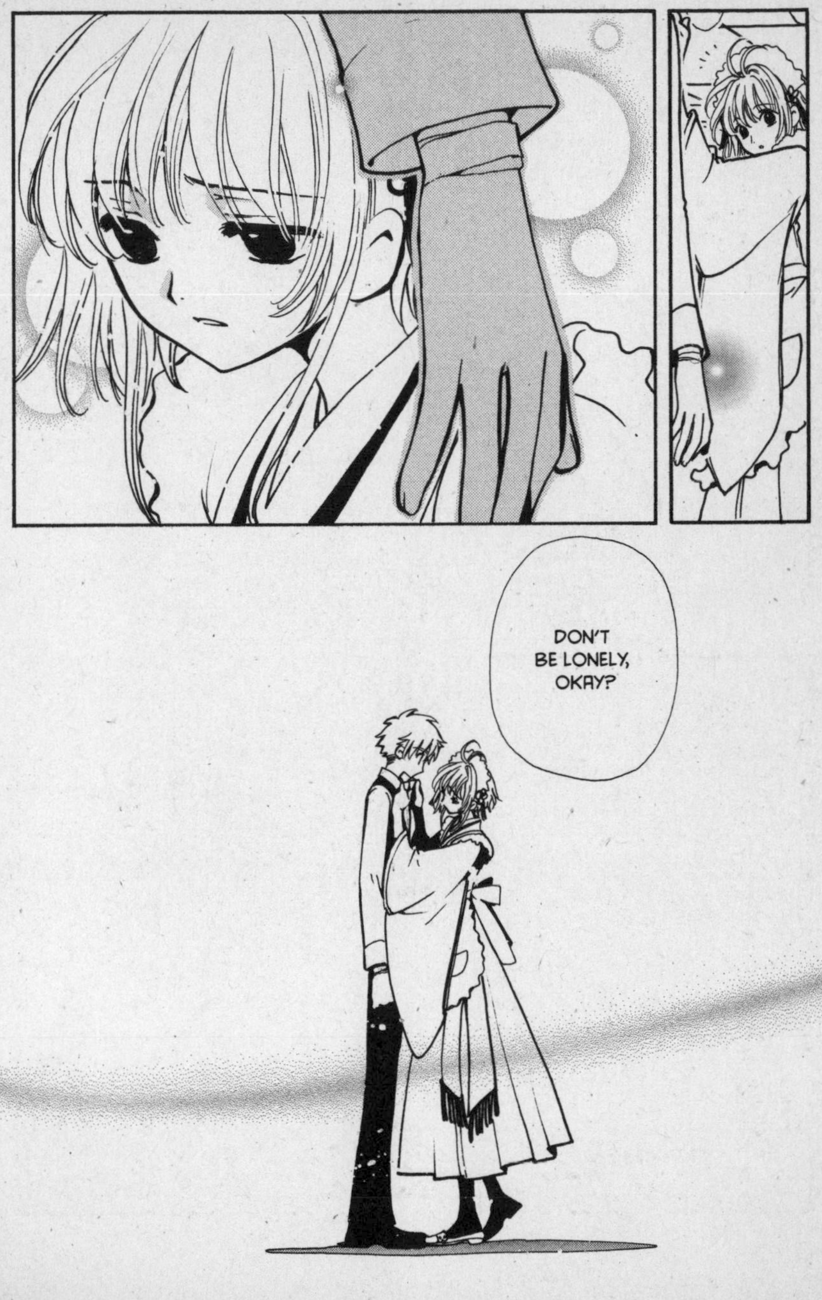
DON'T BE LONELY, OKAY?

EH?!

NOTHING! NOTHING!

LET'S DO OUR BEST WITH THE CAFÉ WHILE FAI-SAN IS GONE!

I GAVE THEM THE MAP

I WONDER IF FAI-SAN, KUROGANE-SAN, AND MOKONA ARE ALREADY AT THE BAR.

AH!

YES, MA'AM!

AND KUROGANE-SAN SAID THAT HE COULD READ A LITTLE OF THIS COUNTRY'S LANGUAGE.

AND IT LOOKS LIKE I CAN'T ENTER PLACES SERVING ALCOHOL IN THIS COUNTRY.

EXCUSE US...

JING

OH! THIS IS THE PLACE!

DOOM

STARE

THANK YOU VERY MUCH!

WELCOME TO OUR CAFÉ!

28

29

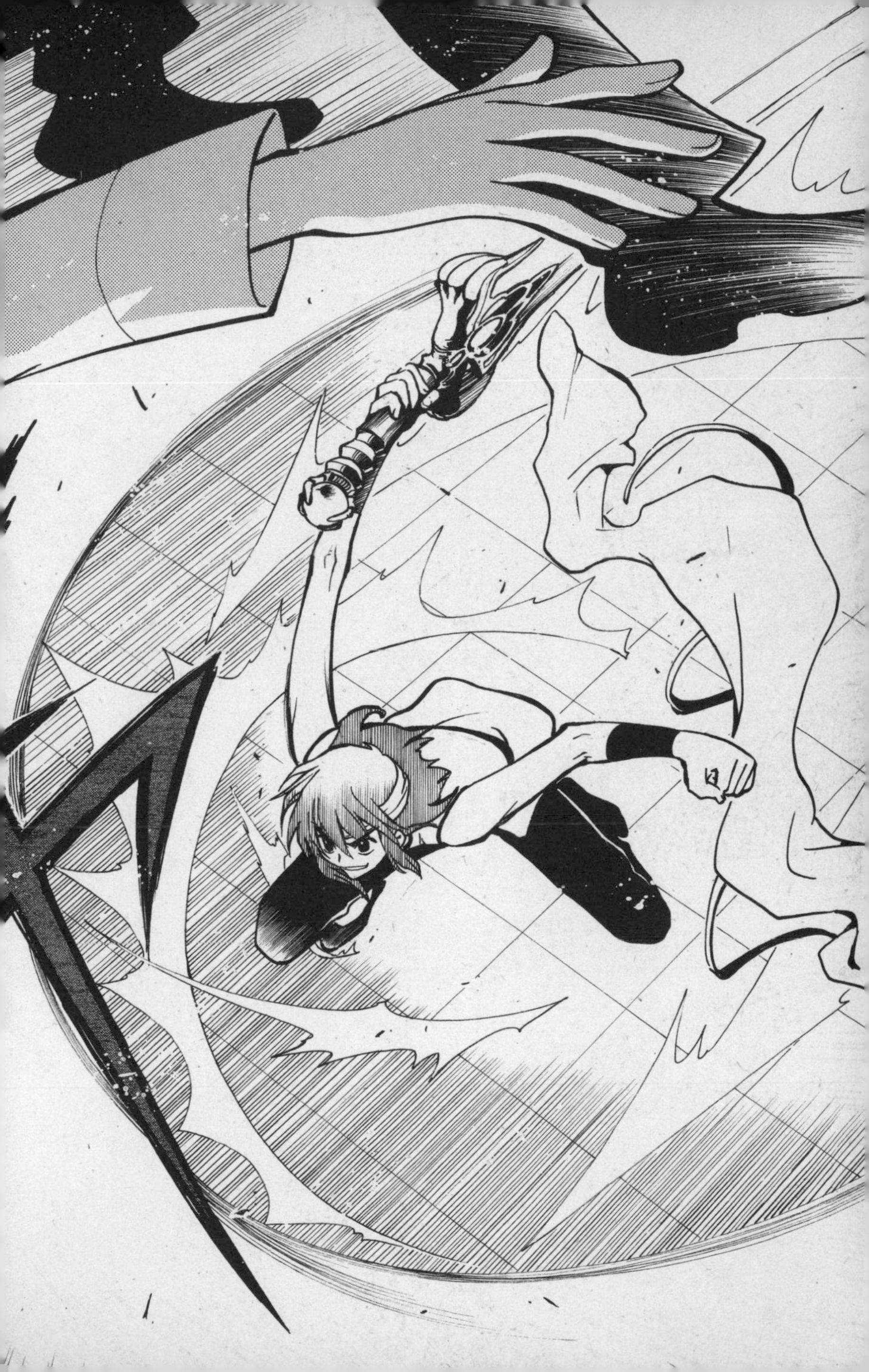

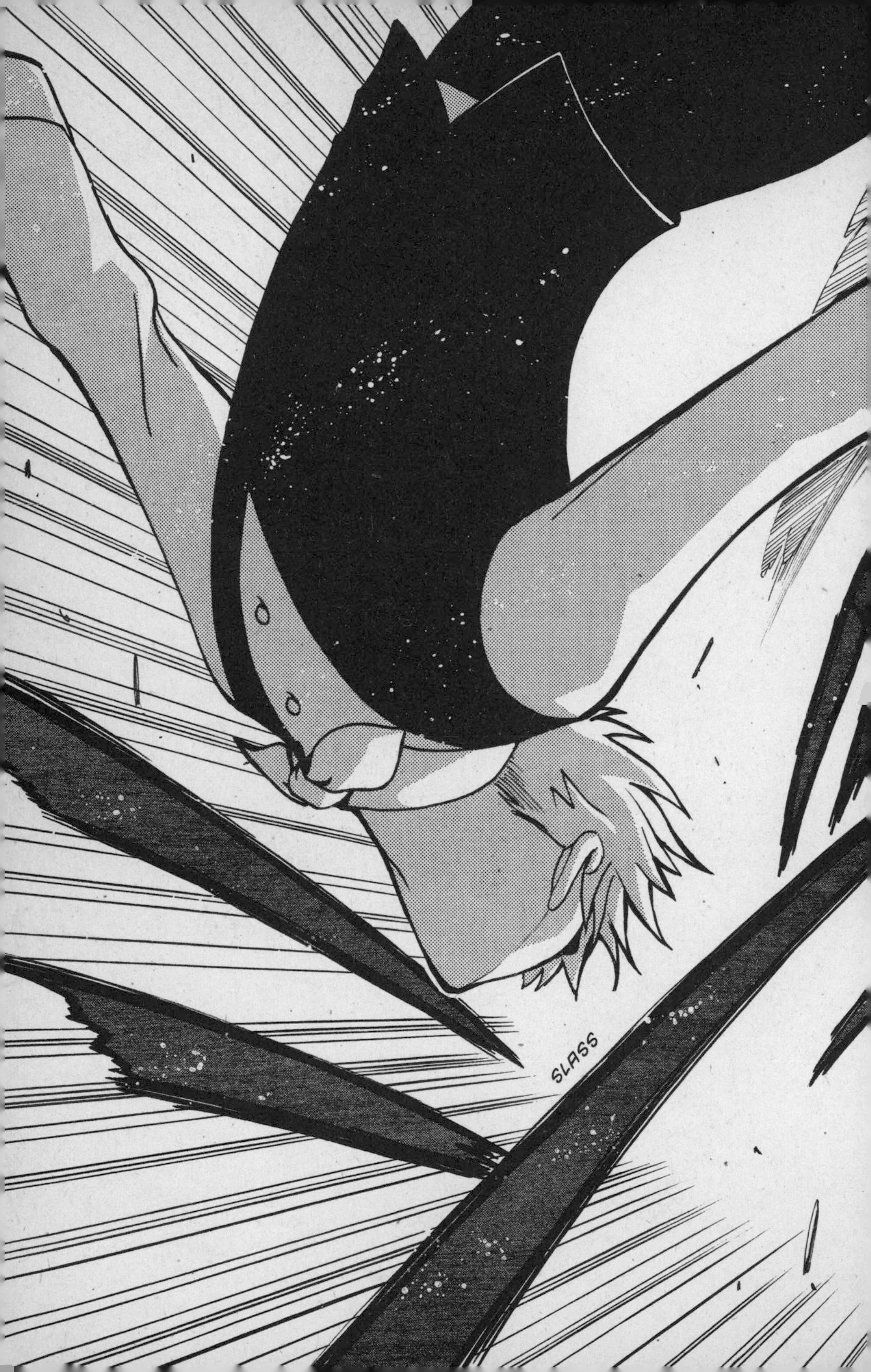
SLASS

32

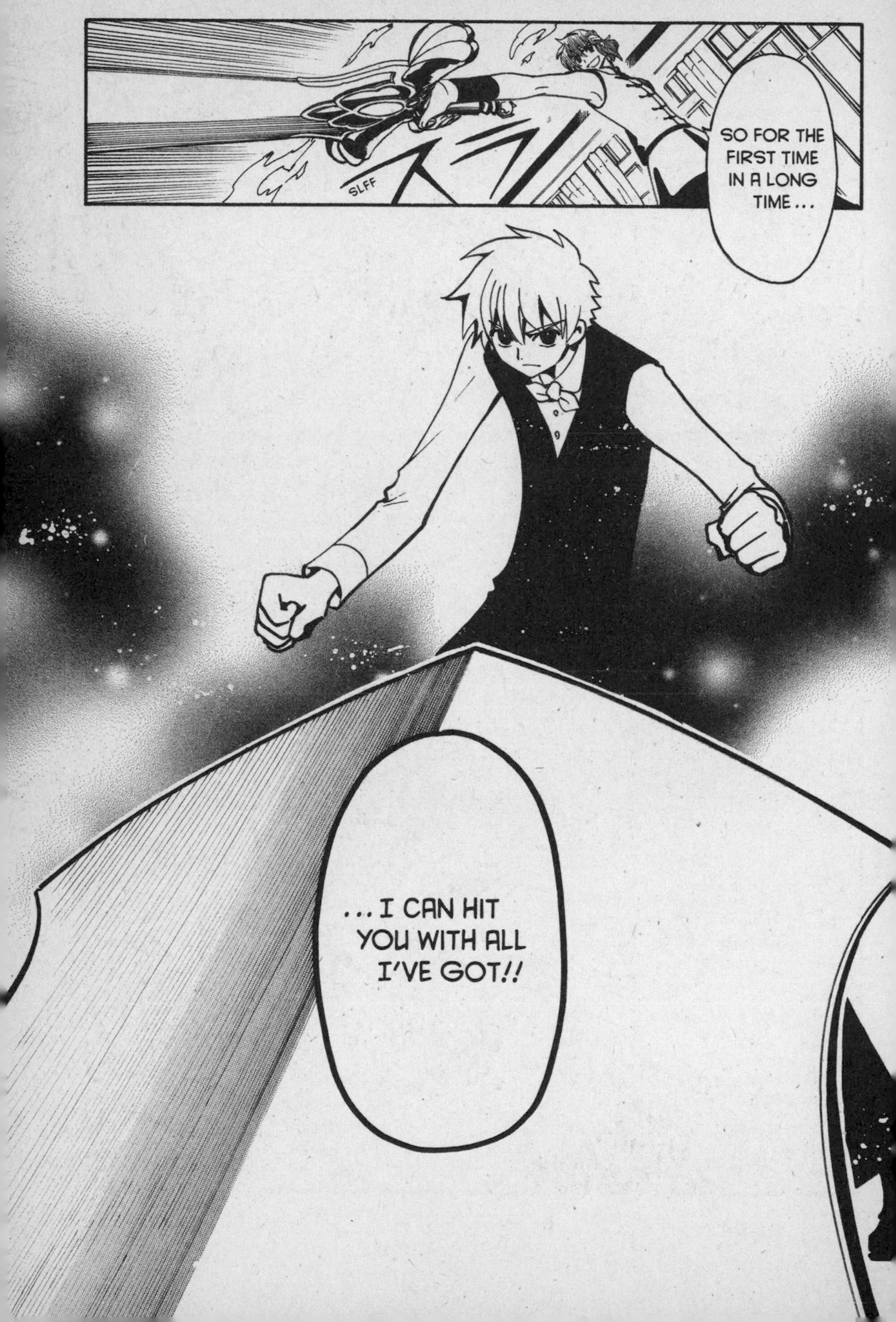
SO FOR THE FIRST TIME IN A LONG TIME...
SLFF
...I CAN HIT YOU WITH ALL I'VE GOT!!

34

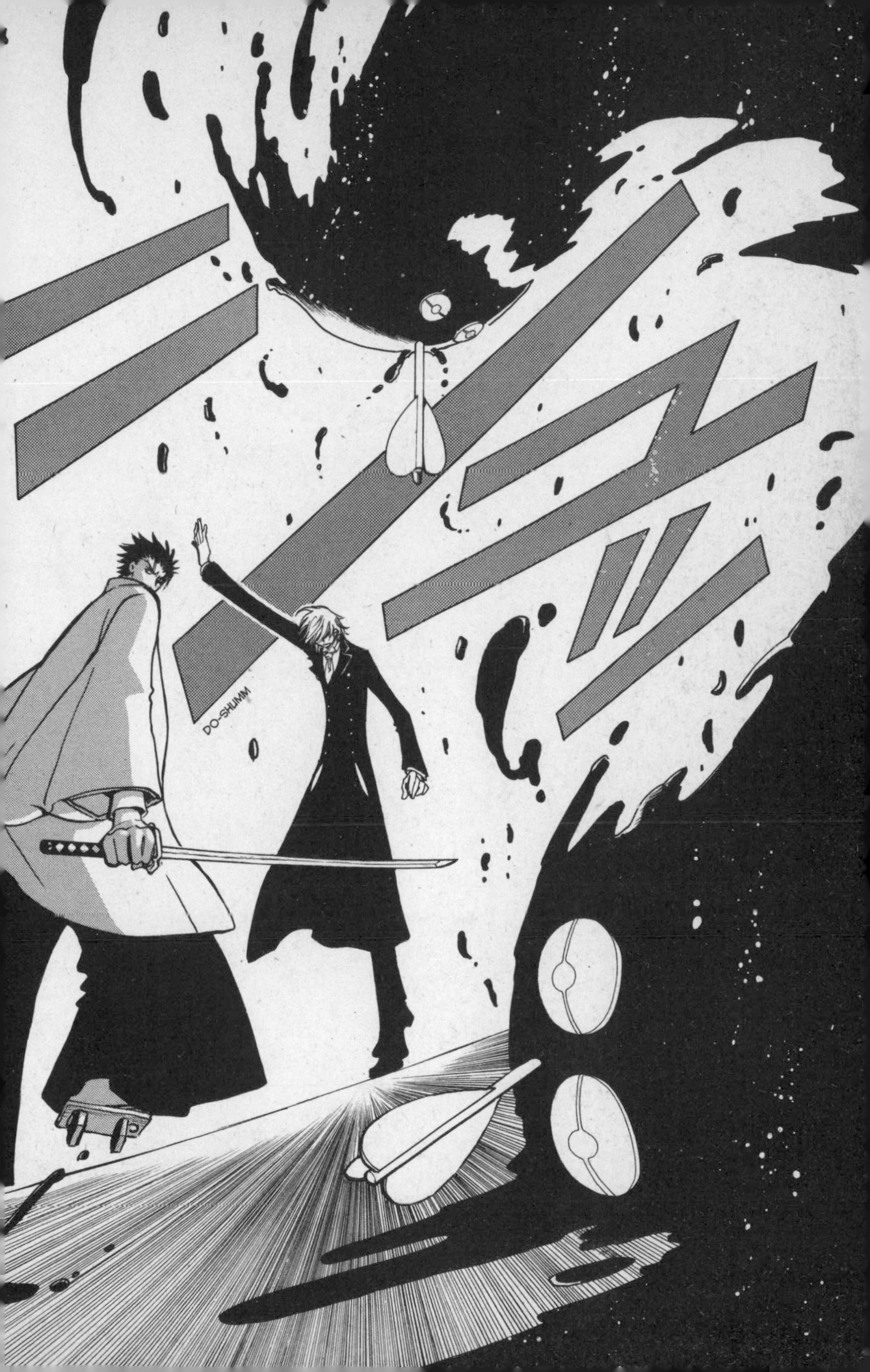
DO-SHUMM

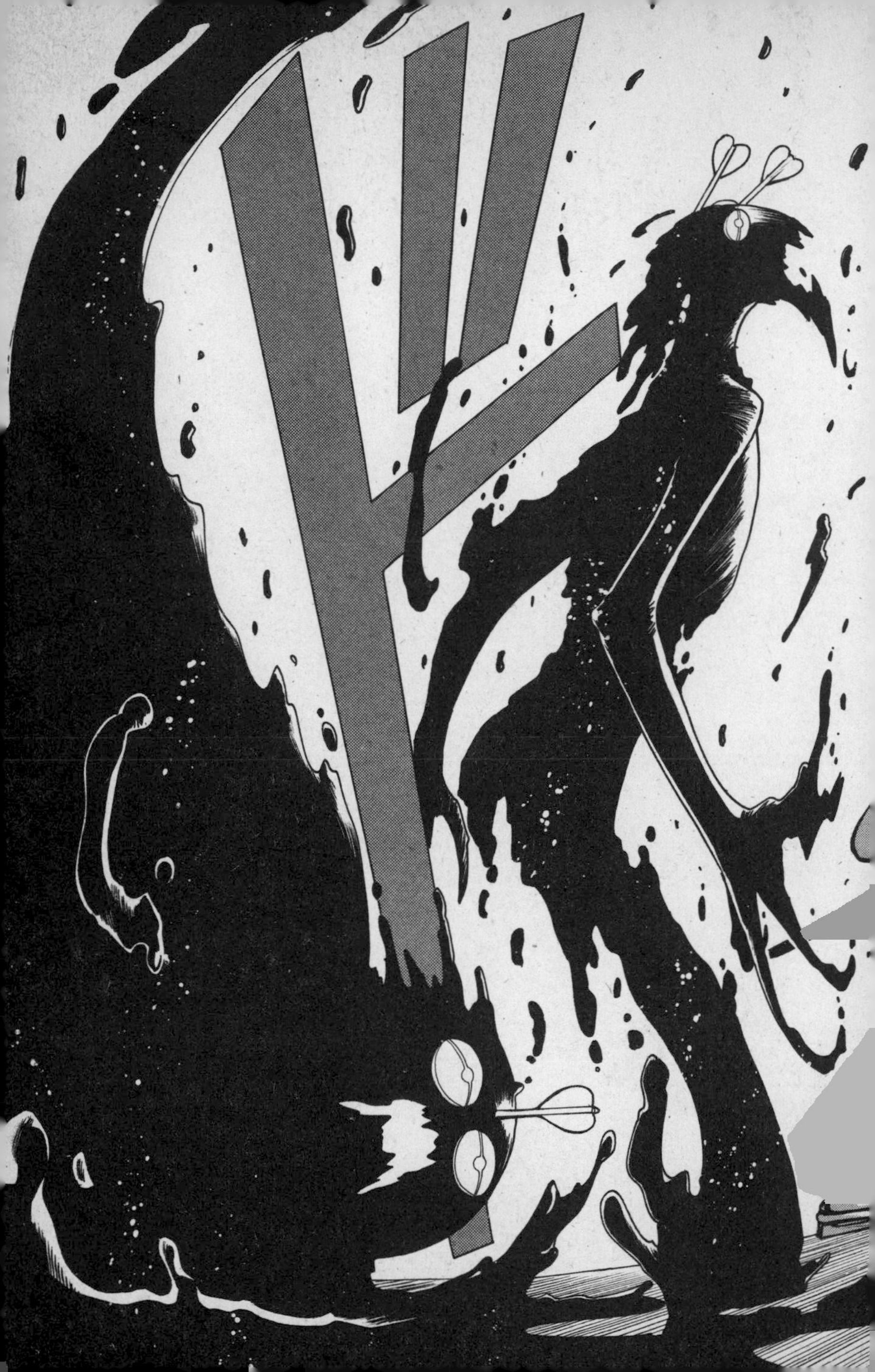

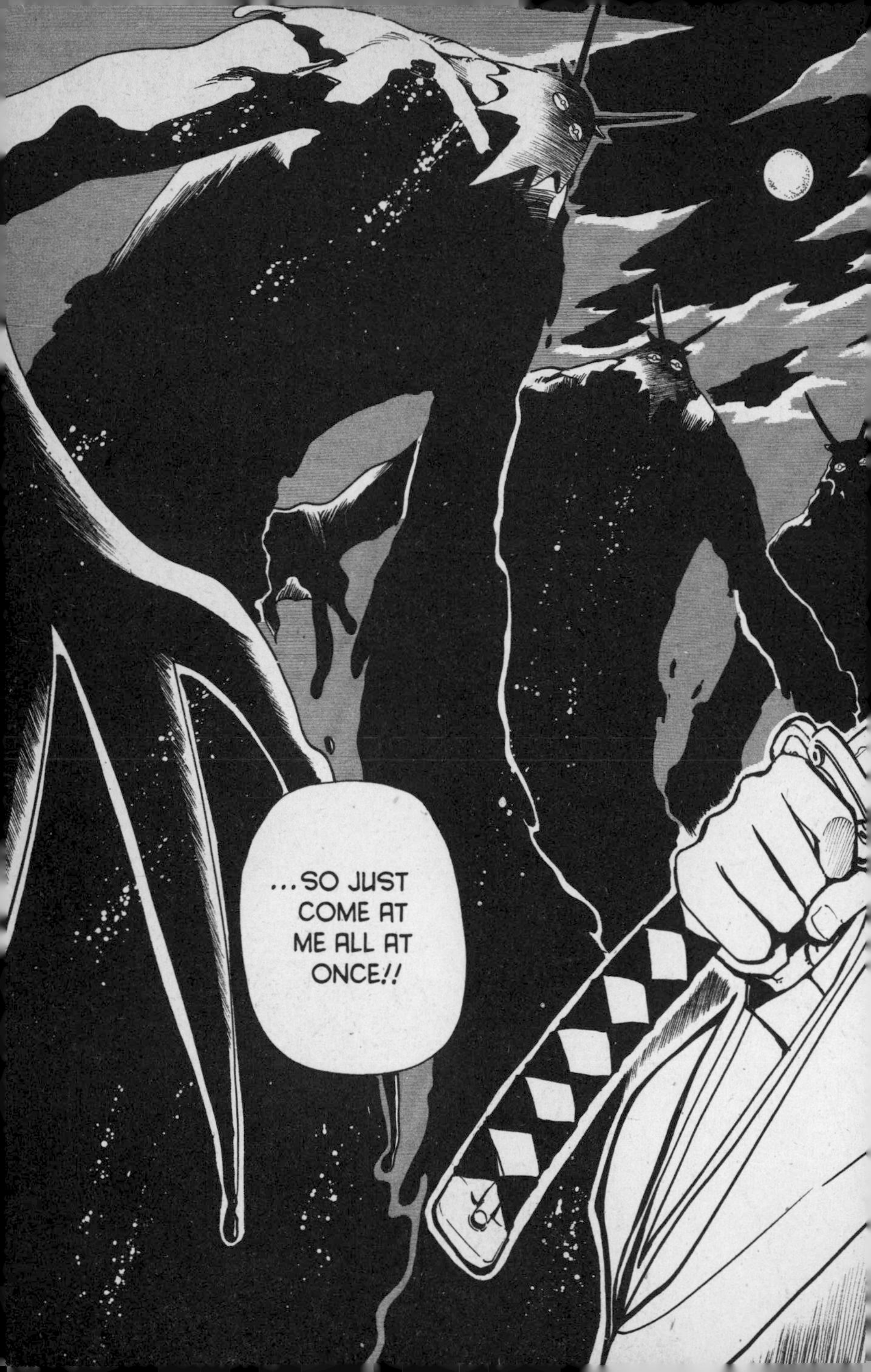
...SO JUST COME AT ME ALL AT ONCE!!

ツバサ

RESERVoir CHRoNiCLE

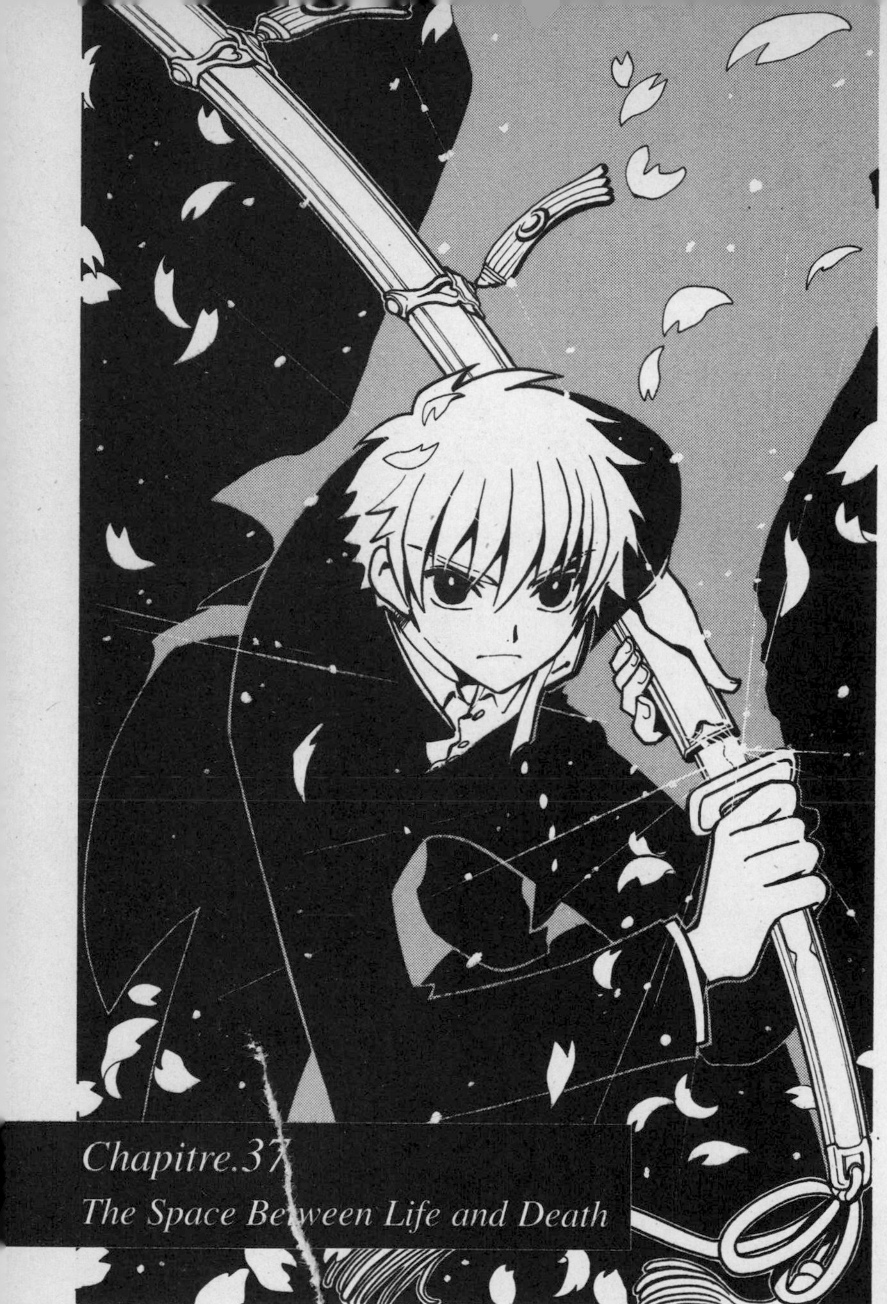
Chapitre.37
The Space Between Life and Death

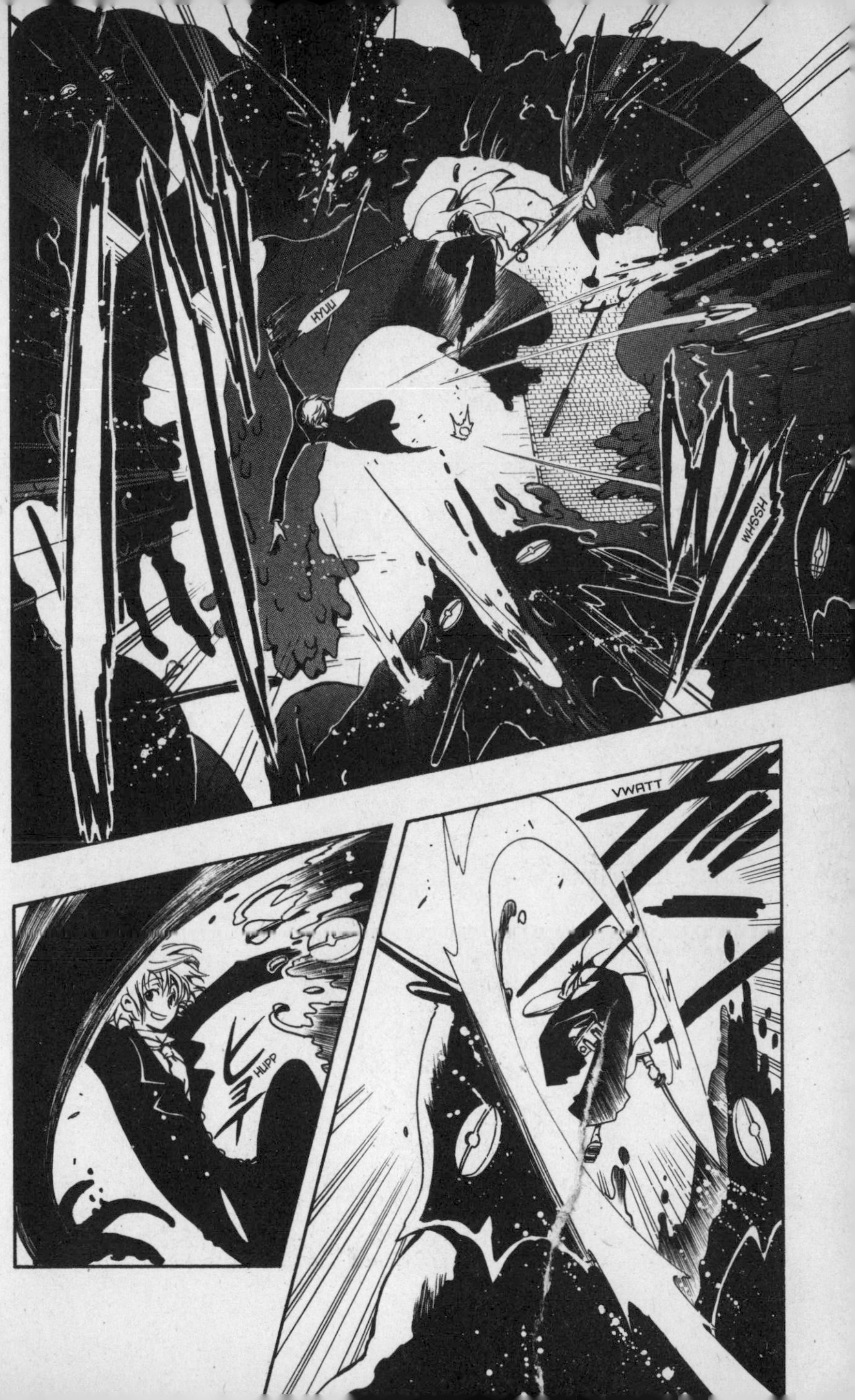
HYUU
WHSSH
VWATT
HUPP

SHKK

BUT...

DON'T JUST TRY TO AVOID THEM!

TAKE THEM DOWN!!

SO I THOUGHT I'D JUST LEAVE IT TO THE EXPERT.

IF I DO THAT, ONI-SAN HERE WILL JUST COME BACK!

MY DARTS TURN OUT TO BE JUST PLAYTHINGS.

STOP THAT!

THOSE STUPID NAMES YOU USED TO CALL ME ARE BETTER!

RIGHT, BIG PUPPY?

ZM

I HATE THEM ALL!!

TMP

YOU REALLY THINK SO?

TELL ME! WHICH ONE DID YOU LIKE BEST?

KURO-TAN? KURO-RIN? KURO-PIPI?

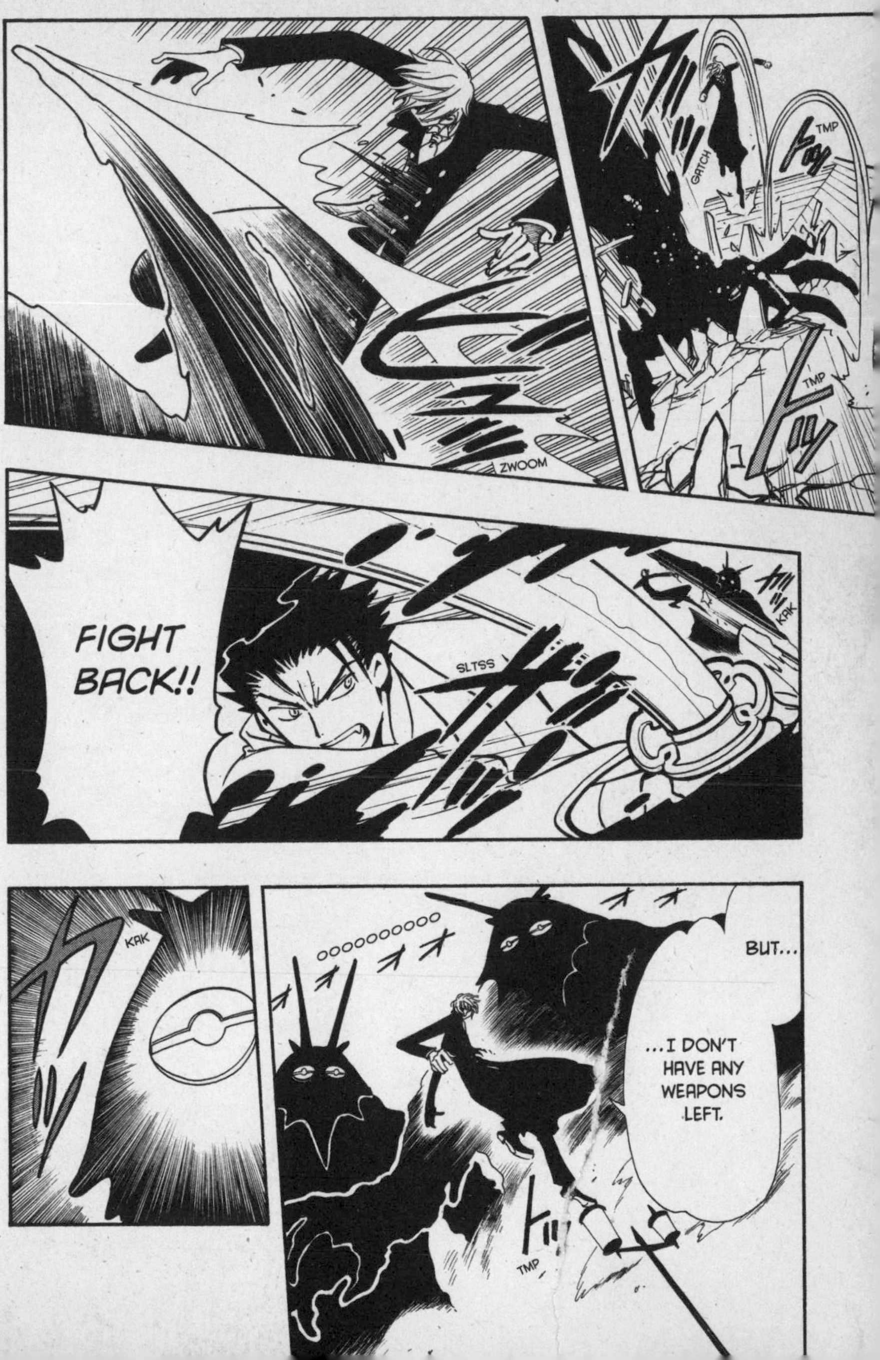
TMP
GATCH
TMP
ZWOOM
KAK
SLTSS
FIGHT BACK!!
BUT...
...I DON'T HAVE ANY WEAPONS LEFT.
OOOOOOOOOO
TMP
KAK

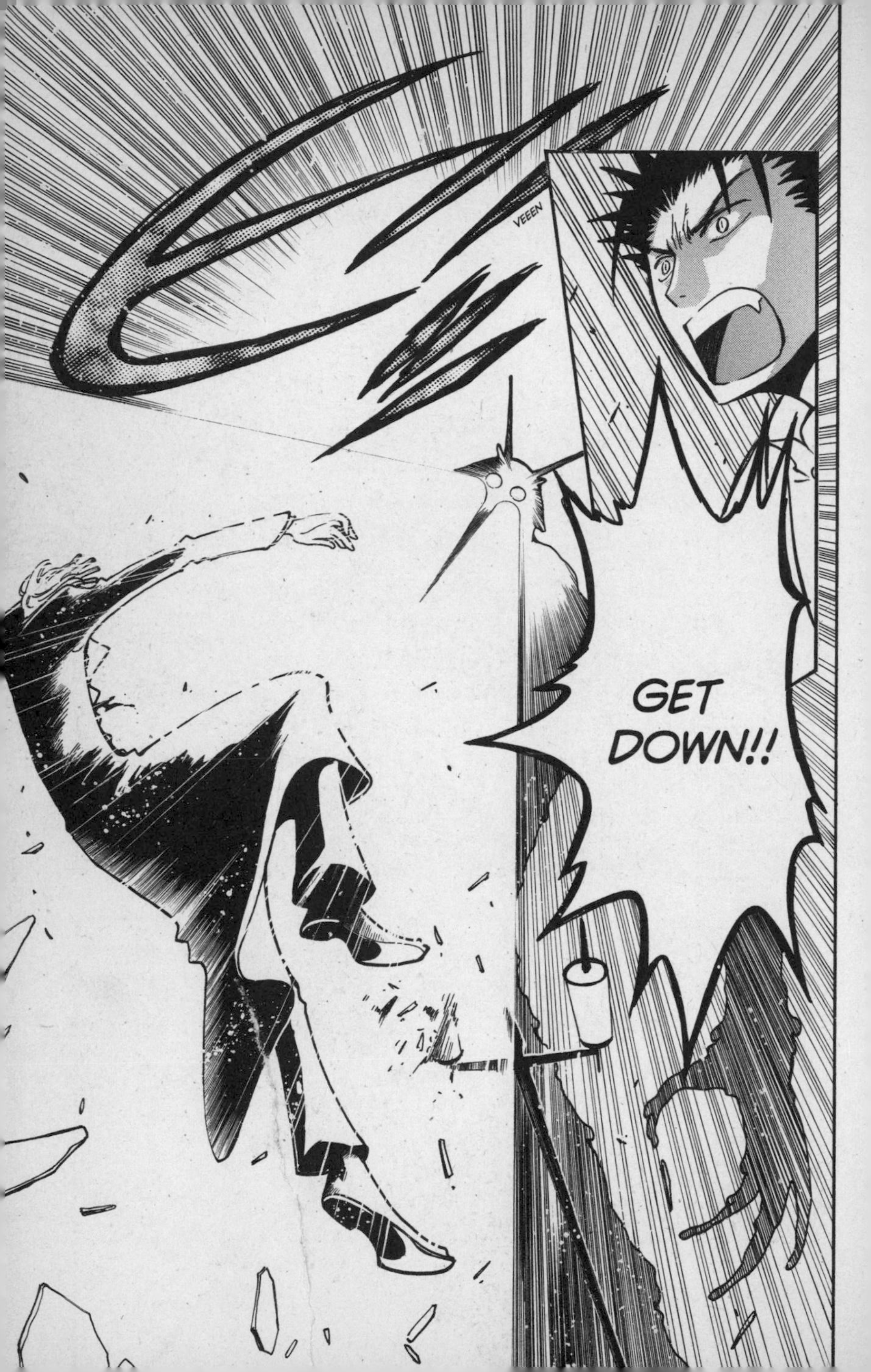
VEEEN
GET DOWN!!

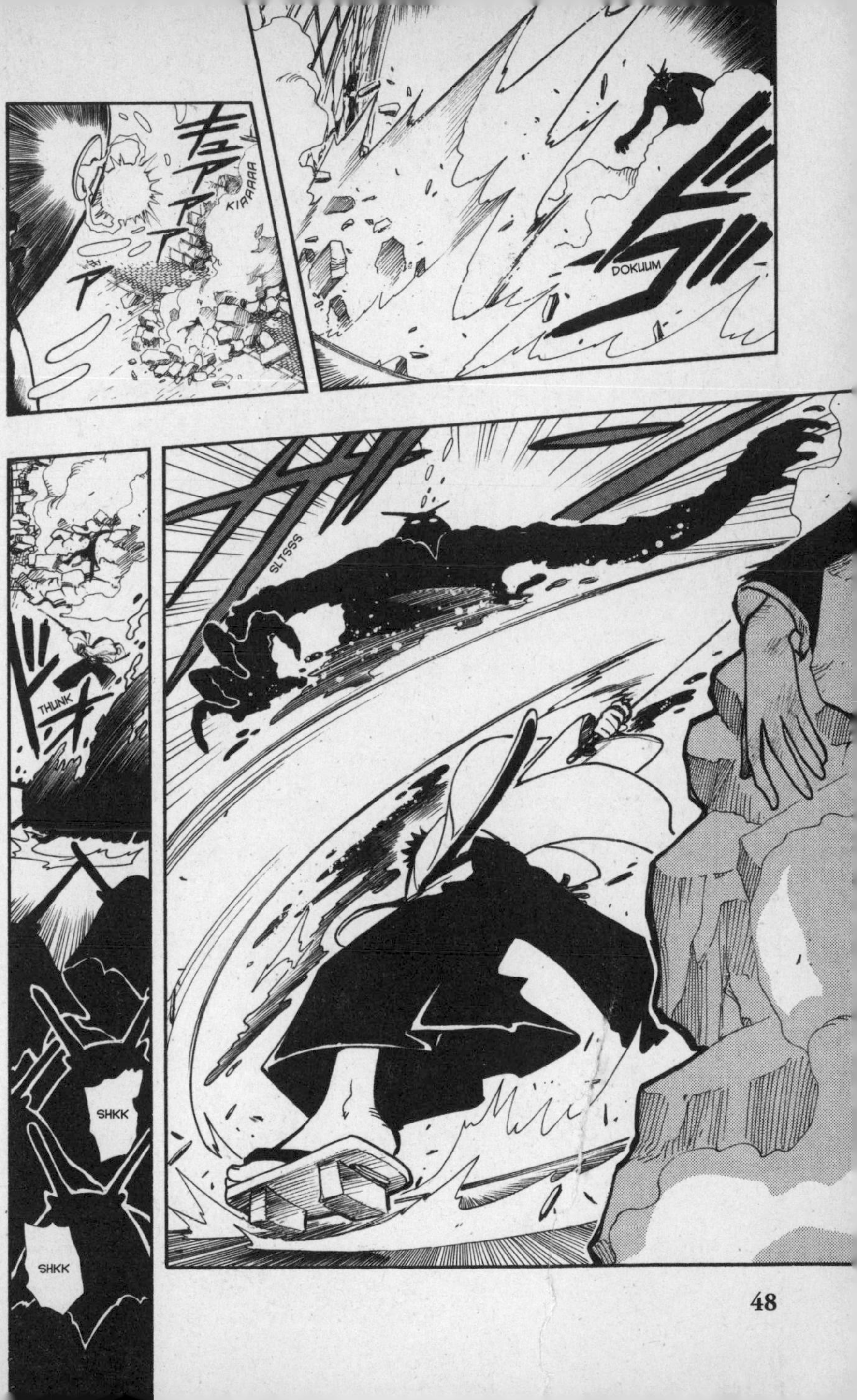
DOKUUM
KIRAAAA
SLTSSS
THUNK
SHKK
SHKK

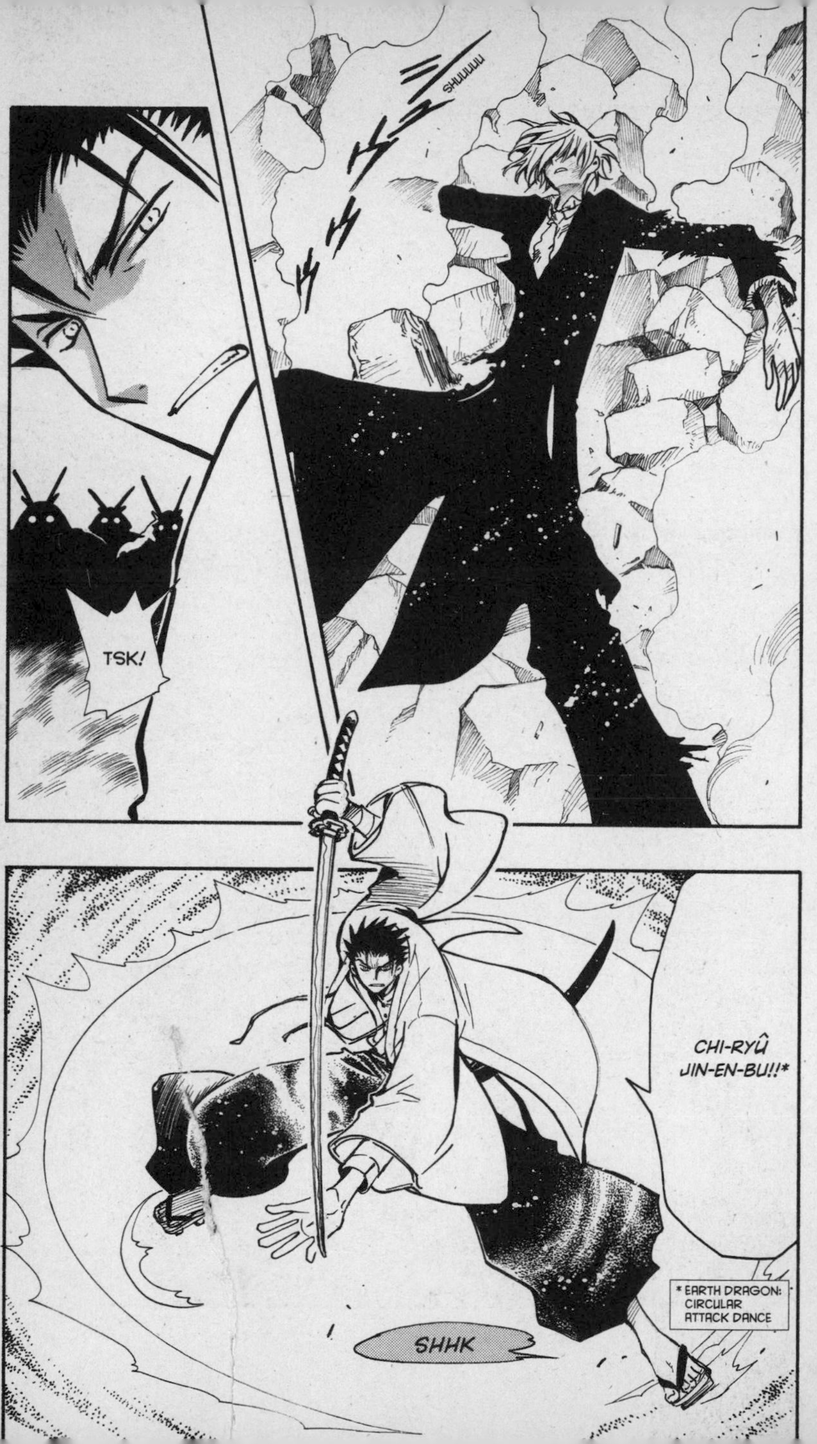
SHUUUUU
TSK!
CHI-RYÛ JIN-EN-BU!!*
* EARTH DRAGON: CIRCULAR ATTACK DANCE
SHHK

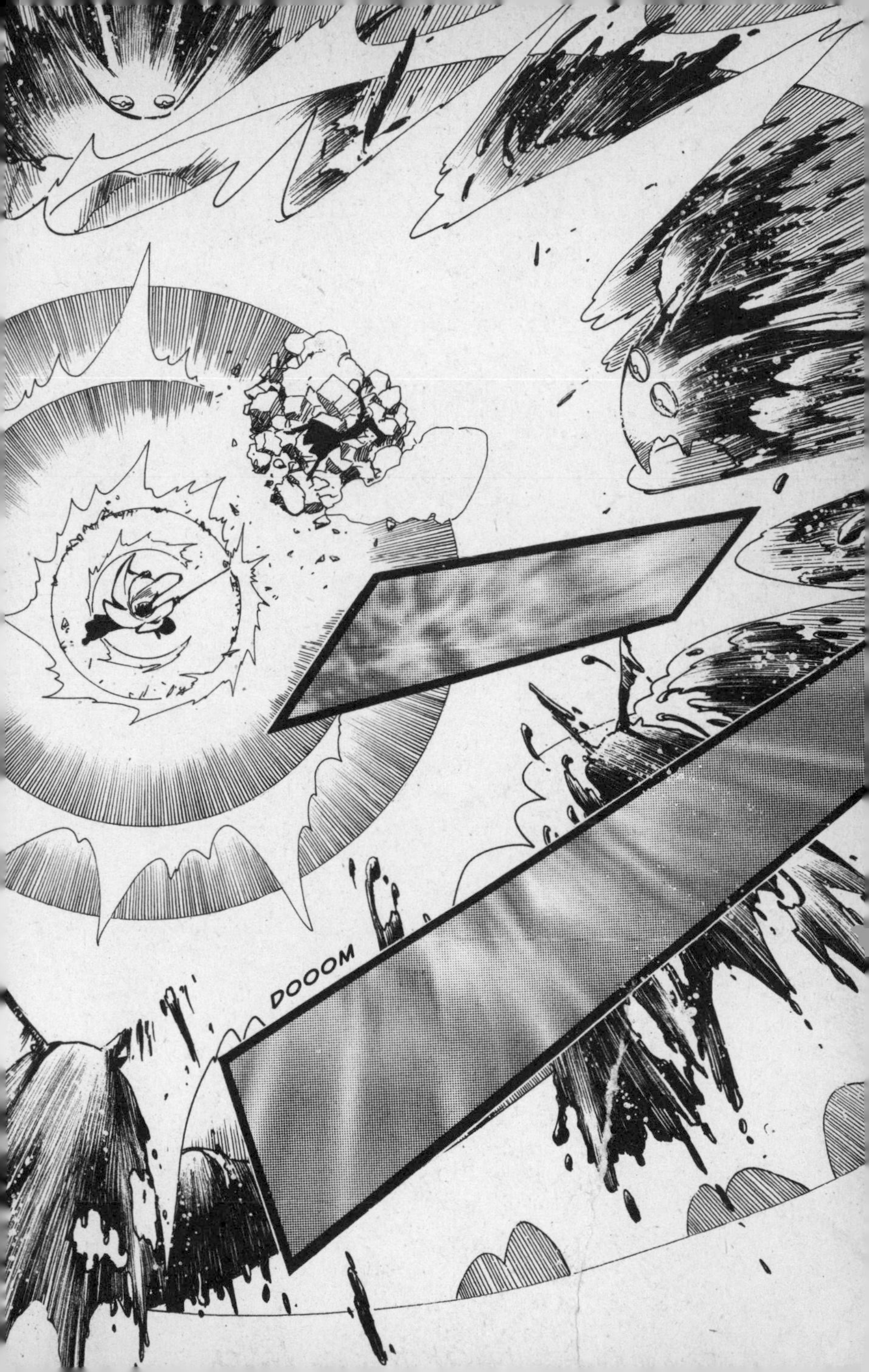
DOOOM

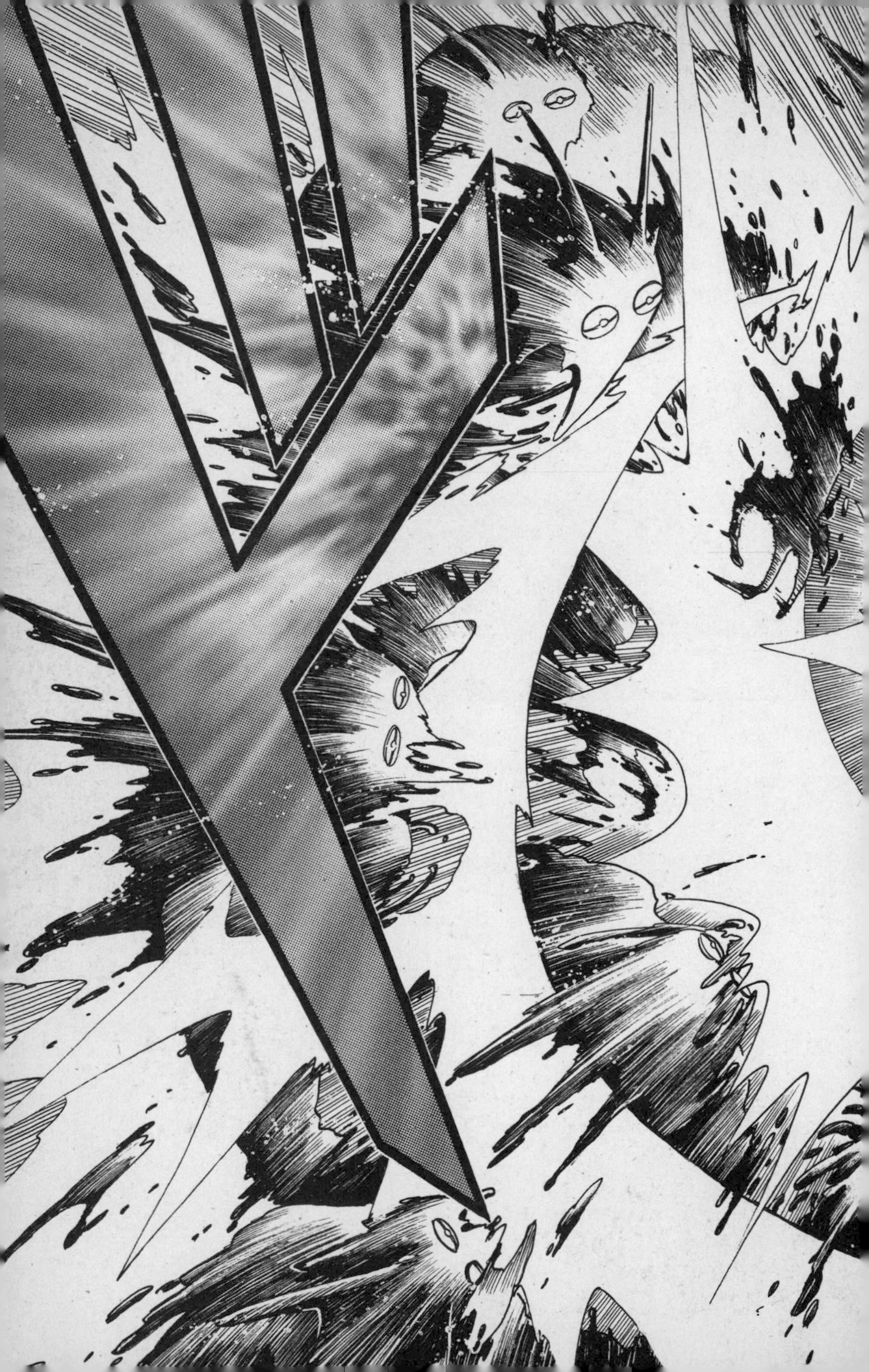

SHARAAA

CHAKL

BUT A WOUND THIS SLIGHT WON'T KILL ME.

SOMETHING'S A LITTLE WEIRD WITH MY LEGS.

MM?

ZHAAN

I KNEW IT! I KNEW THIS SWORD WAS TOO CHEAP FOR THAT TECHNIQUE!

KLAP KLAP KLAP KLAP

WAY TO GO, KURO-SAMA!

53

54

CLOVER
白詰草
クローバー
4

HEY! HEY!

NO PRIVATE FIGHTS SO CLOSE TO OUR DOORS!

EXCUSE US!

WOULD YOU HAPPEN TO KNOW OF A BAR NAMED "CLOVER"?

YOU MEAN THIS BAR HERE?

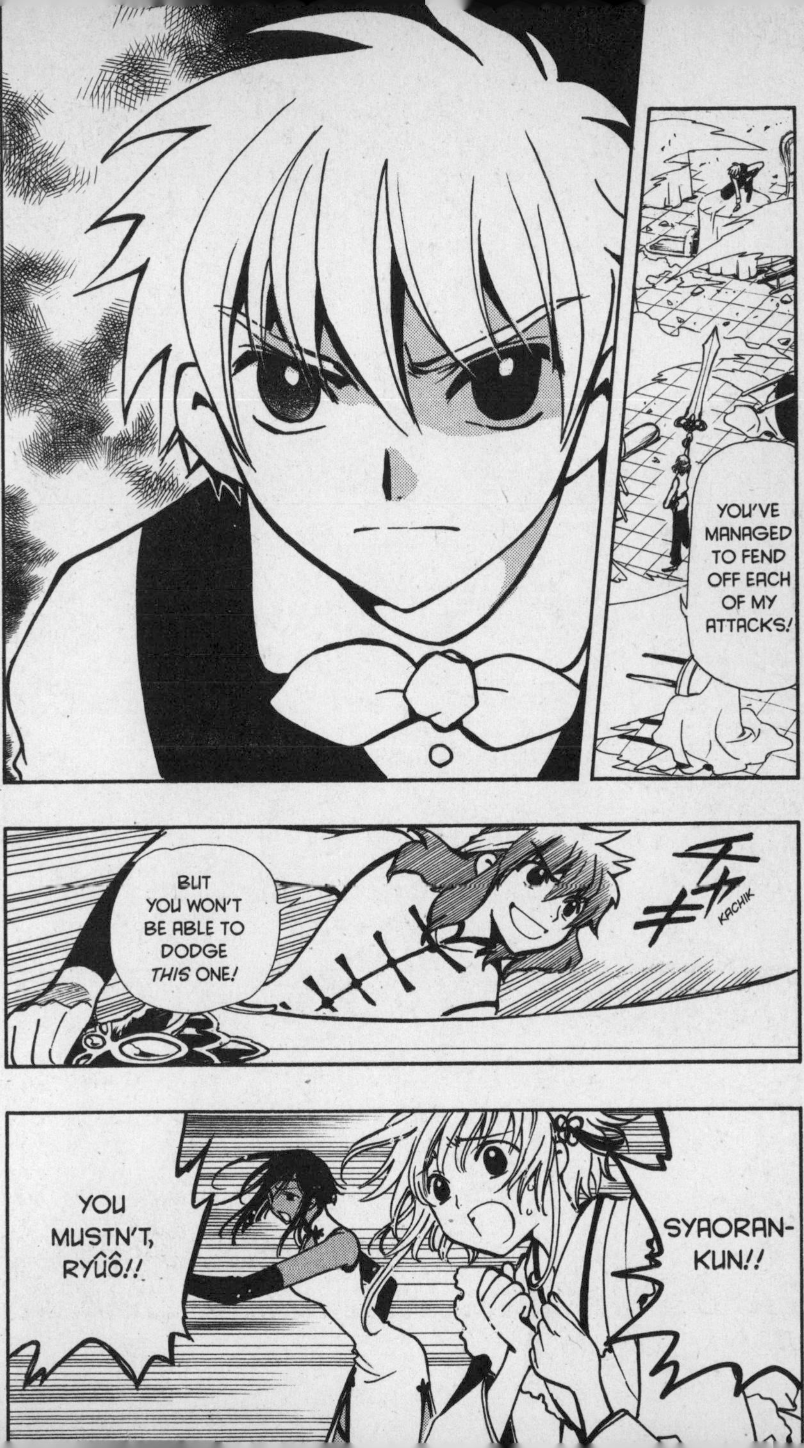
YOU'VE MANAGED TO FEND OFF EACH OF MY ATTACKS!
BUT YOU WON'T BE ABLE TO DODGE *THIS* ONE!
KACHIK
SYAORAN-KUN!!
YOU MUSTN'T, RYÛÔ!!

57

NAW, IT'S MY FAULT!

...FOR BEING UNABLE TO STOP RYÛO...

BOW

PLEASE ACCEPT MY HUMBLE APOLOGY...

WHEN WE FOUND THIS GREAT CAFÉ, I WAS TELLING RYÛO ABOUT HOW GOOD THE FOOD WAS, BUT I ALSO MENTIONED WHAT GOOD FIGHTERS WERE HERE, TOO.

THIS IS GOOD!

SO GOOD!

THAT NOISE JUST NOW WAS SO SHOCKING THAT MOKONA HAD TO COME DOWN FROM THE 2ND FLOOR TO CHECK!

THANK YOU. I WILL.

PLEASE HAVE SOME BEFORE IT GETS COLD.

PAAA

AND RYÛO CAN'T SEEM TO HELP HIMSELF, HE LOVES TESTING HIS STRENGTH AGAINST OTHERS SO MUCH.

NO... FAI-SA— I MEAN, BIG KITTY MADE IT...

THERE ARE TWO "PUPPIES" AND TWO "KITTIES" LIVING HERE.

IT TRULY IS DELICIOUS!

YOU TWO MADE IT YOURSELVES?

59

60

IT'S NICE TO MEET YOU, LITTLE PUPPY!

URK!

...YOU MEAN THE ONE THE INFORMANT ERII WAS TALKING ABOUT?

YEAH...

NOW THAT I THINK OF IT... HAVE YOU HEARD THE RUMOR?

OH! THE ONE ABOUT THE NEW TYPE OF ONI?!

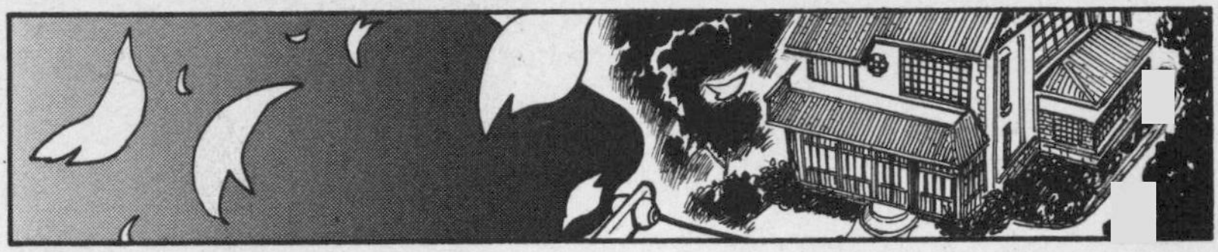

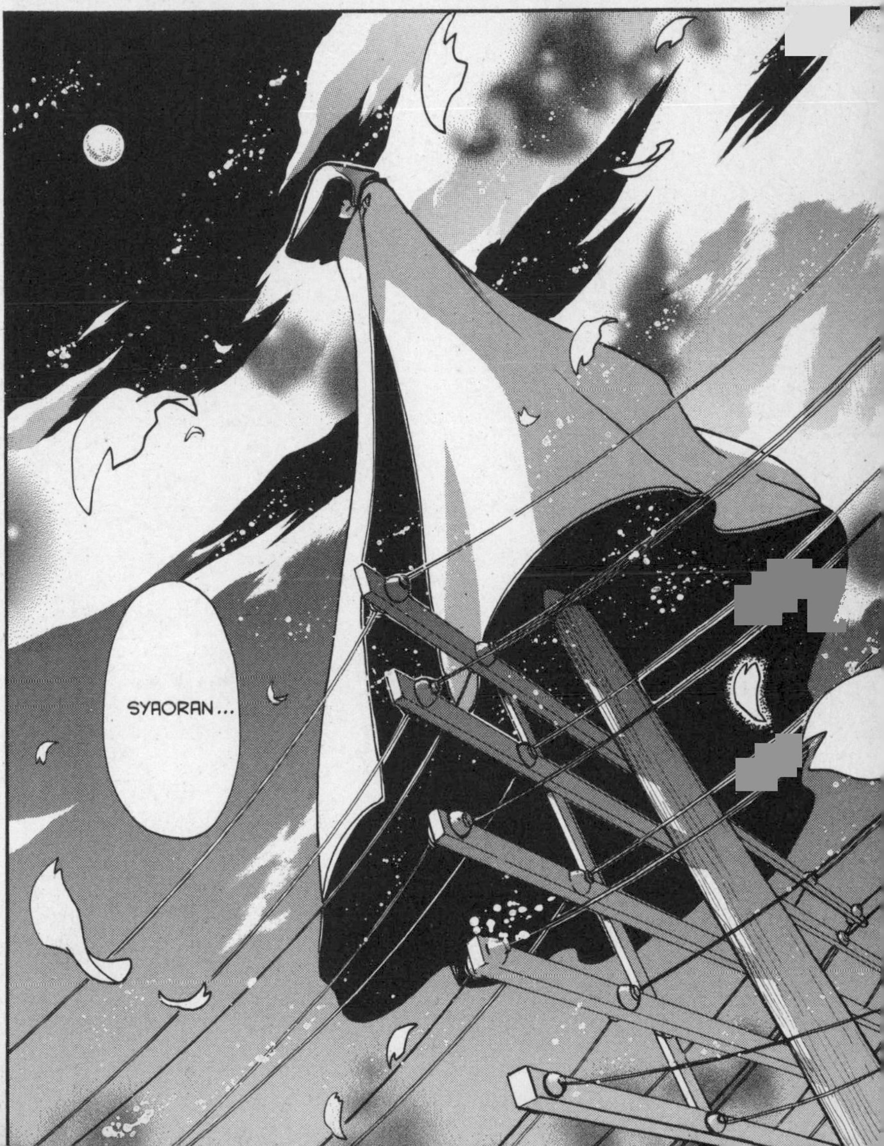
SYAORAN...

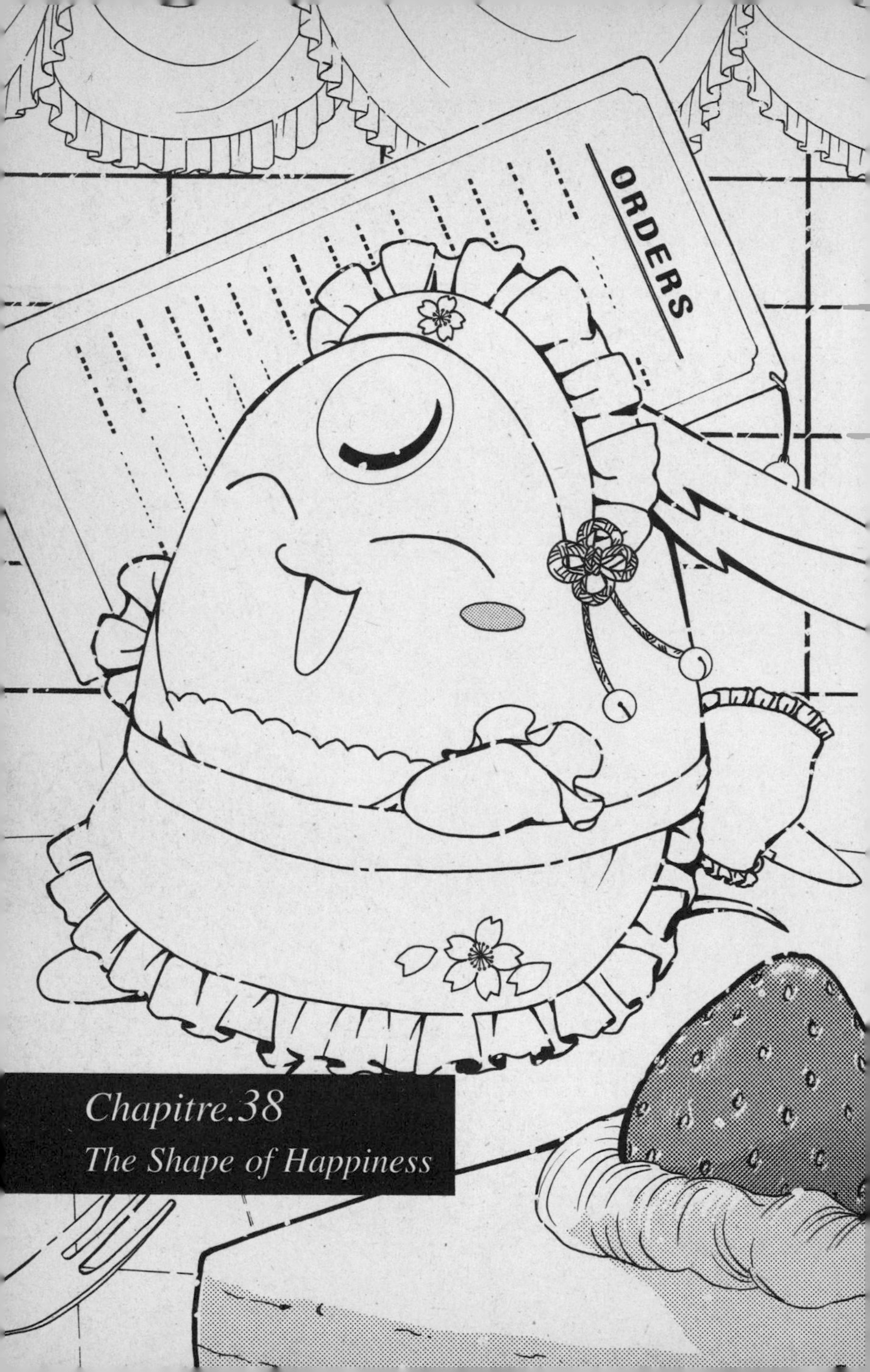
ORDERS
Chapitre.38
The Shape of Happiness

NOBODY'S BEEN ABLE TO DEFEAT ONI OF LEVEL 'RO OR BETTER WITHOUT AN ONI-HUNTING WEAPON.

YES... I'LL MANAGE.

THANKS FOR THE ICE.

WILL YOUR LEG BE OKAY?

YOU GUYS HAVE GONE THROUGH A LOTTA HELL, HUH?

SHAKKA SHAKKA

THIS IS A COCKTAIL THAT ORIGINATED RIGHT HERE AT CLOVER.

IT'S SUCH A BEAUTIFUL SHADE OF GREEN.

IT'S CALLED THE "FOUR LEAF."

I IMAGINE THOSE AREN'T VERY USEFUL.

I HIT AN ONI WITH THEM, AND THEY JUST POPPED BACK TO NORMAL.

NO, THEY WON'T DO ANY DAMAGE.

SST

REALLY? THEN, BARTENDER-SAN...

YOU TALK A LOT LIKE THE PEOPLE FROM THE HANSHIN REPUBLIC.

HMP?

THE BARTENDER THAT ERII TOLD YOU ABOUT IS ME...

SO NOW...

64

65

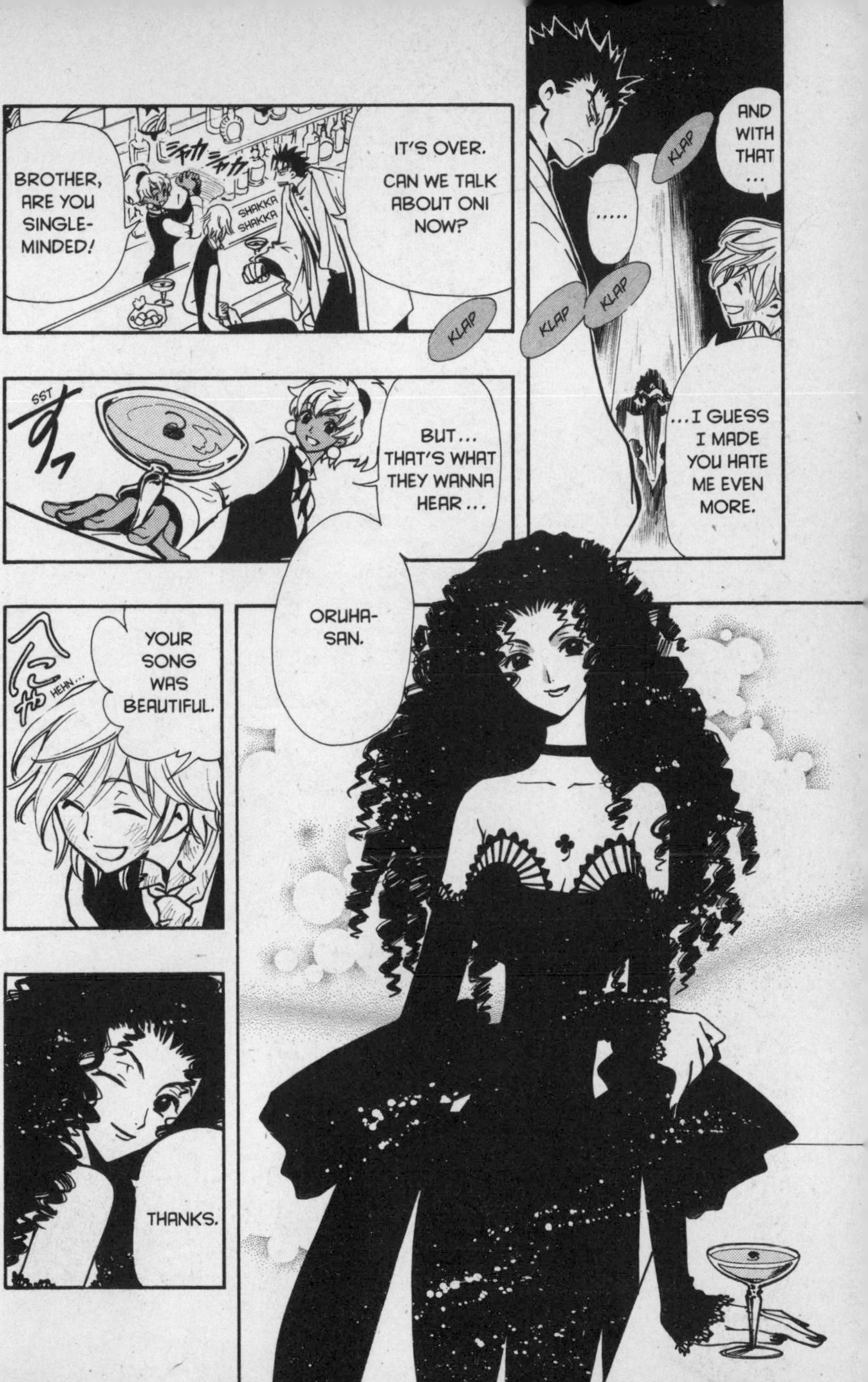
AND WITH THAT ...
KLAP
.....
KLAP
KLAP
KLAP
...I GUESS I MADE YOU HATE ME EVEN MORE.
IT'S OVER.
CAN WE TALK ABOUT ONI NOW?
SHAKKA SHAKKA
BROTHER, ARE YOU SINGLE-MINDED!
BUT... THAT'S WHAT THEY WANNA HEAR...
SST
ORUHA-SAN.
YOUR SONG WAS BEAUTIFUL.
HEHN...
THANKS.

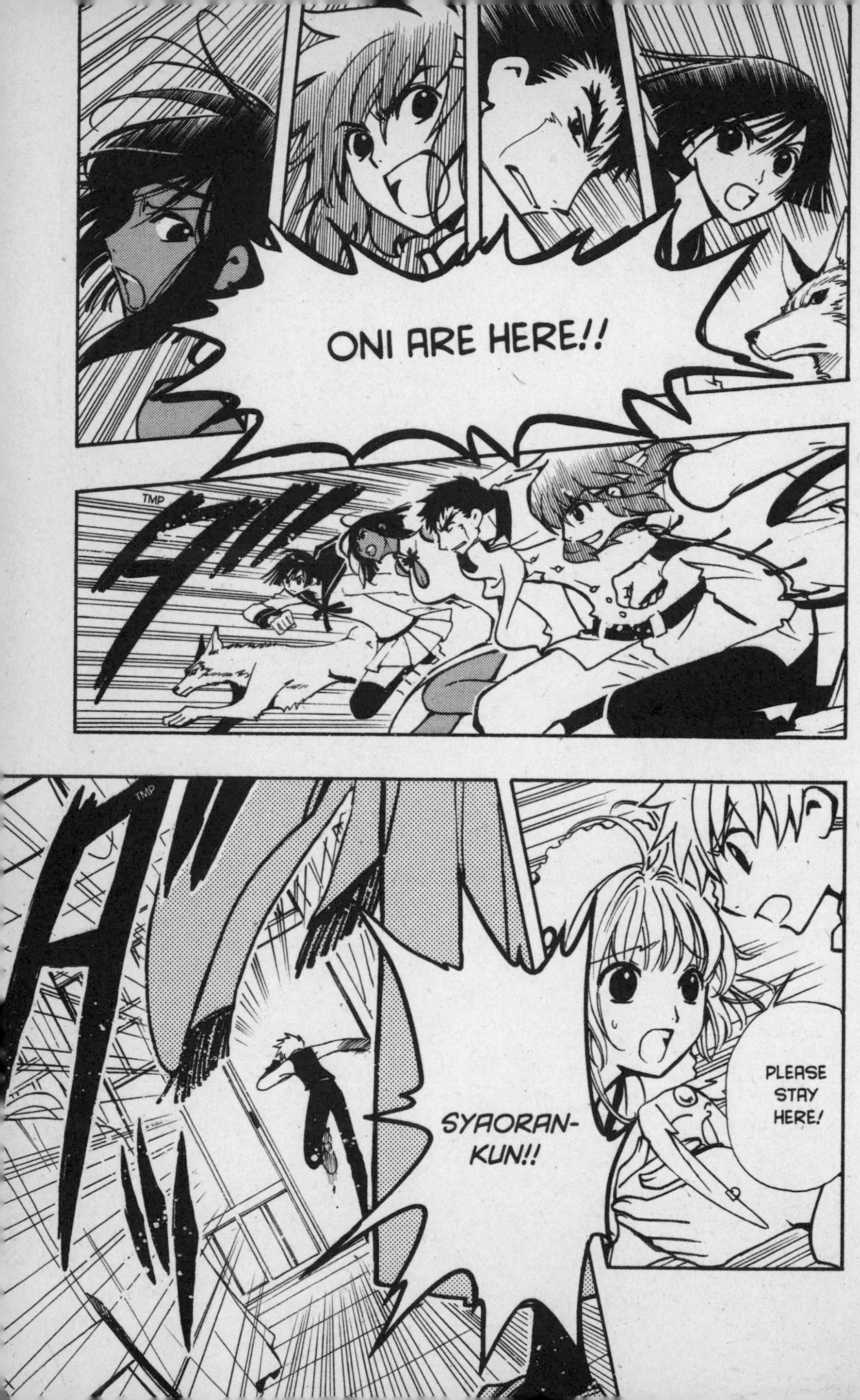
ONI ARE HERE!!
TMP
PLEASE STAY HERE!
SYAORAN-KUN!!
TMP

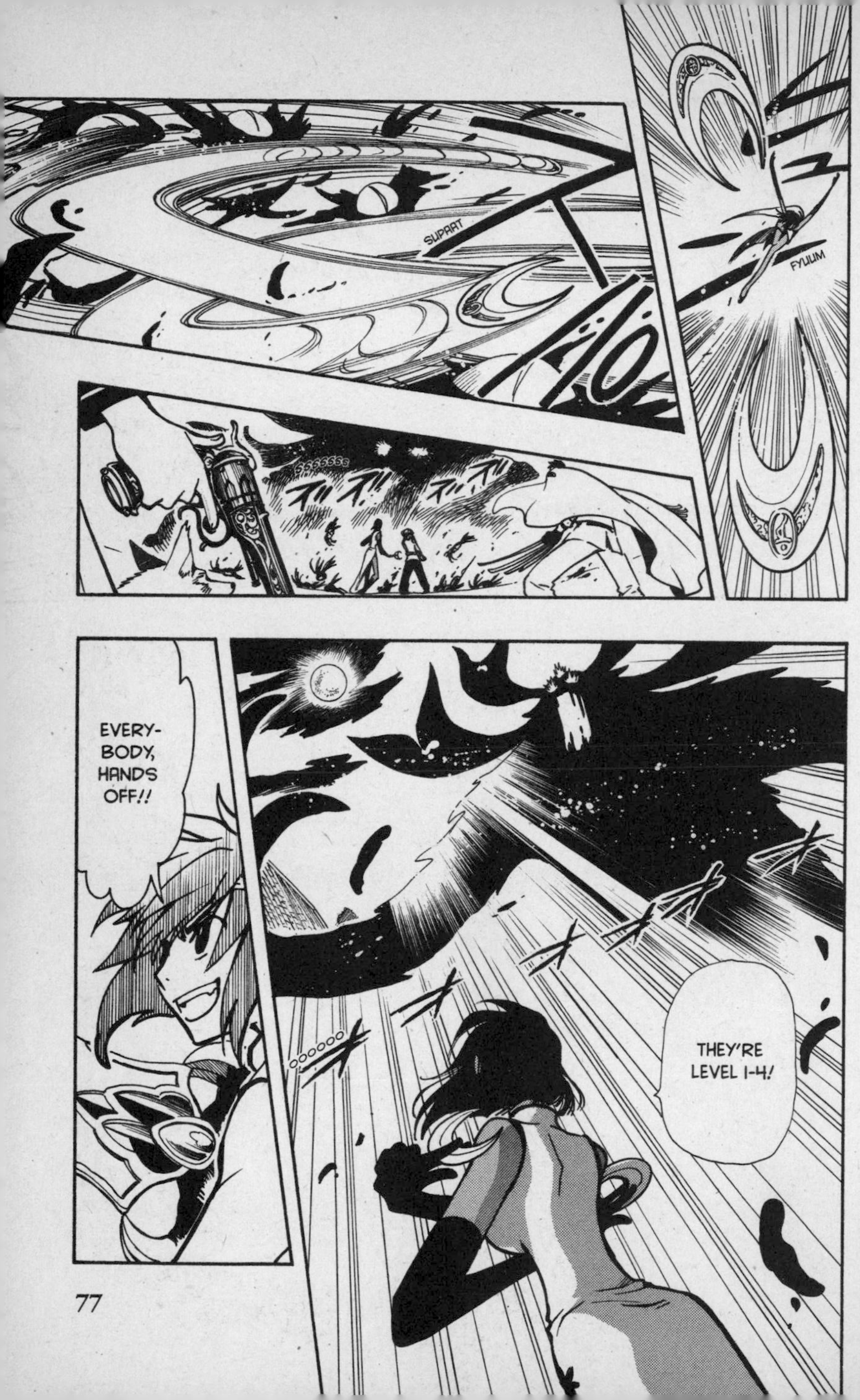
FYUUM
SUPAAT
SSSSSSS
THEY'RE LEVEL 1-4!
OOOOOO
EVERY-BODY, HANDS OFF!!

78

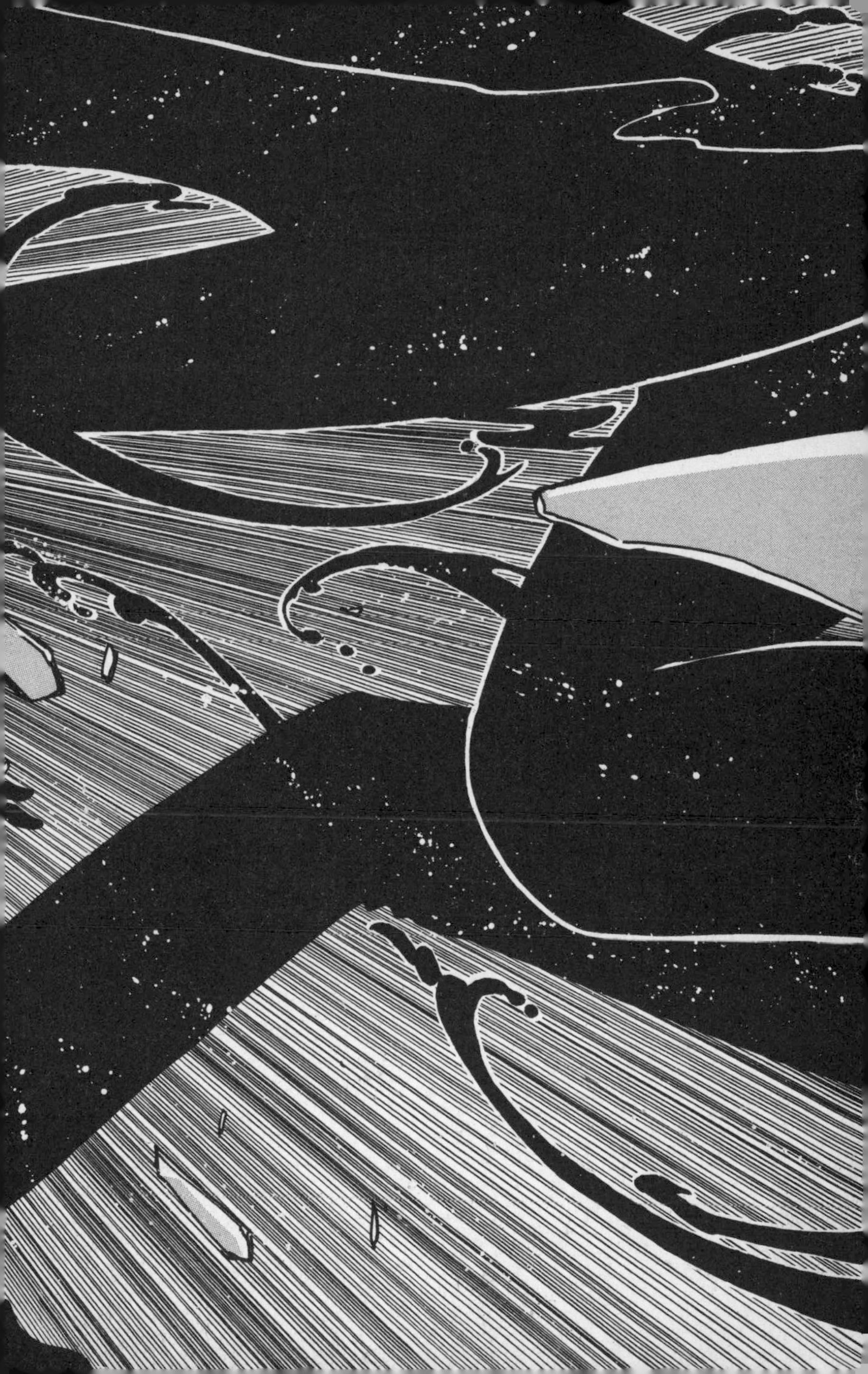

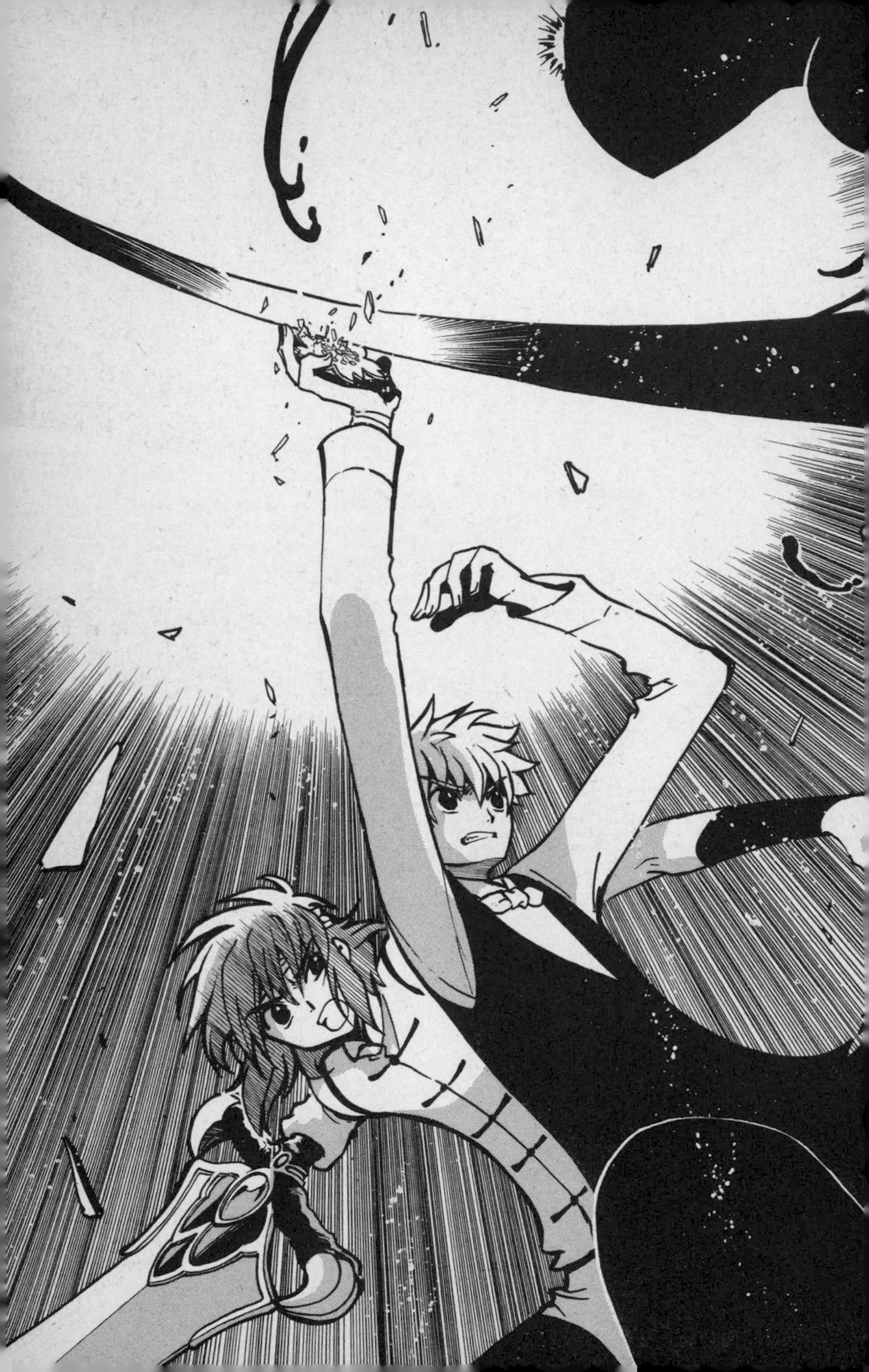

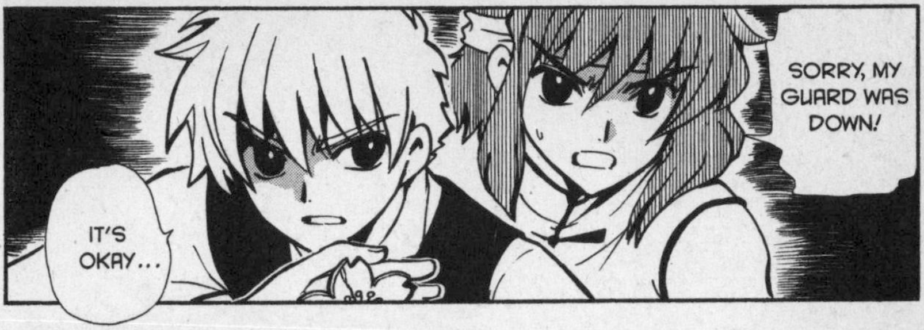
SORRY, MY GUARD WAS DOWN!
IT'S OKAY...

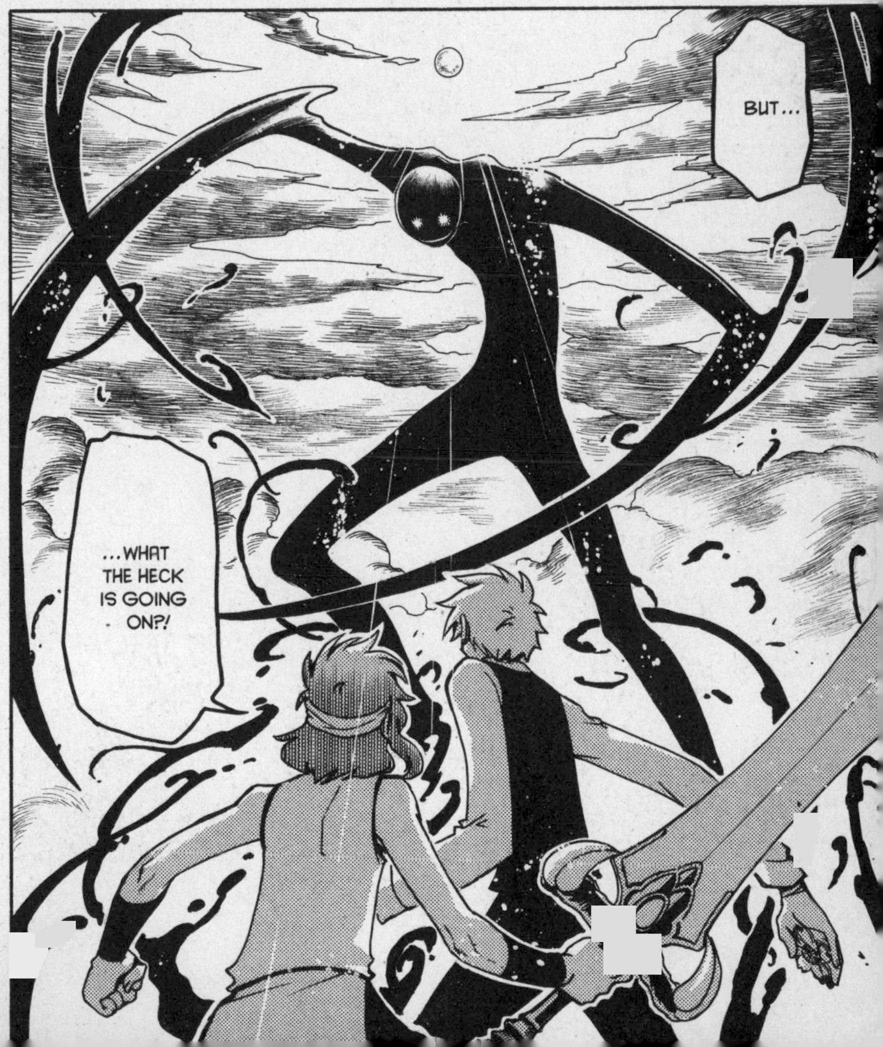
BUT...
...WHAT THE HECK IS GOING ON?!

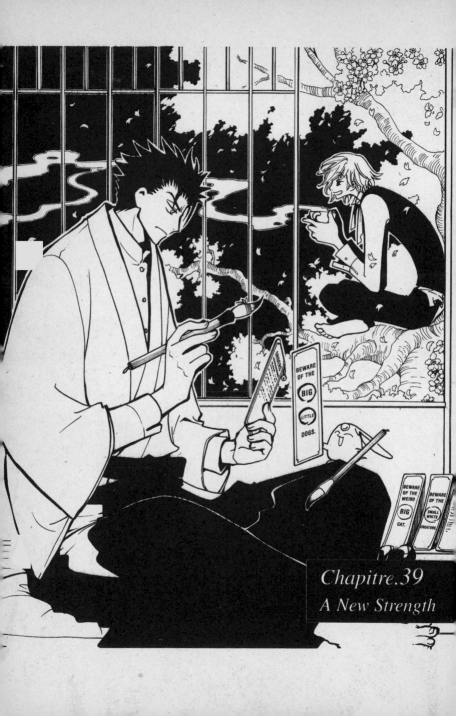

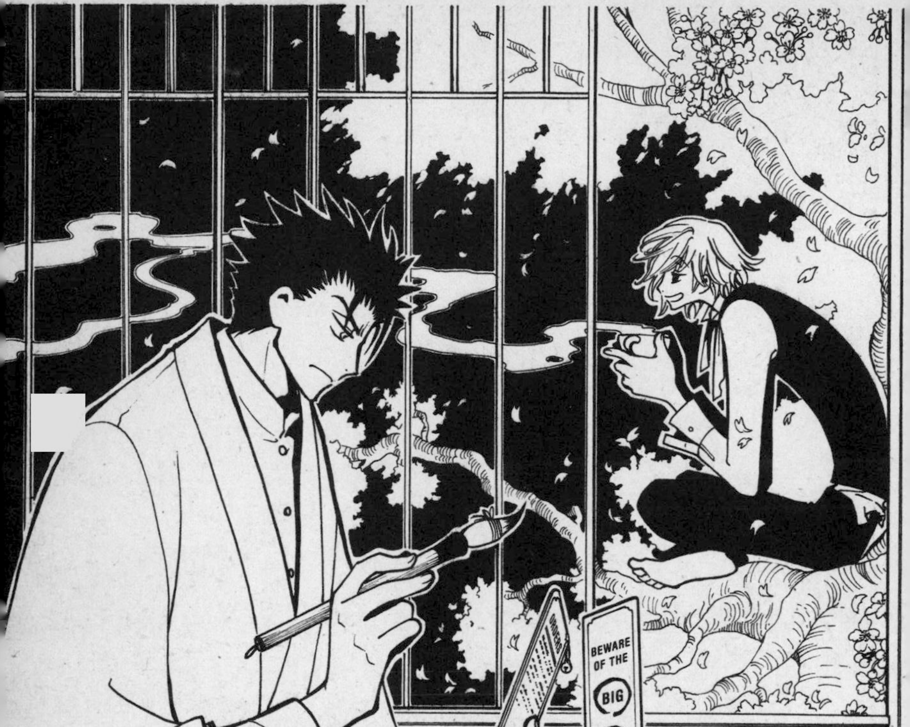
BEWARE OF THE BIG LITTLE DOGS.
BEWARE OF THE WEIRD BIG CAT.
BEWARE OF THE SMALL WHITE CREATURE.

Chapitre.39
A New Strength

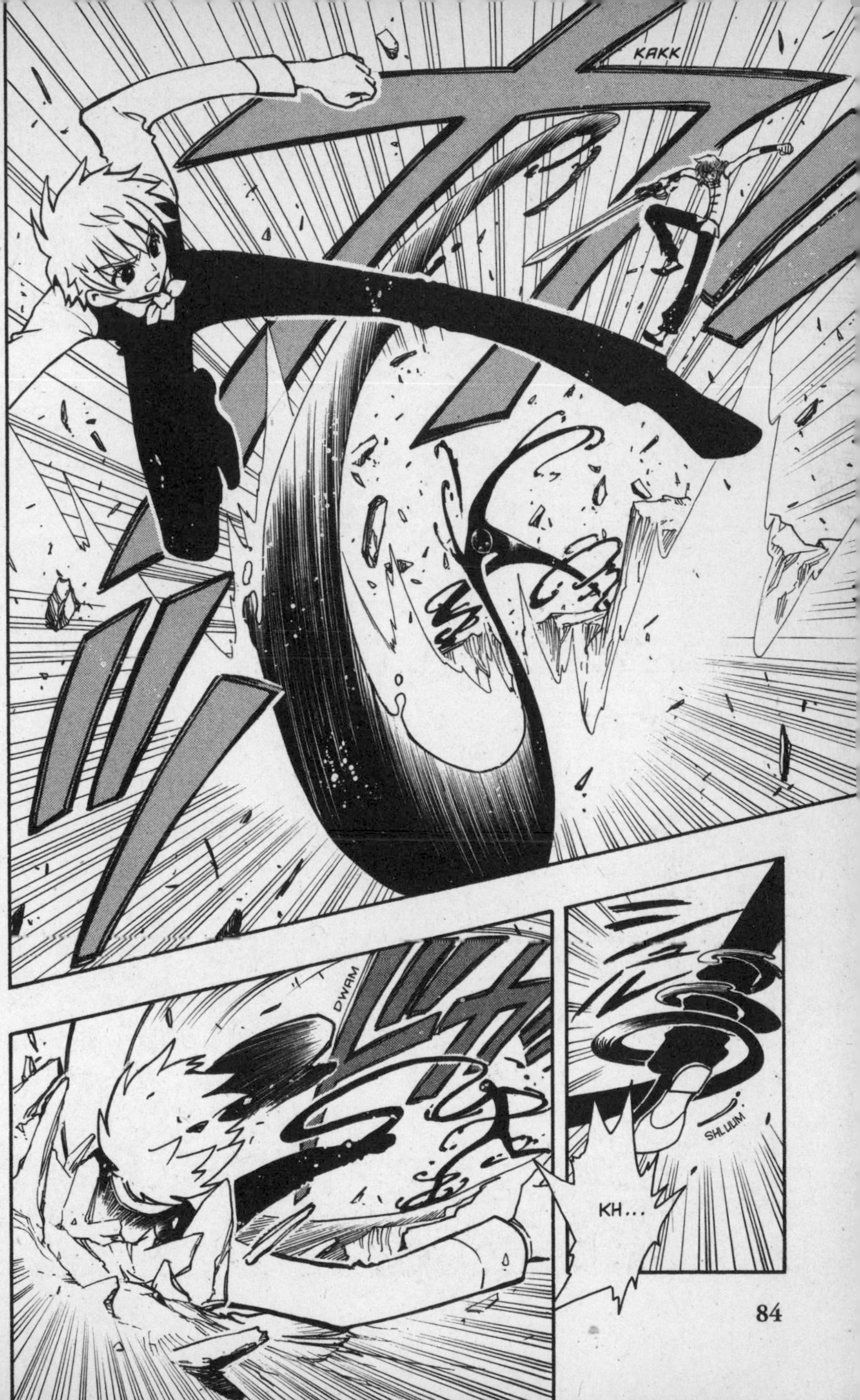
KAKK
SHLUUM
KH...
DWAM

85

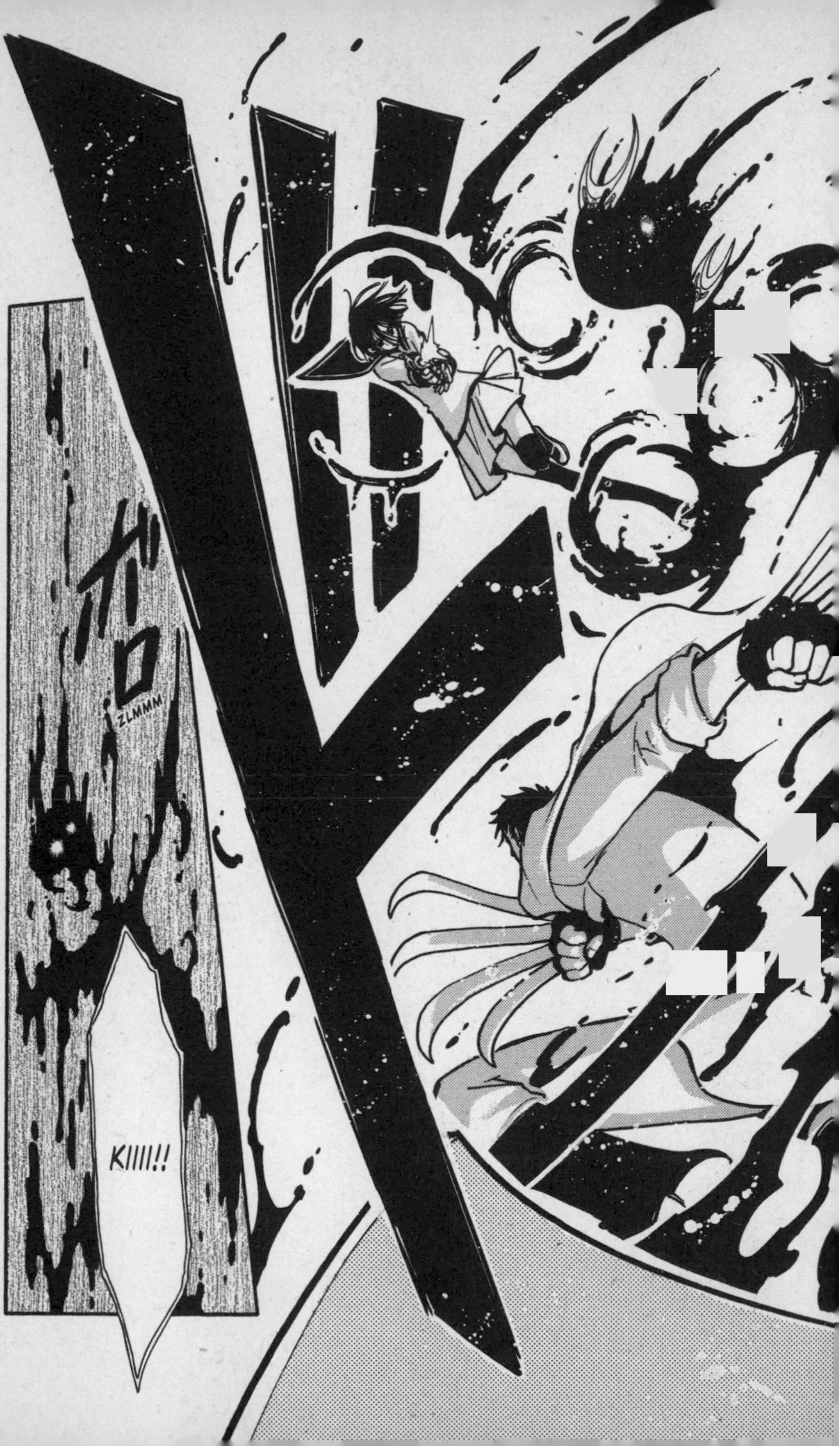
ガロ
ZLMMM
KIIII!!

WE WERE CARELESS AND HAD A RUN-IN WITH SOME ONI.

HMP WE HAVE CUSTOMERS?

FAI-SAN!!

WE'RE HOME!!

WA!

SSLIP

WAAAA...

WHUMP

SÔMA...

SO THERE'S A SÔMA-SAN IN KUROGANE-SAN'S COUNTRY WHO LOOKS EXACTLY LIKE THIS SÔMA-SAN, HUH?

THANK YOU FOR WATCHING THE SHOP.

MOKONA HELPED OUT, TOO!

KLNK

BUT...

SHADDAP!!

AND YOU WERE SO SURPRISED, YOU DROPPED FAI!!

AH HA HA HA HA

IF THAT'S TRUE, WE MAY MEET MORE IN THE FUTURE. MORE PEOPLE WHO EXIST IN OUR ORIGINAL WORLDS...

...I GUESS IT'S TRUE THAT A VARIETY OF WORLDS EXIST.

JUST LIKE THE SPACE-TIME WITCH SAID, THEY'RE THE SAME AND YET NOT THE SAME.

94

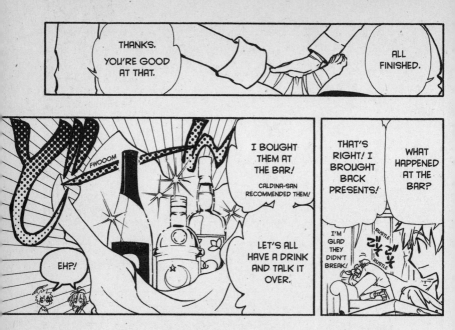

THANKS.

YOU'RE GOOD AT THAT.

ALL FINISHED.

FWOOOM

I BOUGHT THEM AT THE BAR!

CALDINA-SAN RECOMMENDED THEM!

LET'S ALL HAVE A DRINK AND TALK IT OVER.

EH?!

THAT'S RIGHT! I BROUGHT BACK PRESENTS!

WHAT HAPPENED AT THE BAR?

I'M GLAD THEY DIDN'T BREAK!

RUSTLE RUSTLE

UH HU HU!

HU-MEOWW

AH HA HA!

HO-MEOWW

FRA-MEOWW

EH HEH HEH!

...THERE WAS THIS BEAUTIFUL SINGER AND THIS REALLY CUTE BARTENDER THERE AT THE BAR...

AND SO...

AND WE HAD THIS NICE LONG CONVERSATION...

MEOOOW!

MEOW MEOW MEOW MEOW

IF YOU GET DRUNK SO EASILY, DON'T BRING LIQUOR HOME...EVEN IF SOMEBODY *DID* RECOMMEND IT!

I HATE DRUNKS!

MEOW?

HUH? WHAT WAS IT I FOUND SO ODD... MEOW...

BUT THERE WAS SOMETHING ABOUT IT THAT WAS A LITTLE ODD... MEOW...

LISTEN! YÛKO SAID WE JUST *GOTTA* NAME THE CAFÉ "CAT'S EYE"!

MEOW? WE HAVEN'T NAMED IT YET... MEOW...

AH!

AND THEN... I TOLD THEM I RAN A CAFÉ OF MY OWN...

...SOMETHING THEY SAID WHEN I TOLD THEM THE NAME OF THE CAFÉ... MEOW...

96

100

ツバサ

RESERVoir CHRoNiCLE

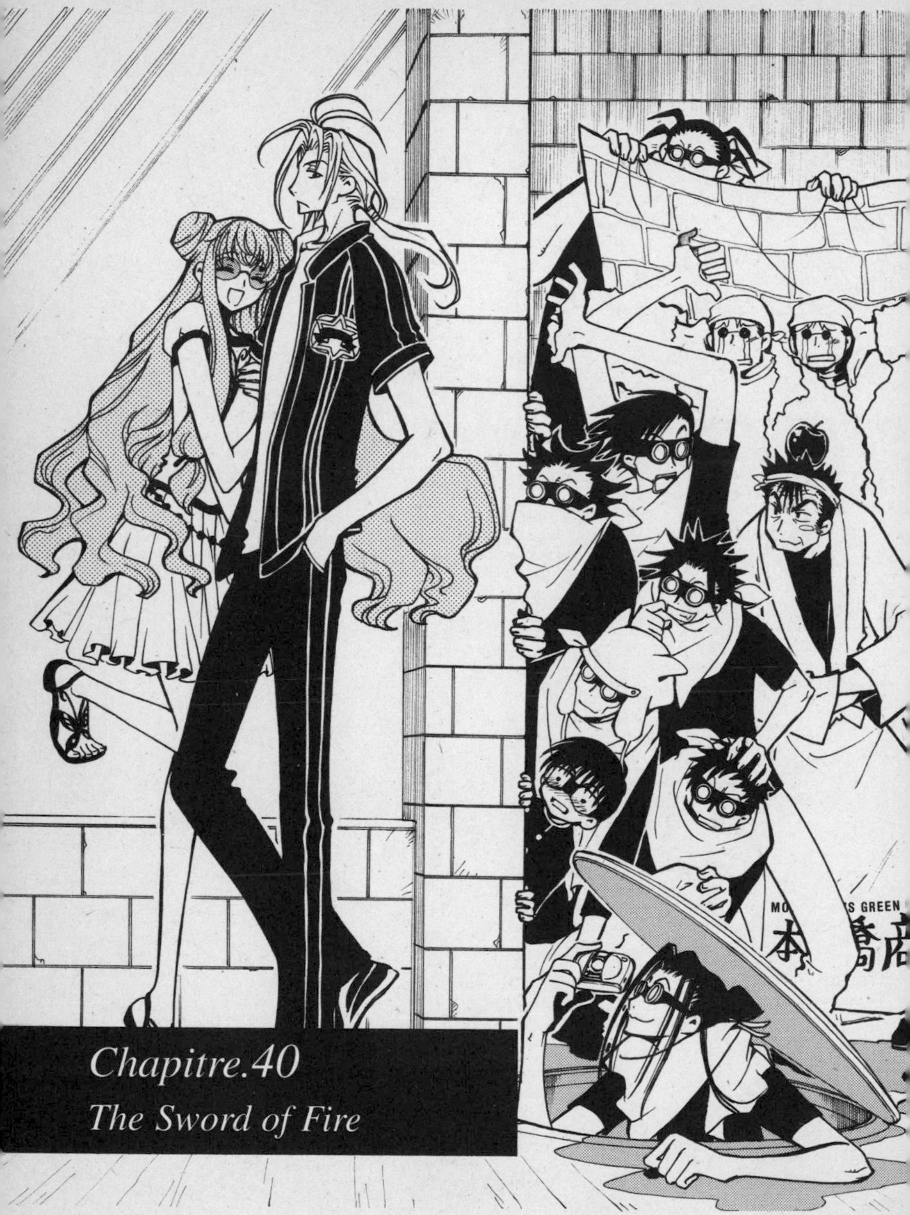

Chapitre.40
The Sword of Fire

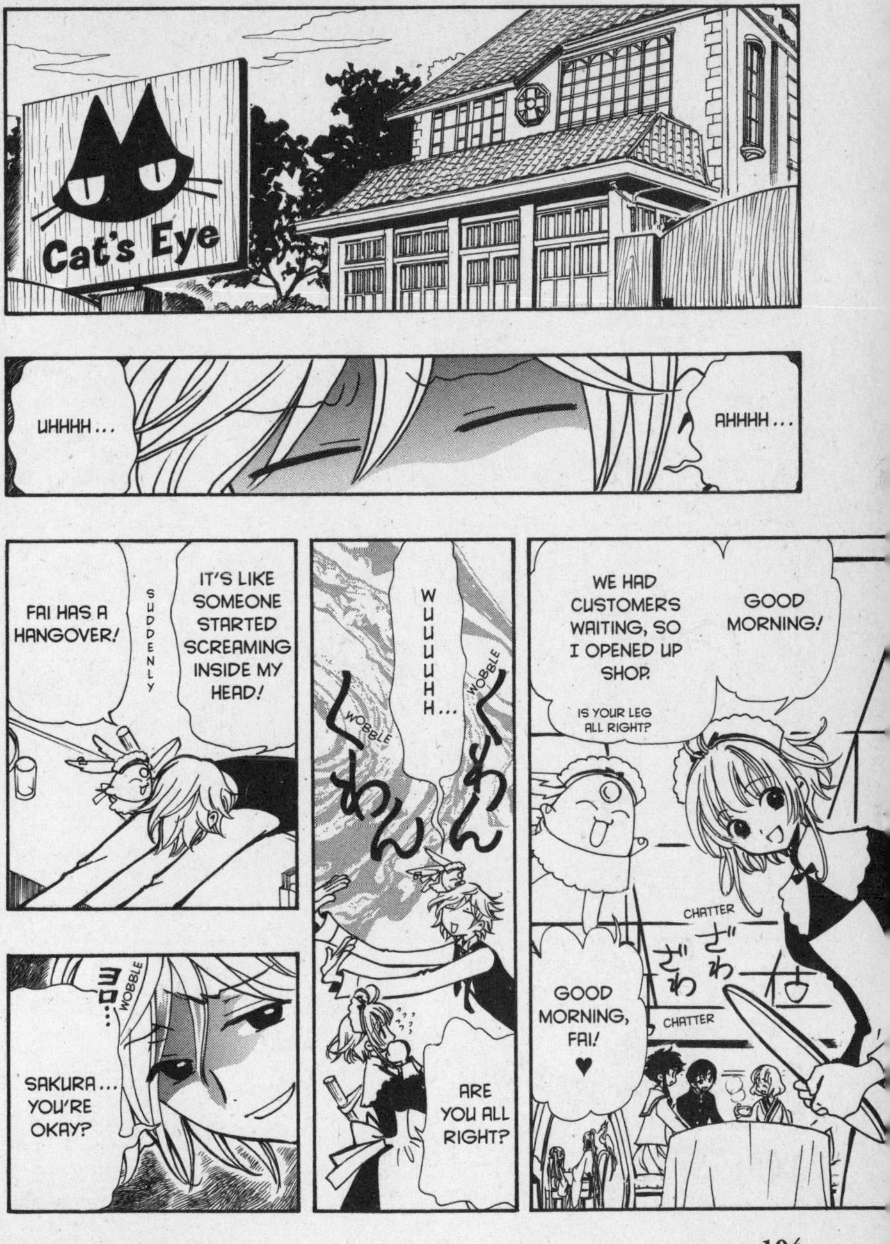
Cat's Eye
AHHHH...
UHHHH...
GOOD MORNING!
WE HAD CUSTOMERS WAITING, SO I OPENED UP SHOP.
IS YOUR LEG ALL RIGHT?
ざわ
CHATTER
ざわ
CHATTER
GOOD MORNING, FAI! ♥
くわん
WOBBLE
WUUUUHH...
くわん
WOBBLE
ARE YOU ALL RIGHT?
IT'S LIKE SOMEONE STARTED SCREAMING INSIDE MY HEAD!
SUDDENLY
FAI HAS A HANGOVER!
ヨロ...
WOBBLE
SAKURA... YOU'RE OKAY?

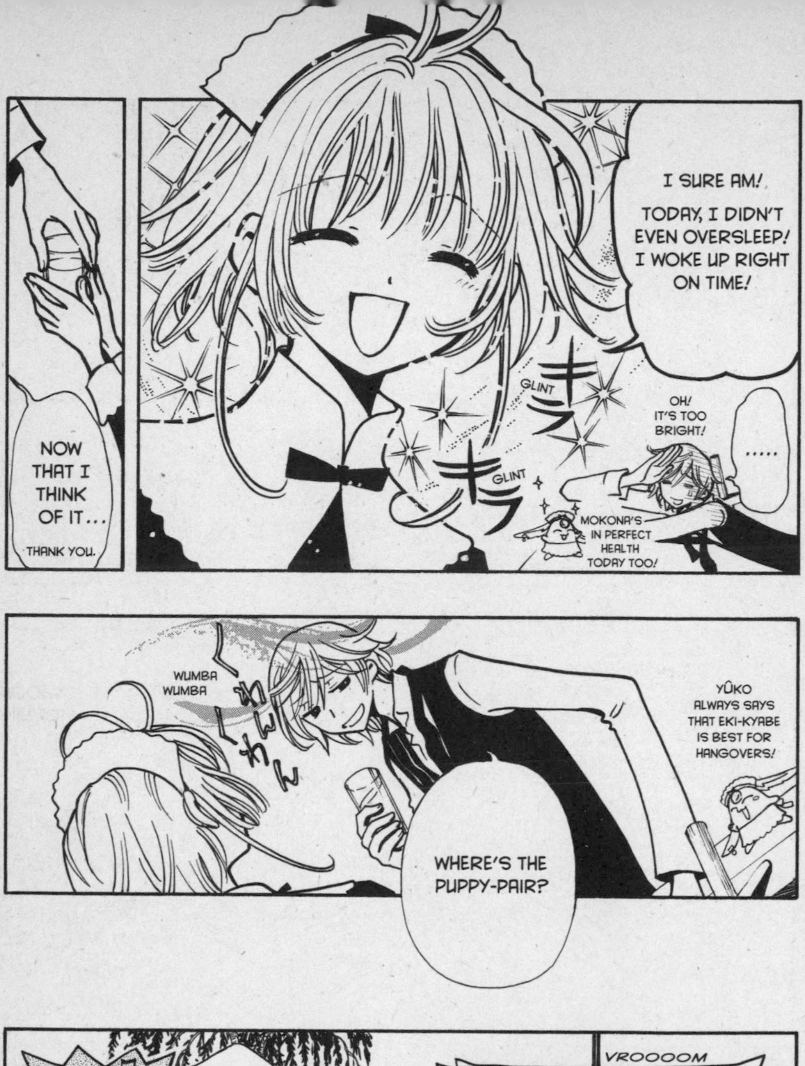
I SURE AM!
TODAY, I DIDN'T EVEN OVERSLEEP! I WOKE UP RIGHT ON TIME!
.....
OH! IT'S TOO BRIGHT!
GLINT
GLINT
MOKONA'S IN PERFECT HEALTH TODAY TOO!
NOW THAT I THINK OF IT...
THANK YOU.
YÛKO ALWAYS SAYS THAT EKI-KYABE IS BEST FOR HANGOVERS!
WHERE'S THE PUPPY-PAIR?
WUMBA WUMBA
VROOOOM
URRGH!
ZHAAN ZHAAN
BEE-BEEEP

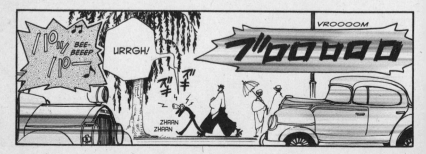

HERE IT IS...

Chanan's

RATTLE

ZHAAN
ZHAAN

THOSE TWO KITTIES WERE ESPECIALLY SLIPPERY— THEY CONSTANTLY RAN AWAY!

YOU HAVE NO IDEA HOW MUCH TROUBLE IT WAS JUST TO GET YOU GUYS TO BED!

THAT MEANS THE THREE OF YOU WON'T BE DRINKING FOR A LONG TIME TO COME, RIGHT?

AH...

R-RIGHT...

ЗOOO...

WOBBBBBLE

WE'RE HERE TO SHOP.

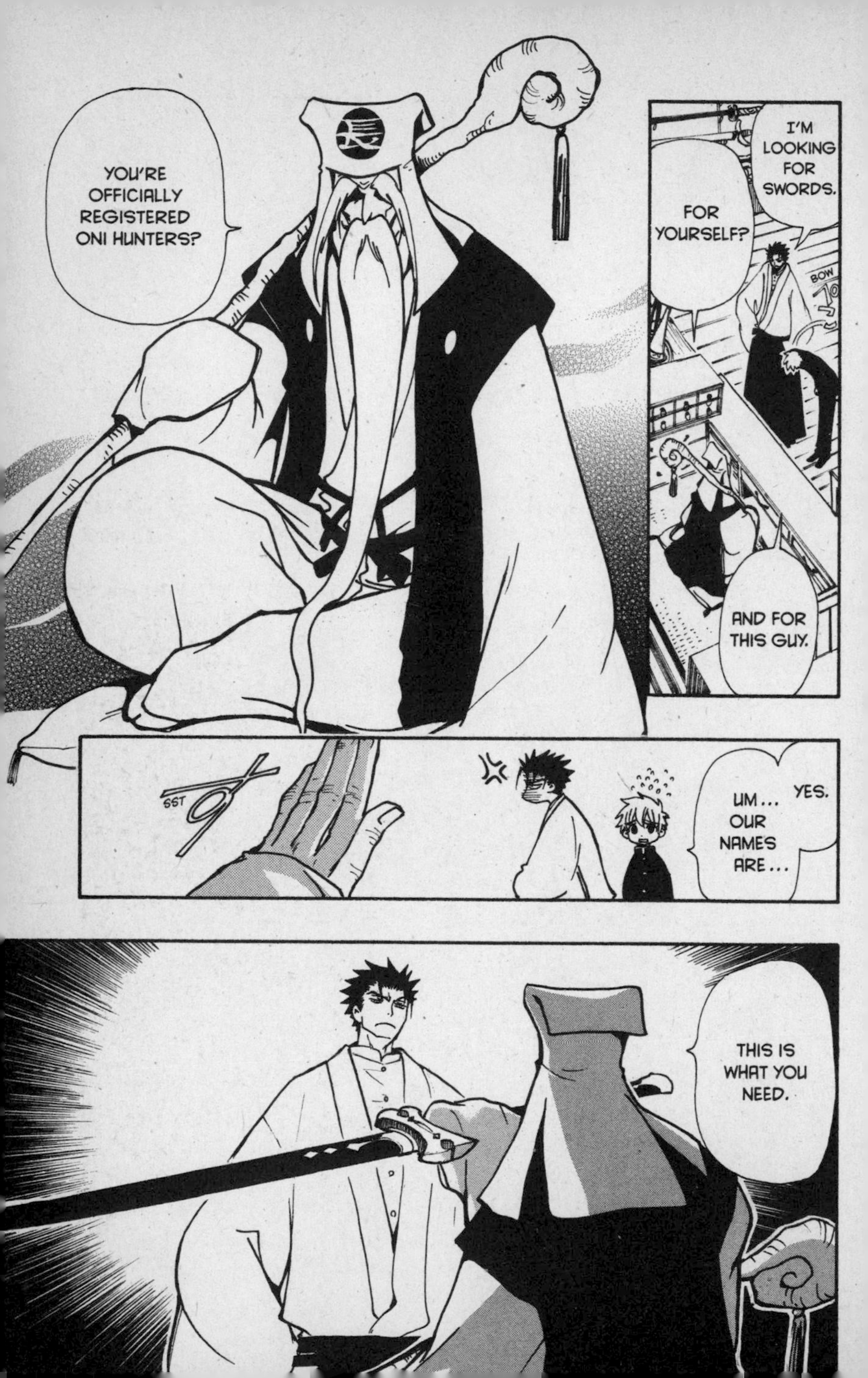
I'M LOOKING FOR SWORDS.
FOR YOURSELF?
BOW
AND FOR THIS GUY.
YOU'RE OFFICIALLY REGISTERED ONI HUNTERS?
YES.
UM... OUR NAMES ARE...
SST
THIS IS WHAT YOU NEED.

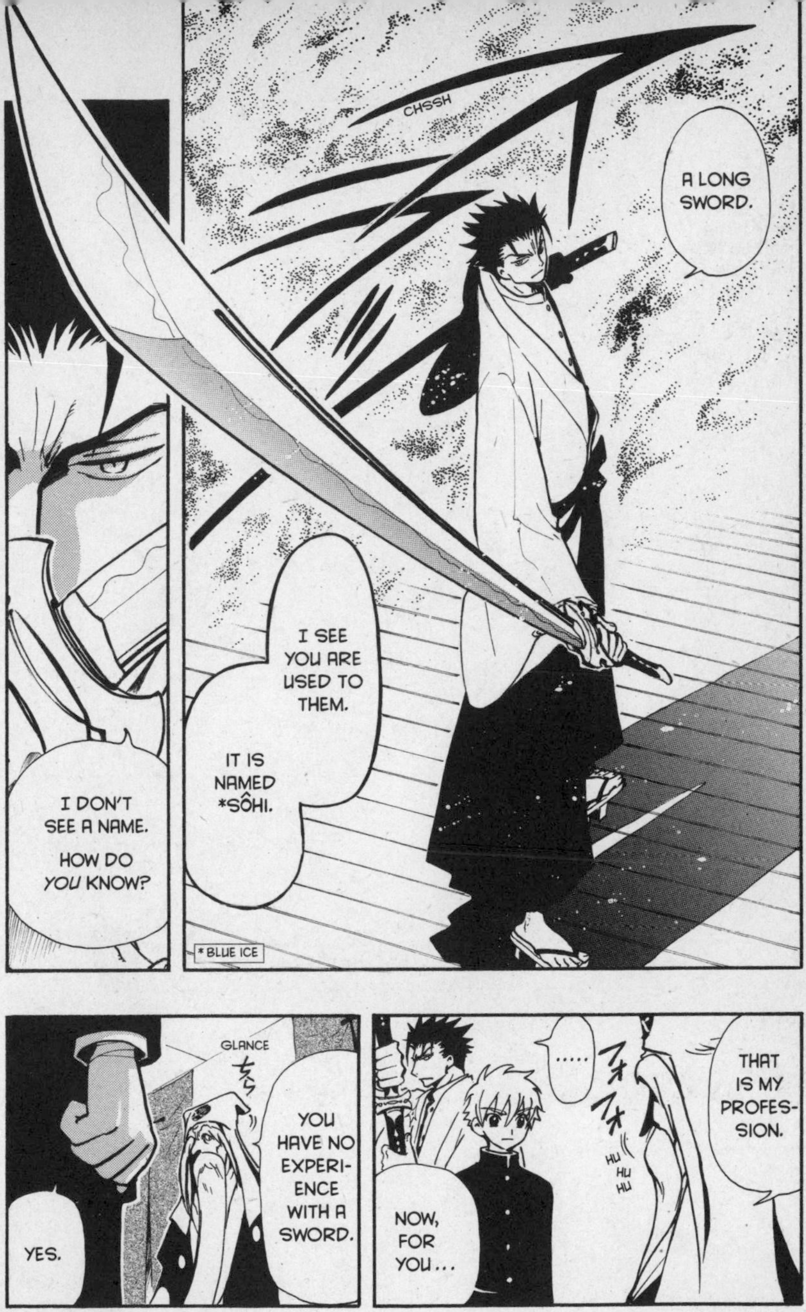
CHSSH
A LONG SWORD.
I SEE YOU ARE USED TO THEM.
IT IS NAMED *SÔHI.
I DON'T SEE A NAME.
HOW DO *YOU* KNOW?
*BLUE ICE
THAT IS MY PROFES-SION.
フォフォ
HU HU HU
......
NOW, FOR YOU...
GLANCE
ちら
YOU HAVE NO EXPERI-ENCE WITH A SWORD.
YES.

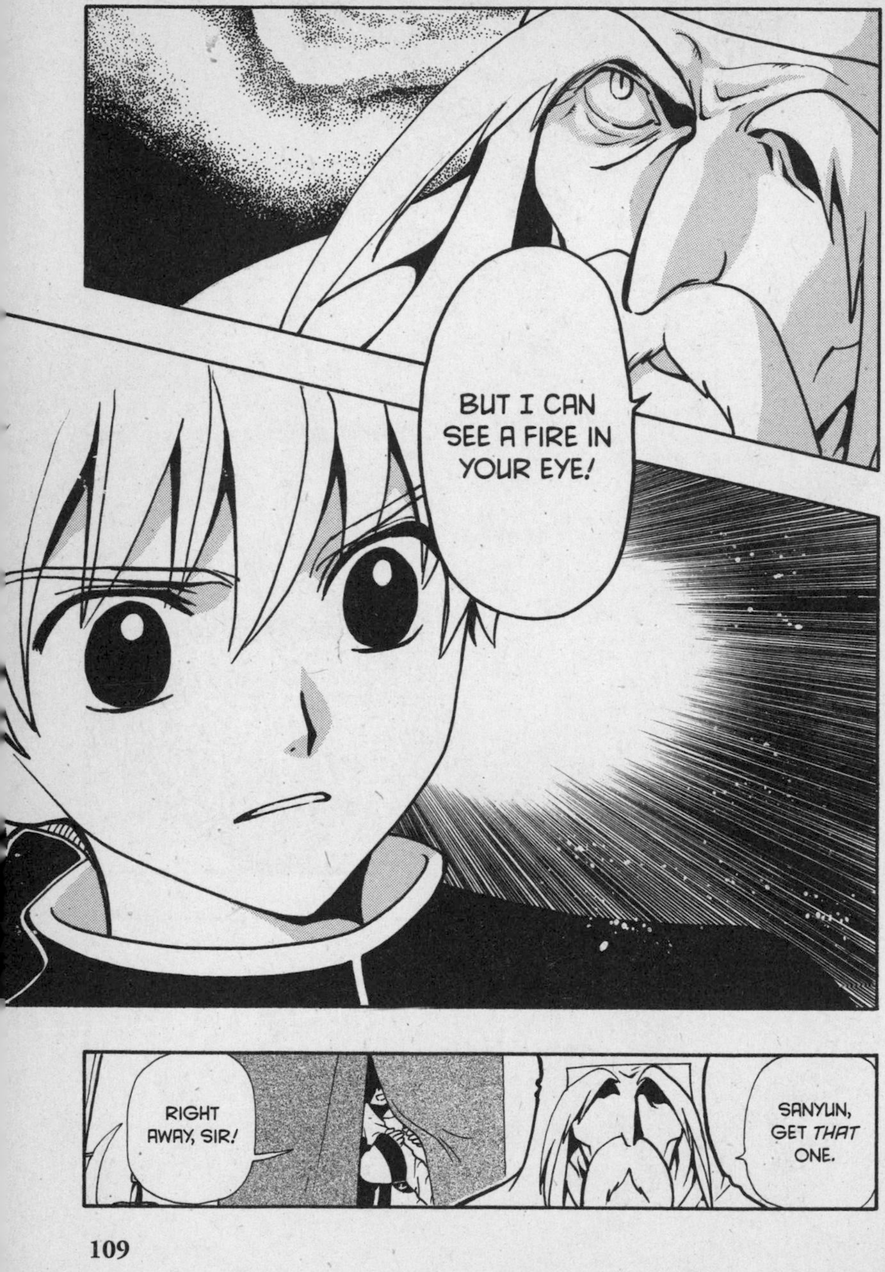
BUT I CAN SEE A FIRE IN YOUR EYE!
SANYUN, GET *THAT* ONE.
RIGHT AWAY, SIR!

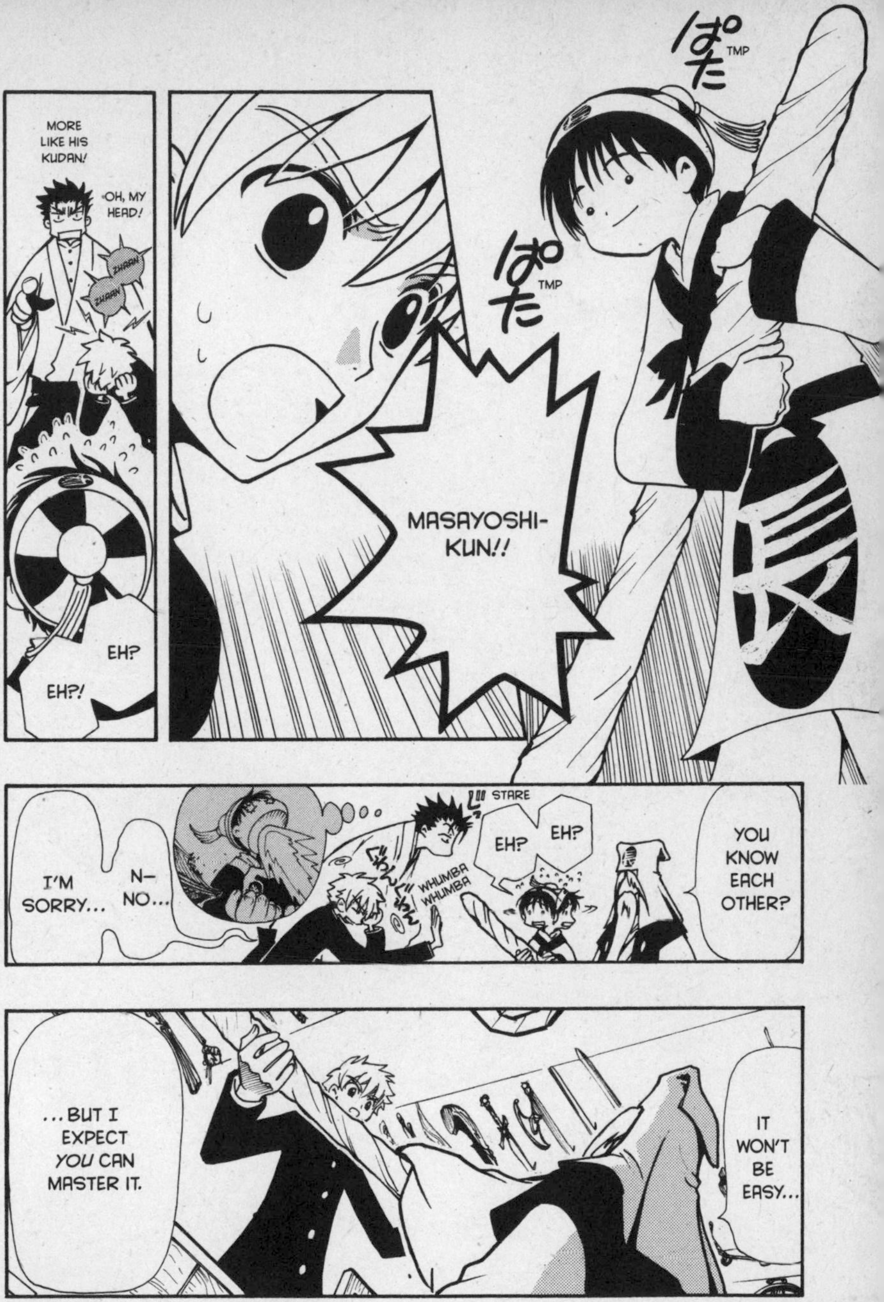

ぱた
TMP
ぱた
TMP
MASAYOSHI-KUN!!
MORE LIKE HIS KUDAN!
OH, MY HEAD!
ZHAAN
ZHAAN
EH?
EH?!
YOU KNOW EACH OTHER?
EH?
EH?
STARE
WHUMBA WHUMBA
N— NO...
I'M SORRY...
IT WON'T BE EASY...
...BUT I EXPECT *YOU* CAN MASTER IT.

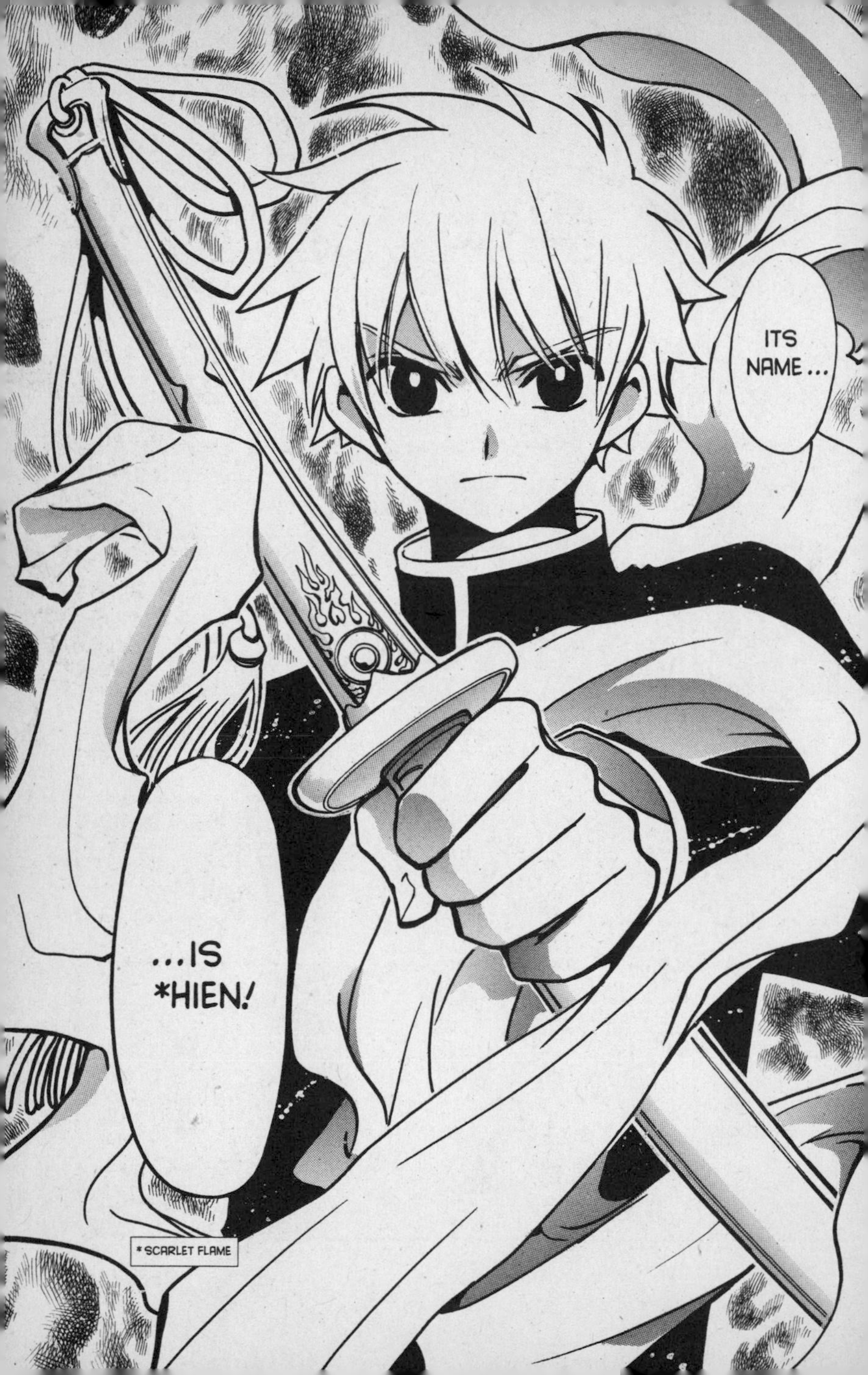
ITS NAME...
...IS *HIEN!
* SCARLET FLAME

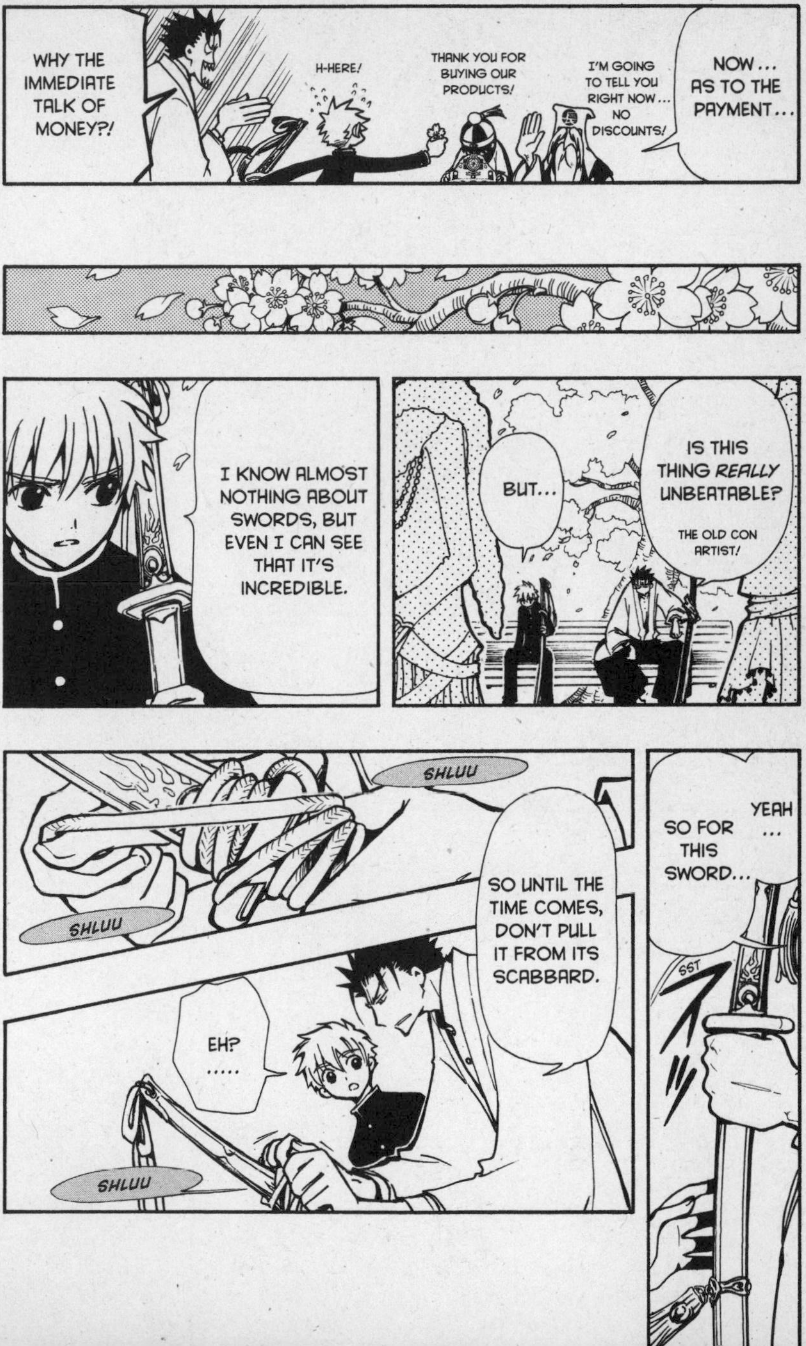
NOW... AS TO THE PAYMENT...
I'M GOING TO TELL YOU RIGHT NOW... NO DISCOUNTS!
THANK YOU FOR BUYING OUR PRODUCTS!
H-HERE!
WHY THE IMMEDIATE TALK OF MONEY?!
IS THIS THING *REALLY* UNBEATABLE?
THE OLD CON ARTIST!
BUT...
I KNOW ALMOST NOTHING ABOUT SWORDS, BUT EVEN I CAN SEE THAT IT'S INCREDIBLE.
YEAH ...
SO FOR THIS SWORD...
SST
SHLUU
SO UNTIL THE TIME COMES, DON'T PULL IT FROM ITS SCABBARD.
SHLUU
EH? .....
SHLUU

SO UNTIL YOU ARE READY TO CUT THE THINGS YOU *WANT* TO CUT...

...DON'T DRAW THE SWORD.

ALL RIGHT.

A SWORD DOESN'T CHOOSE ITS OWNER.

...HIMSELF, FOR EXAMPLE.

IF THE ONE WHO USES IT ISN'T READY, THE UNREADY SWORDSMAN MAY CUT SOMETHING HE WASN'T PREPARED TO CUT...

...THE ONE HE'S PROTECTING, FOR EXAMPLE...

...THE THINGS YOU NEED TO DO TO DRAW THAT SWORD.

NOW, LET'S BEGIN...

SHUUM

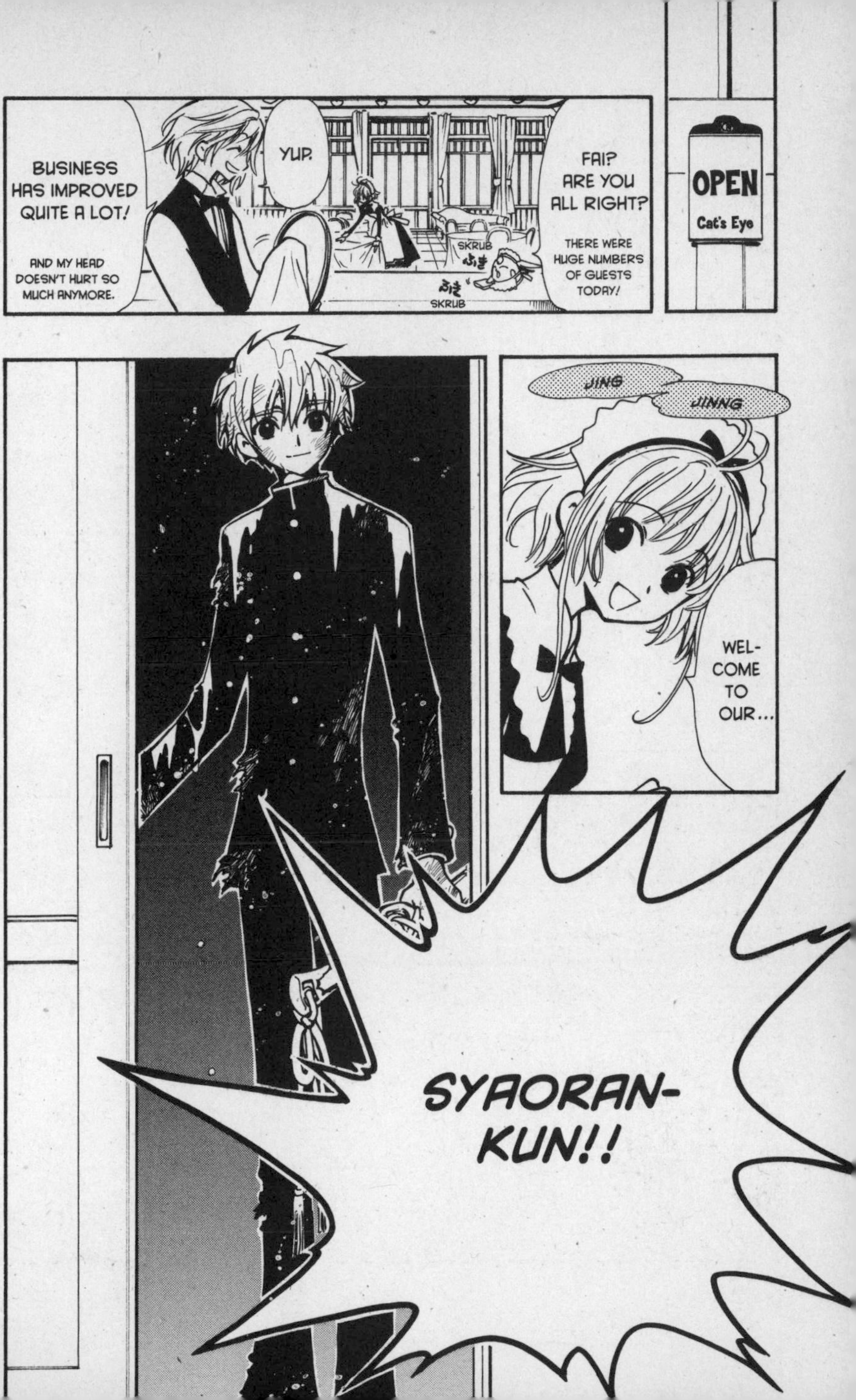
OPEN
Cat's Eye
FAI? ARE YOU ALL RIGHT?
THERE WERE HUGE NUMBERS OF GUESTS TODAY!
SKRUB ふき
ふき SKRUB
YUP.
BUSINESS HAS IMPROVED QUITE A LOT!
AND MY HEAD DOESN'T HURT SO MUCH ANYMORE.
JING
JINNG
WEL-COME TO OUR...
SYAORAN-KUN!!

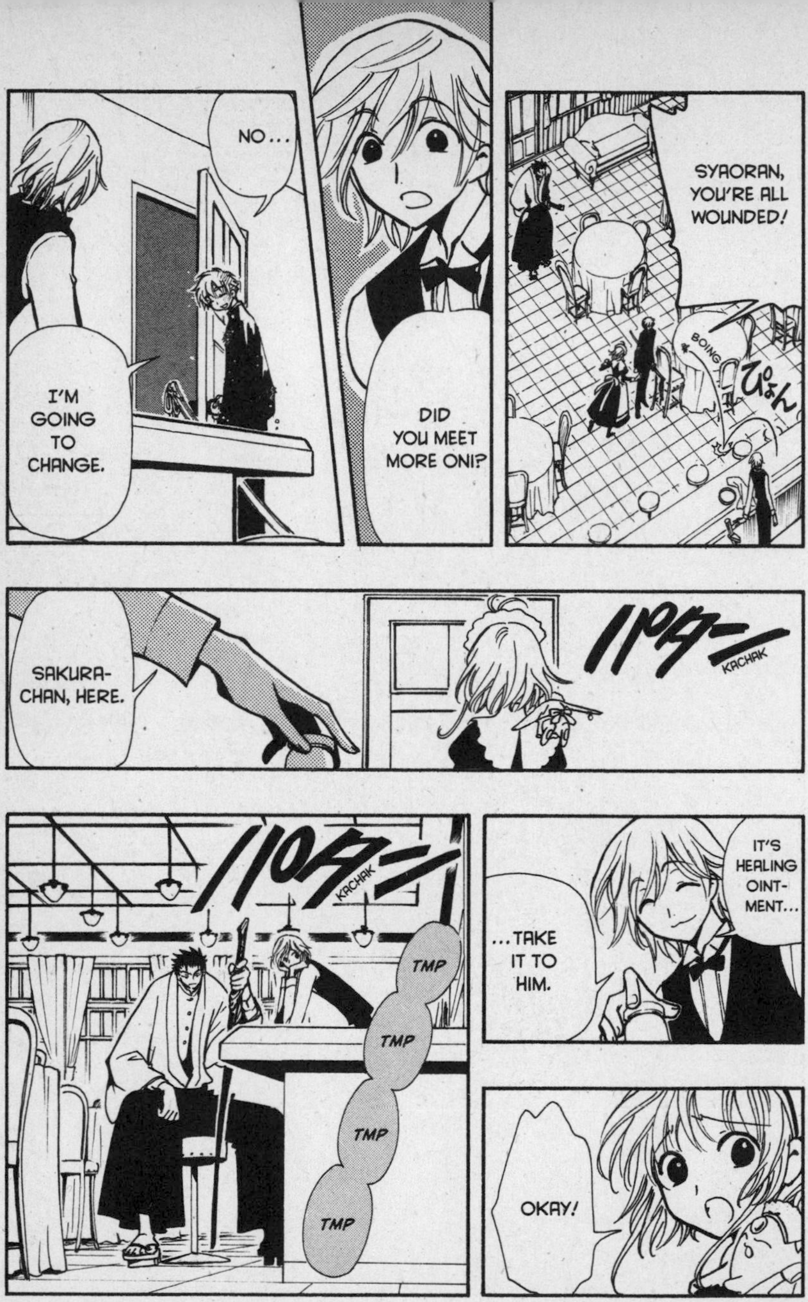
SYAORAN, YOU'RE ALL WOUNDED!
BOING
ぴょん
DID YOU MEET MORE ONI?
NO...
I'M GOING TO CHANGE.
KACHAK
SAKURA-CHAN, HERE.
IT'S HEALING OINT-MENT...
...TAKE IT TO HIM.
OKAY!
KACHAK
TMP
TMP
TMP
TMP

MRFFL
MRFFL
?

I STILL HAD A LITTLE USE OF MY WITS.

BUT WHEN I WOKE UP LATER, I WAS ALREADY IN BED.

AH HA HA HA

あはは

THAT WAS SWORD PRACTICE?

WEREN'T YOU DRUNK?

REMEMBER WHAT ORUHA-SAN SAID ...

"THE ONI IN THE COUNTRY OF ÔTO ALL HAVE ODD SHAPES, AND SO THE ONI HUNTERS HAVE NO TROUBLE DIFFERENTIATING ONI FROM THE CITIZENS, AND NO INNOCENT GETS HURT."

MAYBE ... AND IT'S PROBABLY TRUE THAT HE NEEDS TO RUSH.

KATUNK

YOU WERE A PRETTY STRICT MASTER RIGHT OFF THE BAT.

THAT'S WHAT THE KID WANTED.

116

WHAT I'M WONDERING IS...

...ARE THE ONI... CREATED ON PURPOSE?

DESPITE ALL THAT...

...RECENTLY THE ONI HAVE STARTED TO ACT STRANGE.

DOESN'T IT SEEM LIKE THE ONI IN THIS COUNTRY ARE BEING MANAGED FOR THE BENEFIT OF THE ONI HUNTERS?

THINKING OF IT THAT WAY, I WOULD UNDERSTAND WHY CITY HALL KNOWS ALL OF THE ONIS' MOVEMENTS.

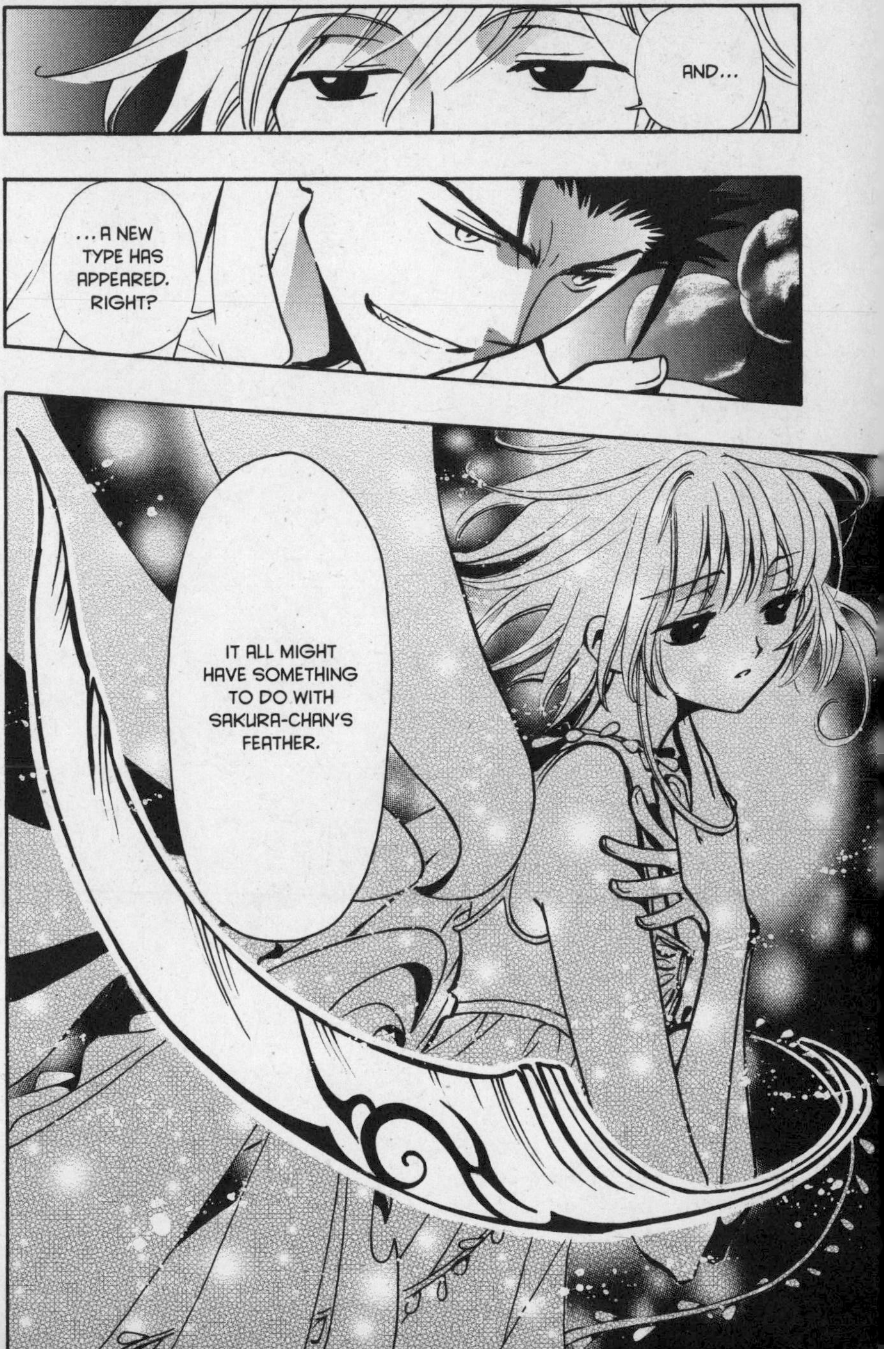
AND...
...A NEW TYPE HAS APPEARED. RIGHT?
IT ALL MIGHT HAVE SOMETHING TO DO WITH SAKURA-CHAN'S FEATHER.

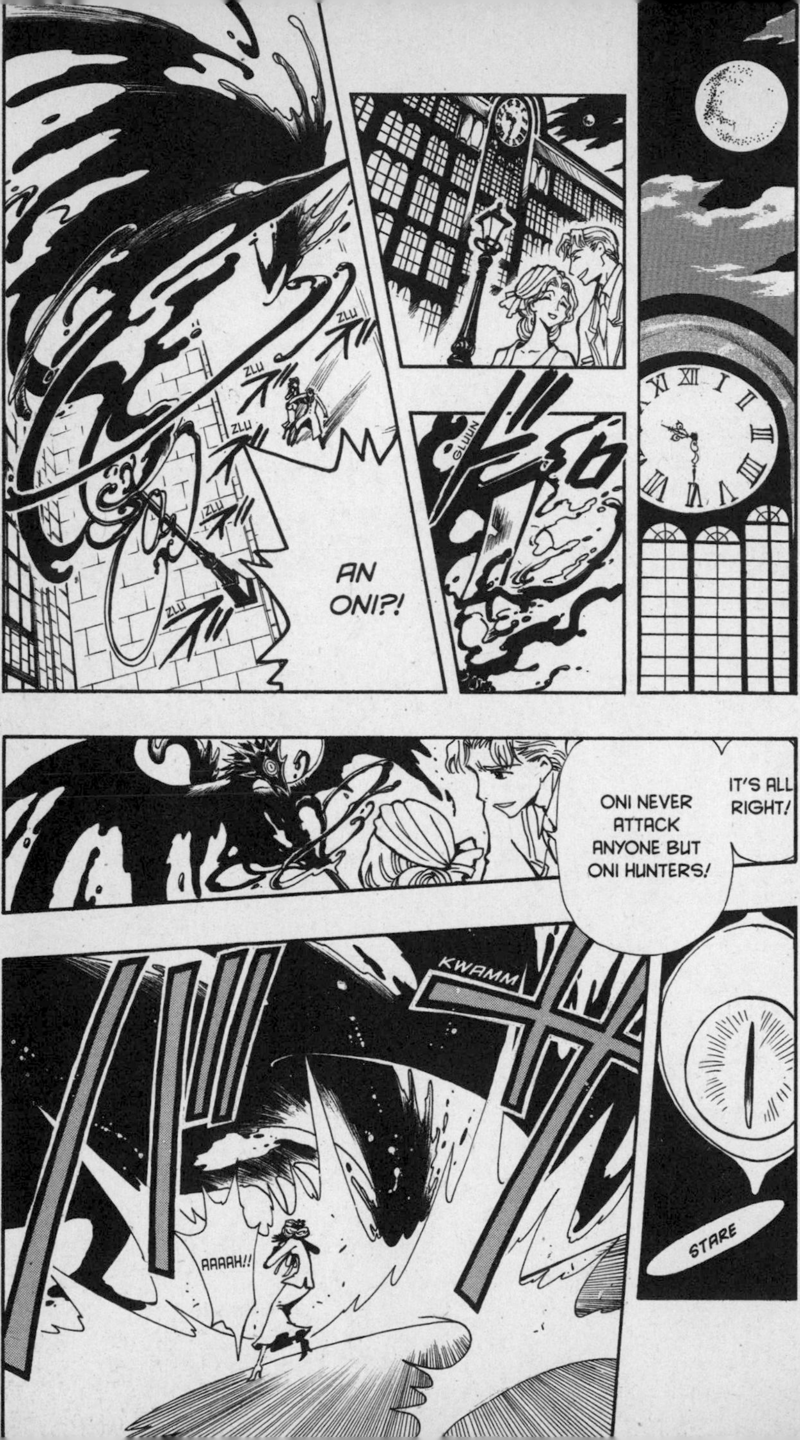
GLUUN
ZLU
ZLU
ZLU
ZLU
ZLU
AN ONI?!
IT'S ALL RIGHT!
ONI NEVER ATTACK ANYONE BUT ONI HUNTERS!
STARE
KWAMM
AAAAH!!

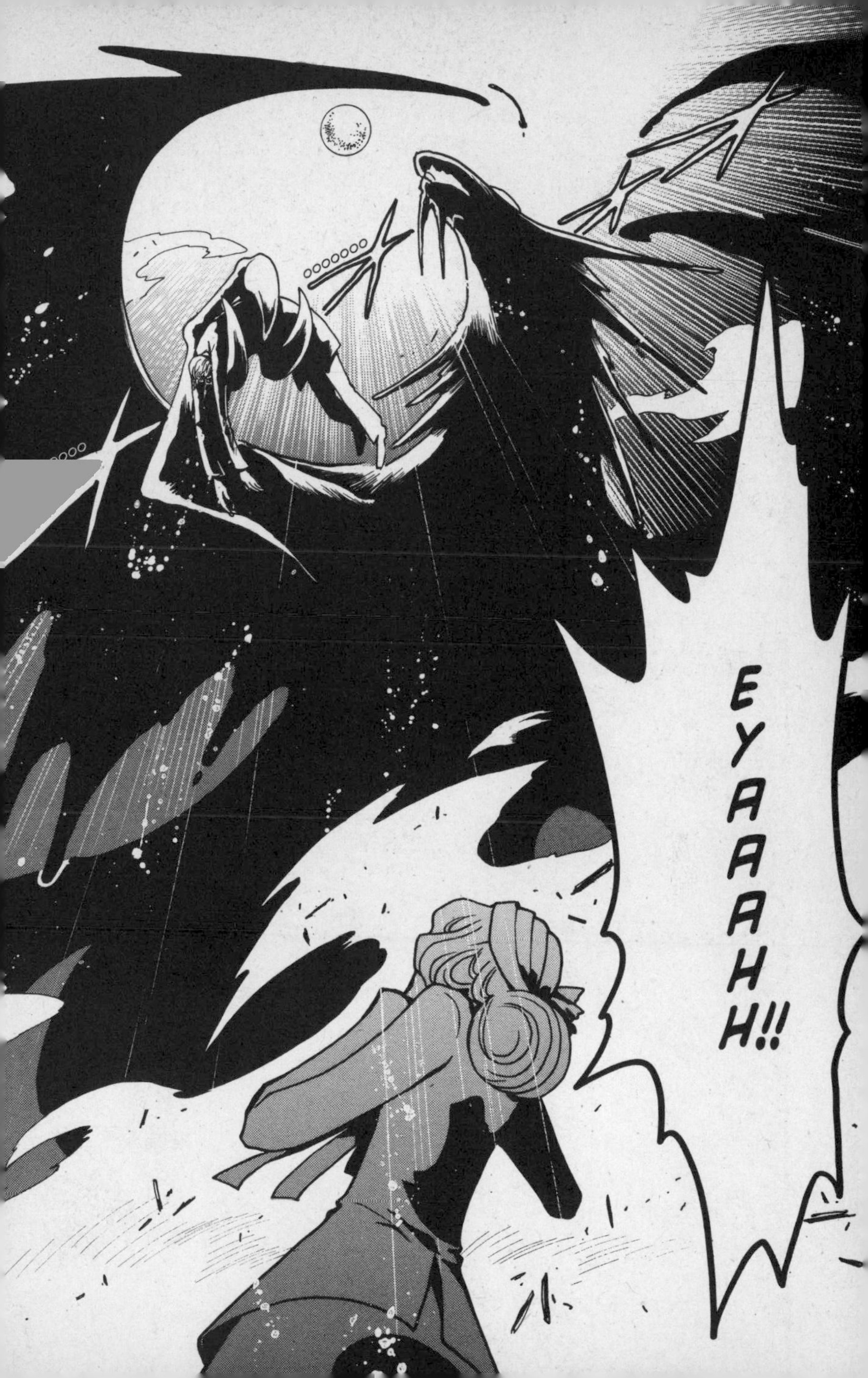
EYAAAAHH!!

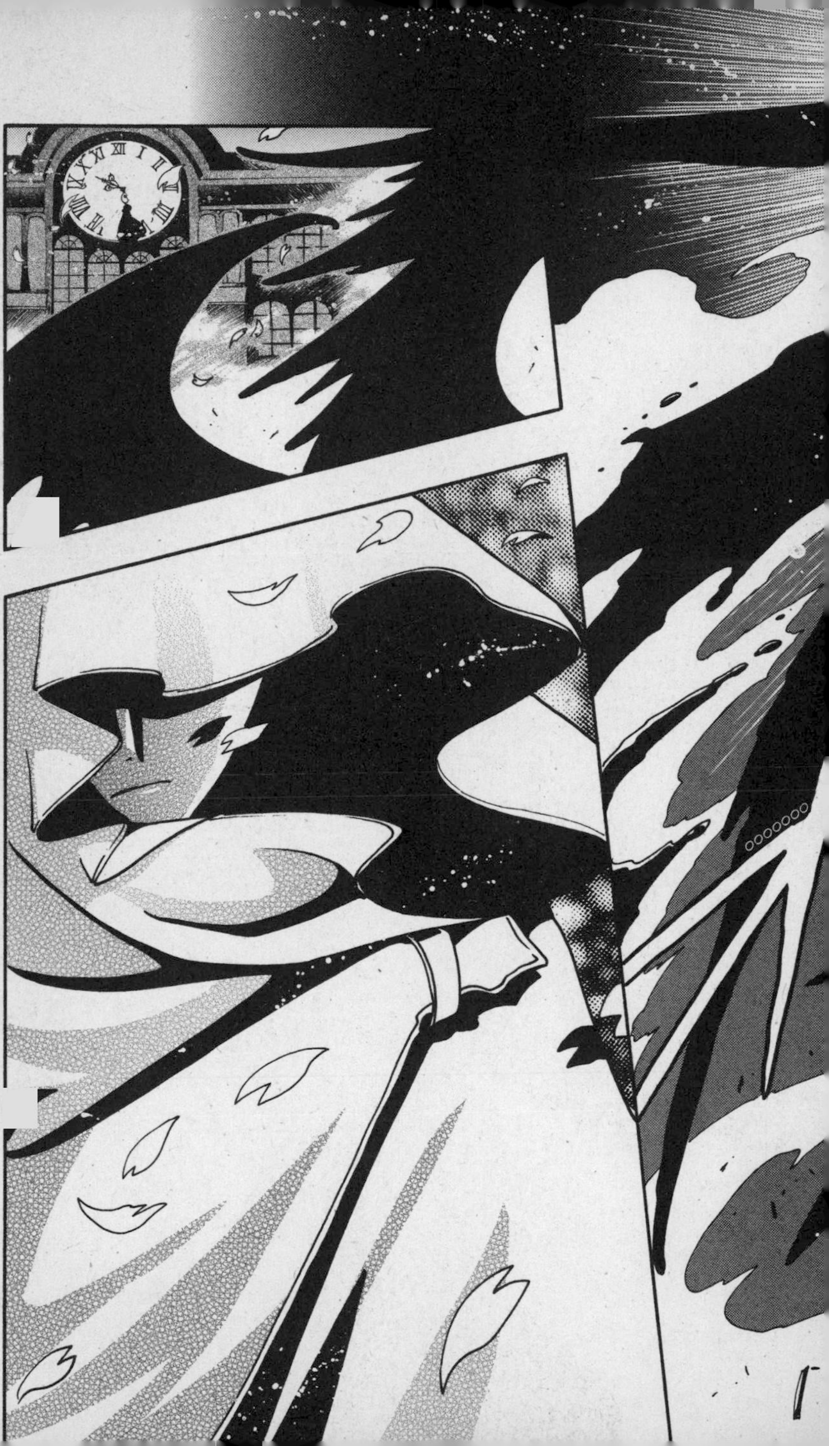

ツバサ

RESERVoir CHRoNiCLE

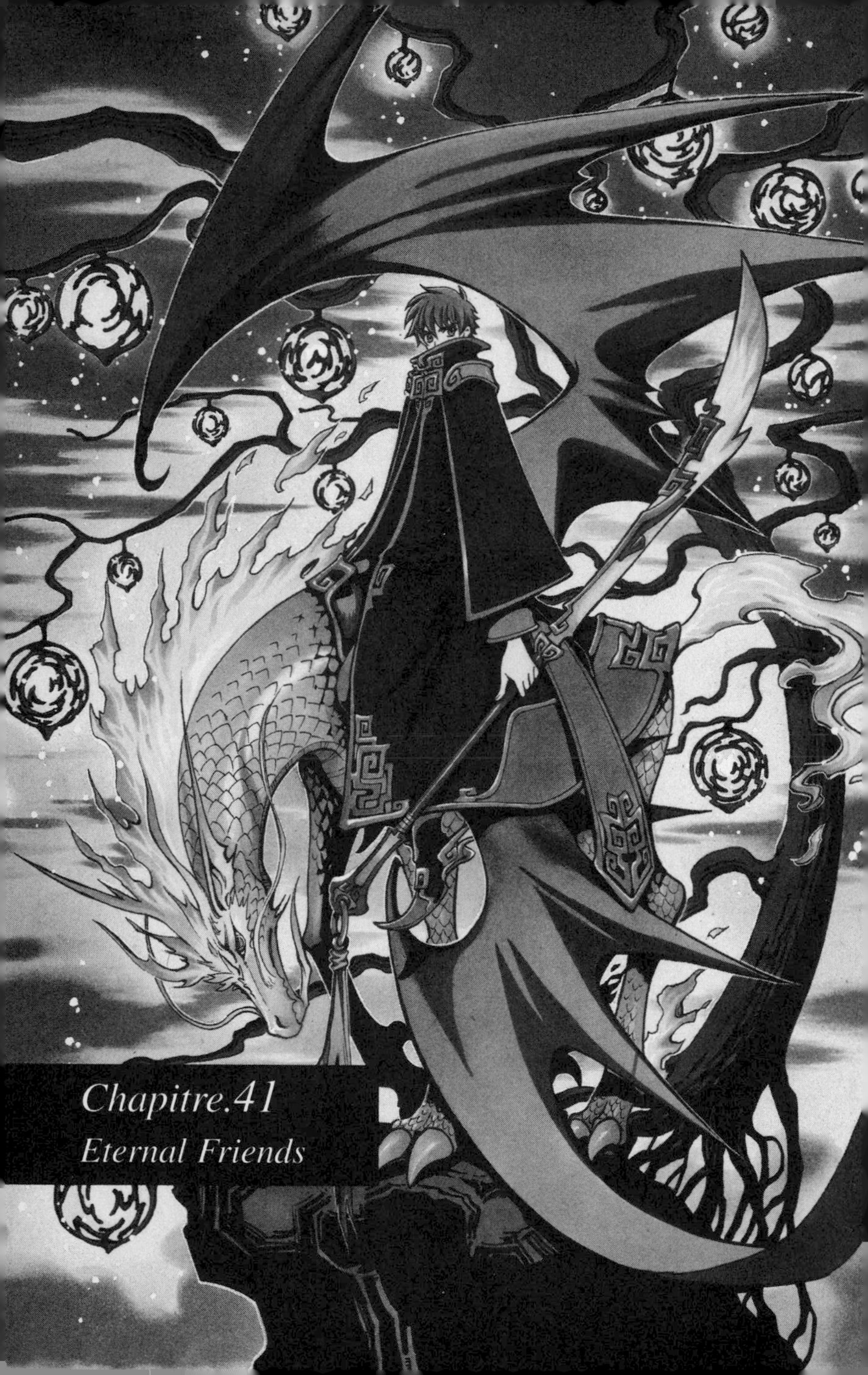

Chapitre.41
Eternal Friends

ツバサ
RESERVoir CHRoNiCLE

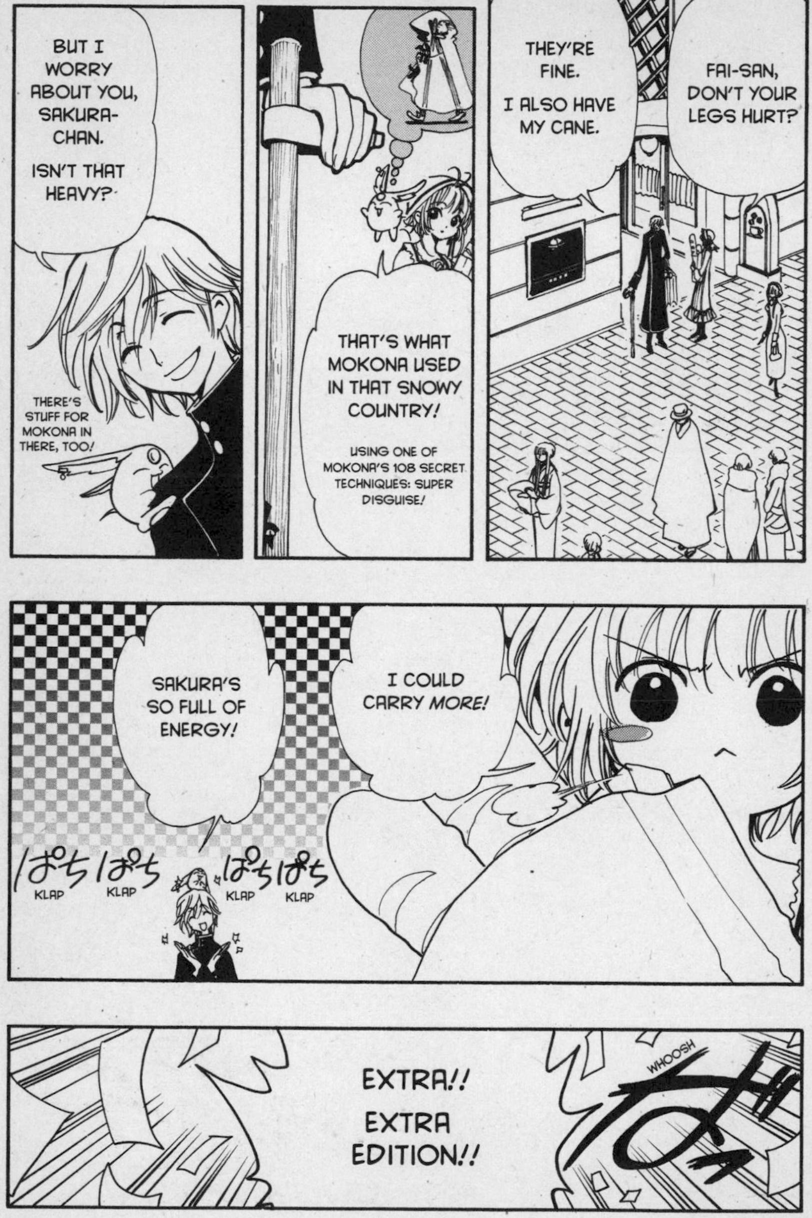
FAI-SAN, DON'T YOUR LEGS HURT?
THEY'RE FINE.
I ALSO HAVE MY CANE.
THAT'S WHAT MOKONA USED IN THAT SNOWY COUNTRY!
USING ONE OF MOKONA'S 108 SECRET TECHNIQUES: SUPER DISGUISE!
BUT I WORRY ABOUT YOU, SAKURA-CHAN.
ISN'T THAT HEAVY?
THERE'S STUFF FOR MOKONA IN THERE, TOO!
I COULD CARRY *MORE!*
SAKURA'S SO FULL OF ENERGY!
ぱちぱち
KLAP KLAP
ぱちぱち
KLAP KLAP
WHOOSH
EXTRA!!
EXTRA EDITION!!

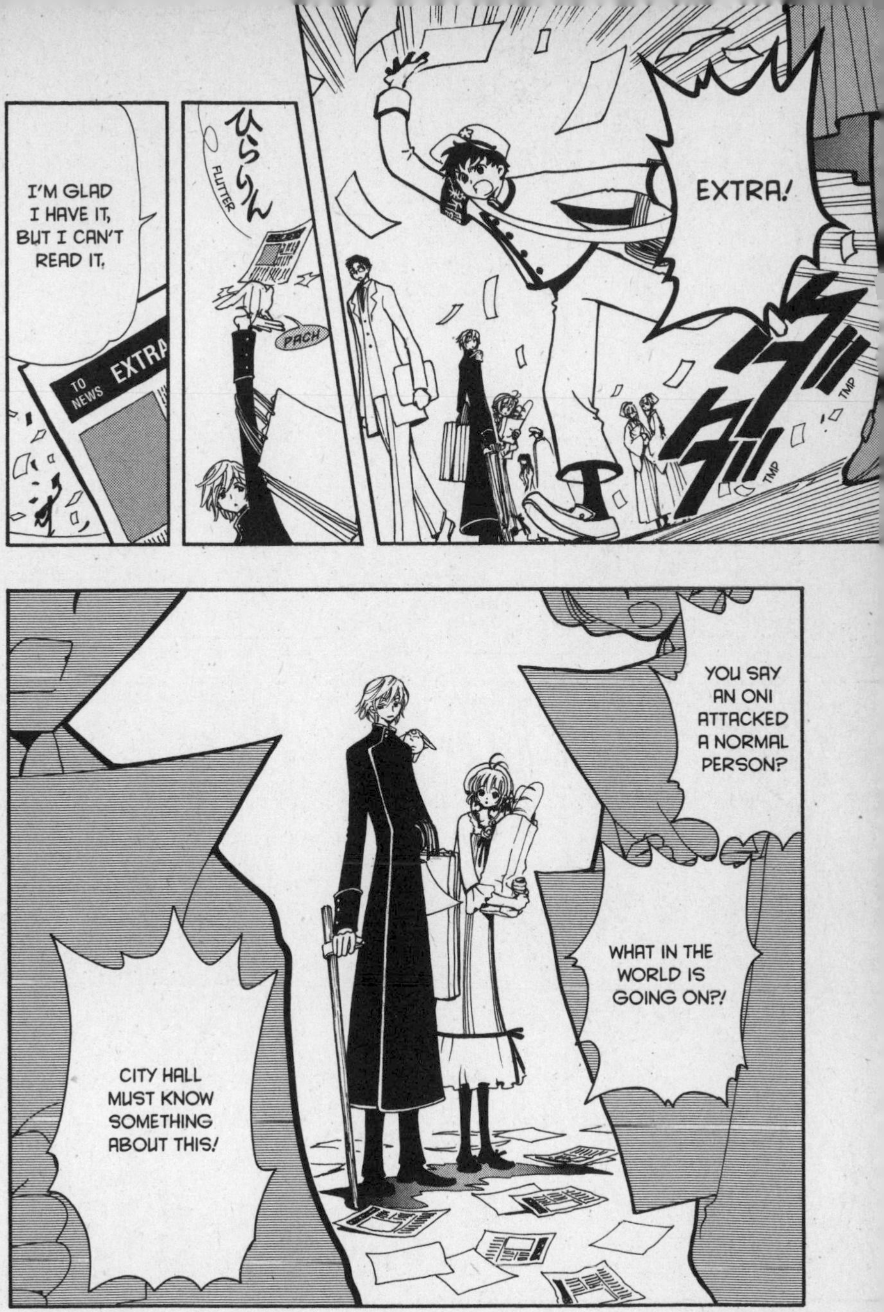
EXTRA!
TMP
TMP
ひらりん
FLUTTER
PACH
I'M GLAD I HAVE IT, BUT I CAN'T READ IT.
TO NEWS
EXTRA
YOU SAY AN ONI ATTACKED A NORMAL PERSON?
WHAT IN THE WORLD IS GOING ON?!
CITY HALL MUST KNOW SOMETHING ABOUT THIS!

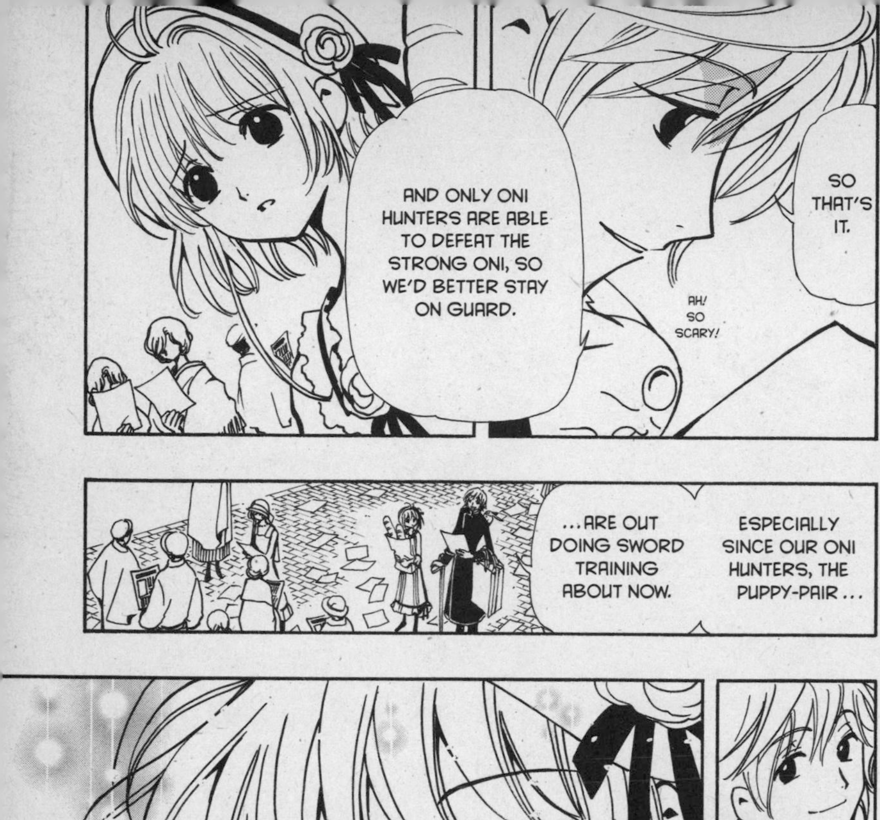

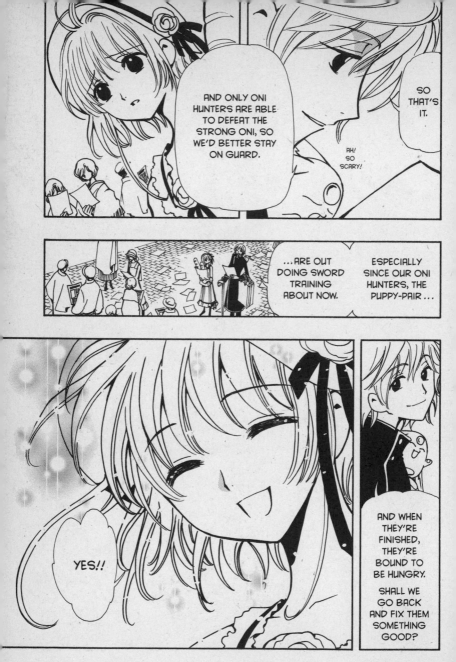

SO THAT'S IT.
AH! SO SCARY!
AND ONLY ONI HUNTERS ARE ABLE TO DEFEAT THE STRONG ONI, SO WE'D BETTER STAY ON GUARD.
ESPECIALLY SINCE OUR ONI HUNTERS, THE PUPPY-PAIR...
...ARE OUT DOING SWORD TRAINING ABOUT NOW.
AND WHEN THEY'RE FINISHED, THEY'RE BOUND TO BE HUNGRY.
SHALL WE GO BACK AND FIX THEM SOMETHING GOOD?
YES!!

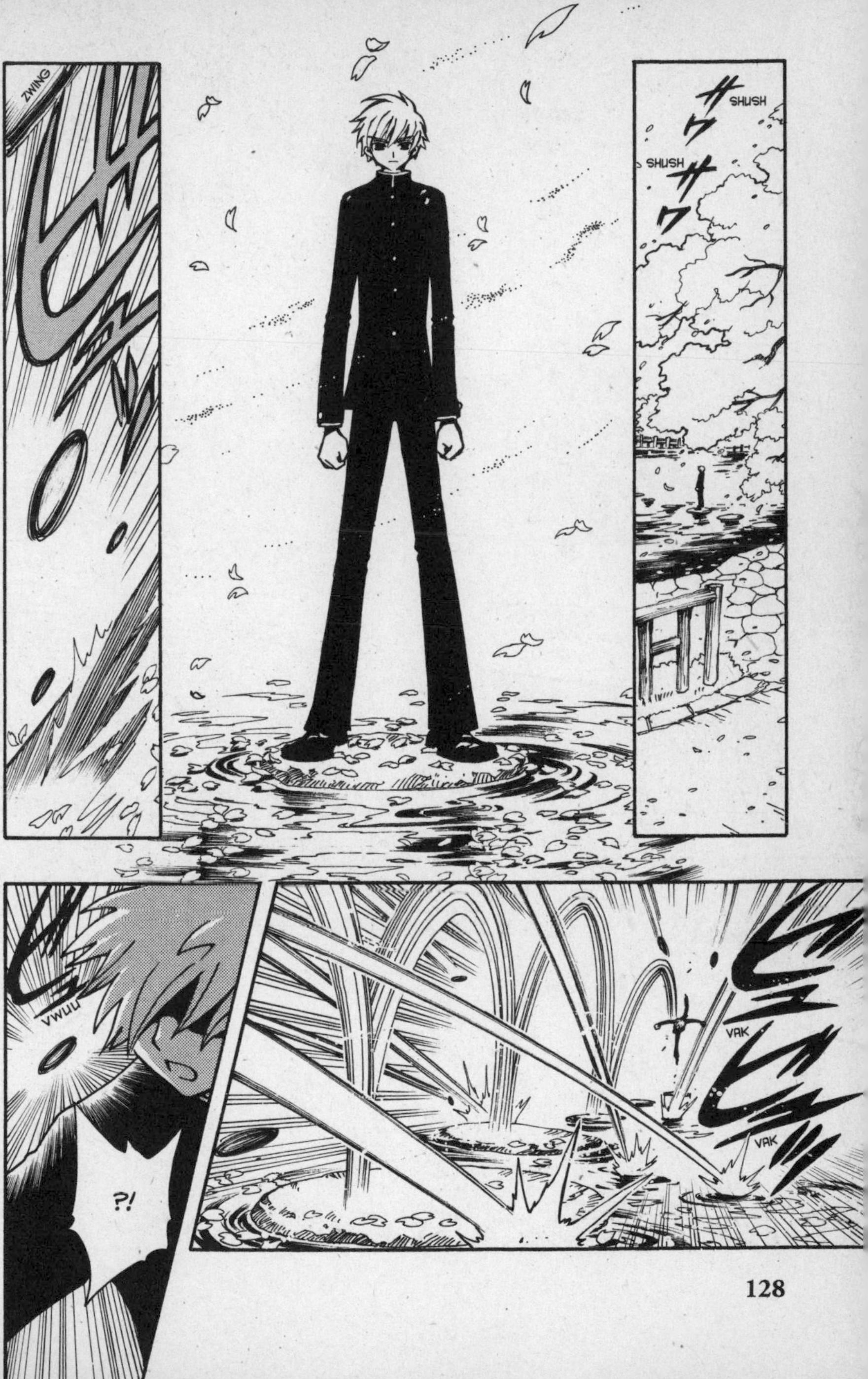
サワ
SHUSH
サワ
SHUSH
ZWING
VAK
VAK
VWUU
?!

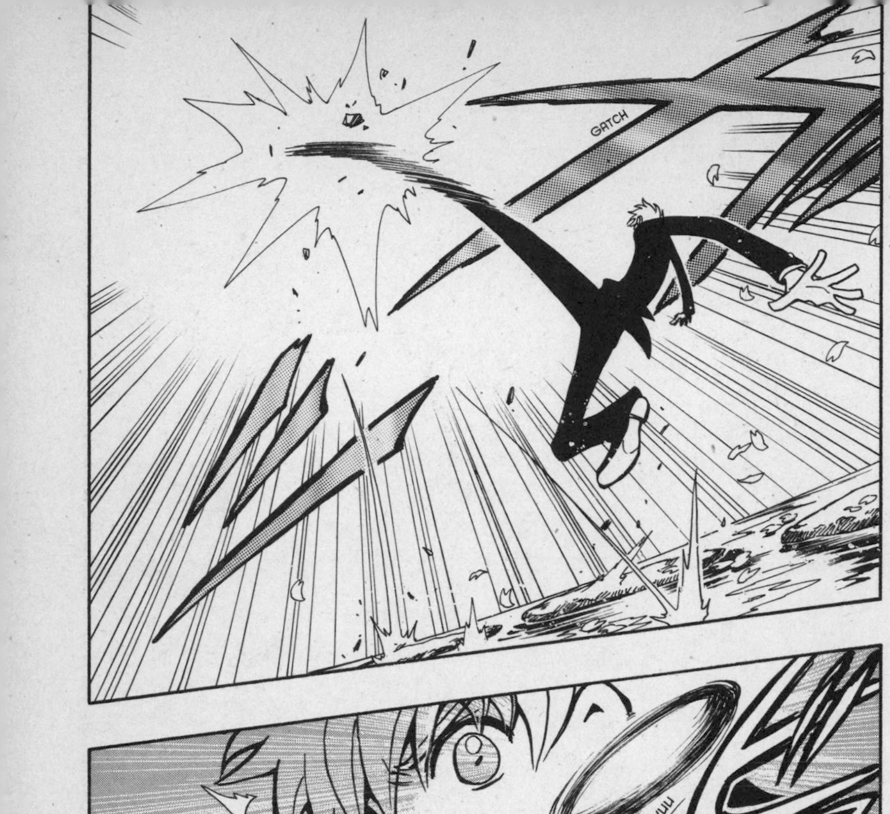

GATCH
VWUU
THWONK
AK!
WOBBLE
SPASSH
I KNEW IT!

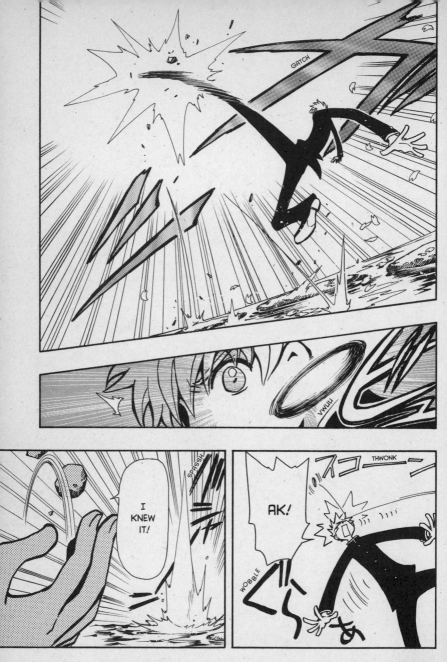

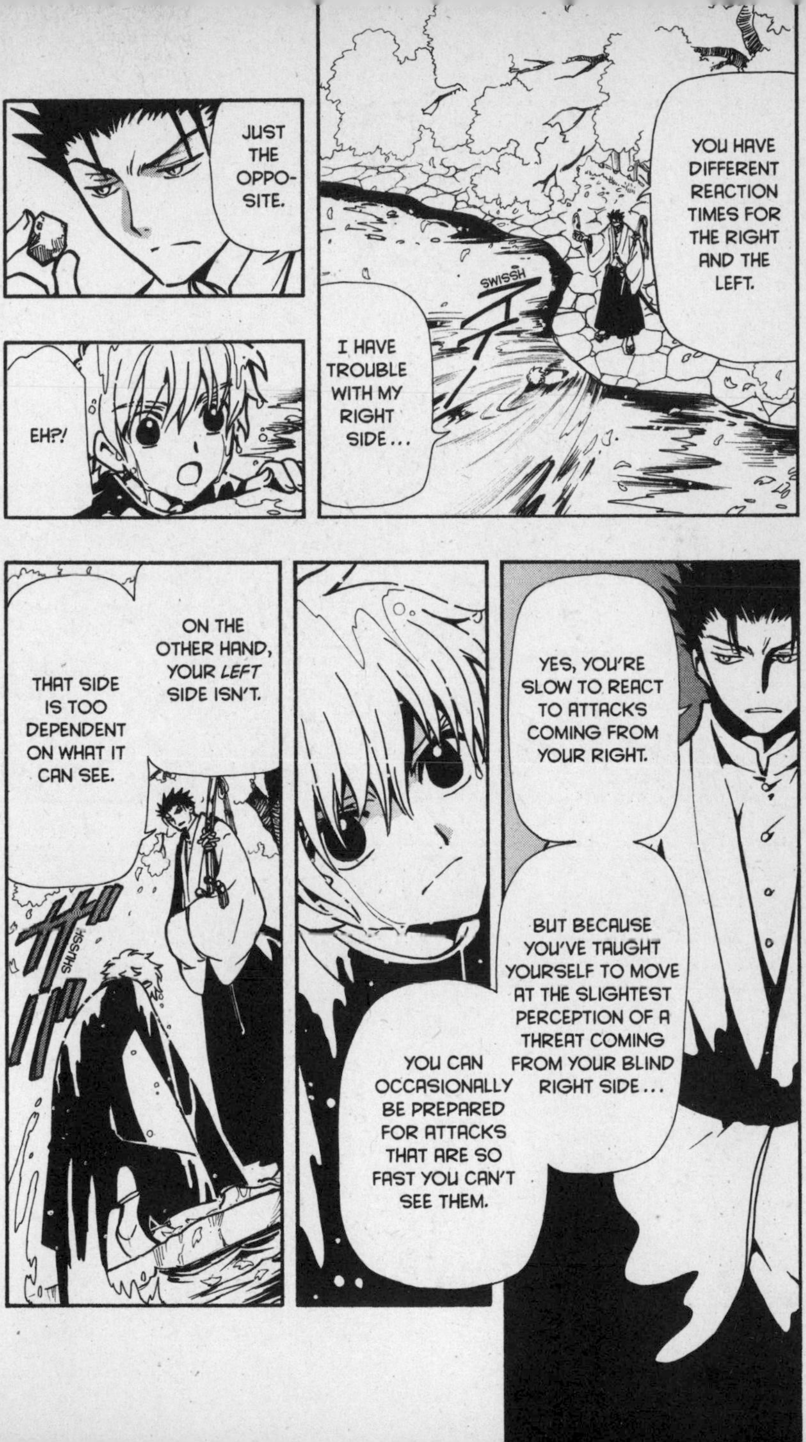
YOU HAVE DIFFERENT REACTION TIMES FOR THE RIGHT AND THE LEFT.
SWISSH
I HAVE TROUBLE WITH MY RIGHT SIDE...
JUST THE OPPO-SITE.
EH?!
YES, YOU'RE SLOW TO REACT TO ATTACKS COMING FROM YOUR RIGHT.
BUT BECAUSE YOU'VE TAUGHT YOURSELF TO MOVE AT THE SLIGHTEST PERCEPTION OF A THREAT COMING FROM YOUR BLIND RIGHT SIDE...
YOU CAN OCCASIONALLY BE PREPARED FOR ATTACKS THAT ARE SO FAST YOU CAN'T SEE THEM.
ON THE OTHER HAND, YOUR *LEFT* SIDE ISN'T.
THAT SIDE IS TOO DEPENDENT ON WHAT IT CAN SEE.
SHUSSH

BLIND YOUR EYES WITH IT AND GO BACK TO THE CAFÉ.

EH?!

PULL OUT THAT THING I GAVE YOU.

OKAY.

YOUR RIGHT SIDE CAN ONLY OCCASIONALLY REACT TO UN-SEEN FORCES.

YOUR LEFT SIDE CAN'T REACT TO THEM AT ALL.

SO YOU'RE GOING TO HAVE TO TRAIN YOURSELF TO BE ABLE TO REACT TO ATTACKS BEFORE YOU SEE THEM ON *BOTH* SIDES.

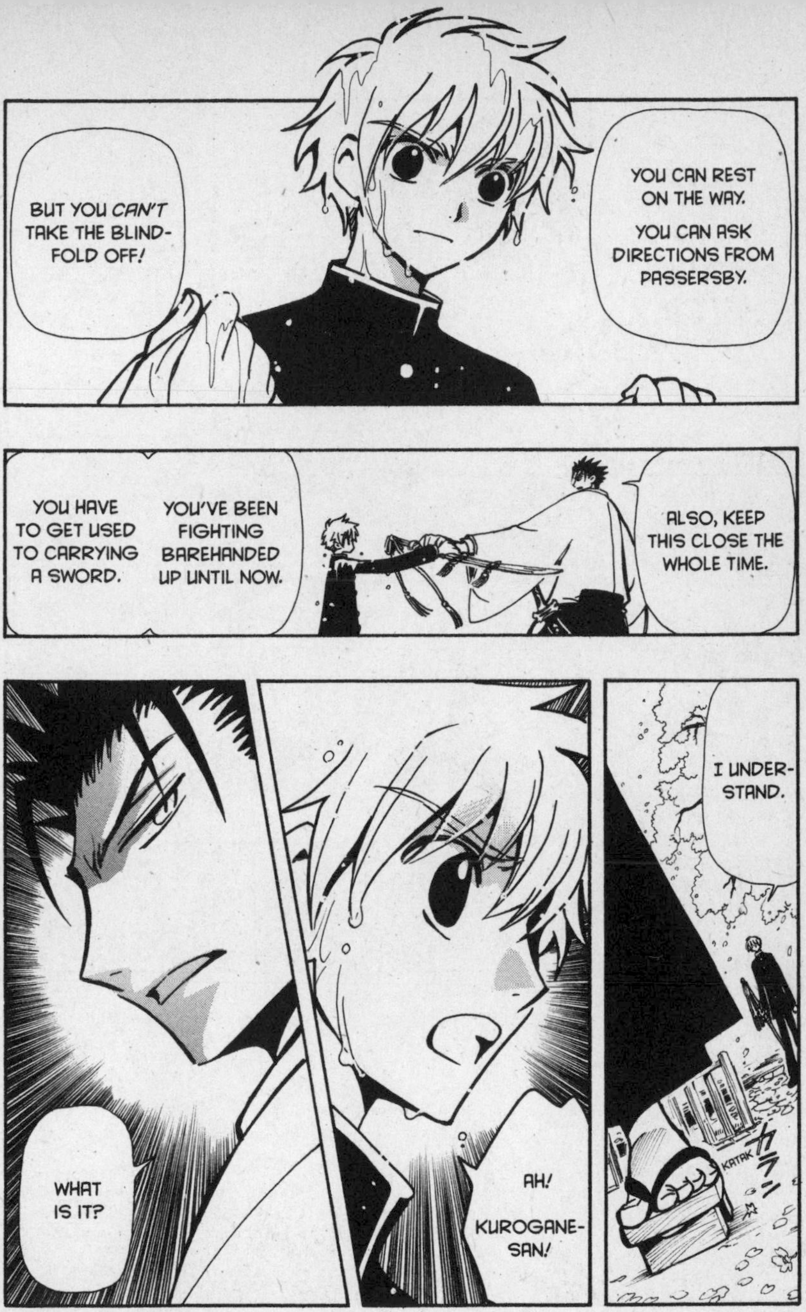
YOU CAN REST ON THE WAY.
YOU CAN ASK DIRECTIONS FROM PASSERSBY.
BUT YOU *CAN'T* TAKE THE BLIND-FOLD OFF!
ALSO, KEEP THIS CLOSE THE WHOLE TIME.
YOU'VE BEEN FIGHTING BAREHANDED UP UNTIL NOW.
YOU HAVE TO GET USED TO CARRYING A SWORD.
I UNDER-STAND.
KATAK
AH!
KUROGANE-SAN!
WHAT IS IT?

FAI ASKED US TO PICK UP SOME WHEAT FLOUR ON THE WAY HOME ...

HE SAID THAT FLOUR BAGS ARE TOO HEAVY FOR HIM.

AM I HIS DAMNED FETCH BOY?!

I'M GOING TO HAVE TO TRAIN MYSELF...

...TO REACT TO UNSEEN ATTACKS ON BOTH SIDES.

I'M SORRY, AND THANK YOU!

WHY DO I HAVE TO BE THE ONE TO GO ALL THE WAY TO THE MARKET AND LUG THEM THE WHOLE WAY HOME P!

BLOW

GWNCH

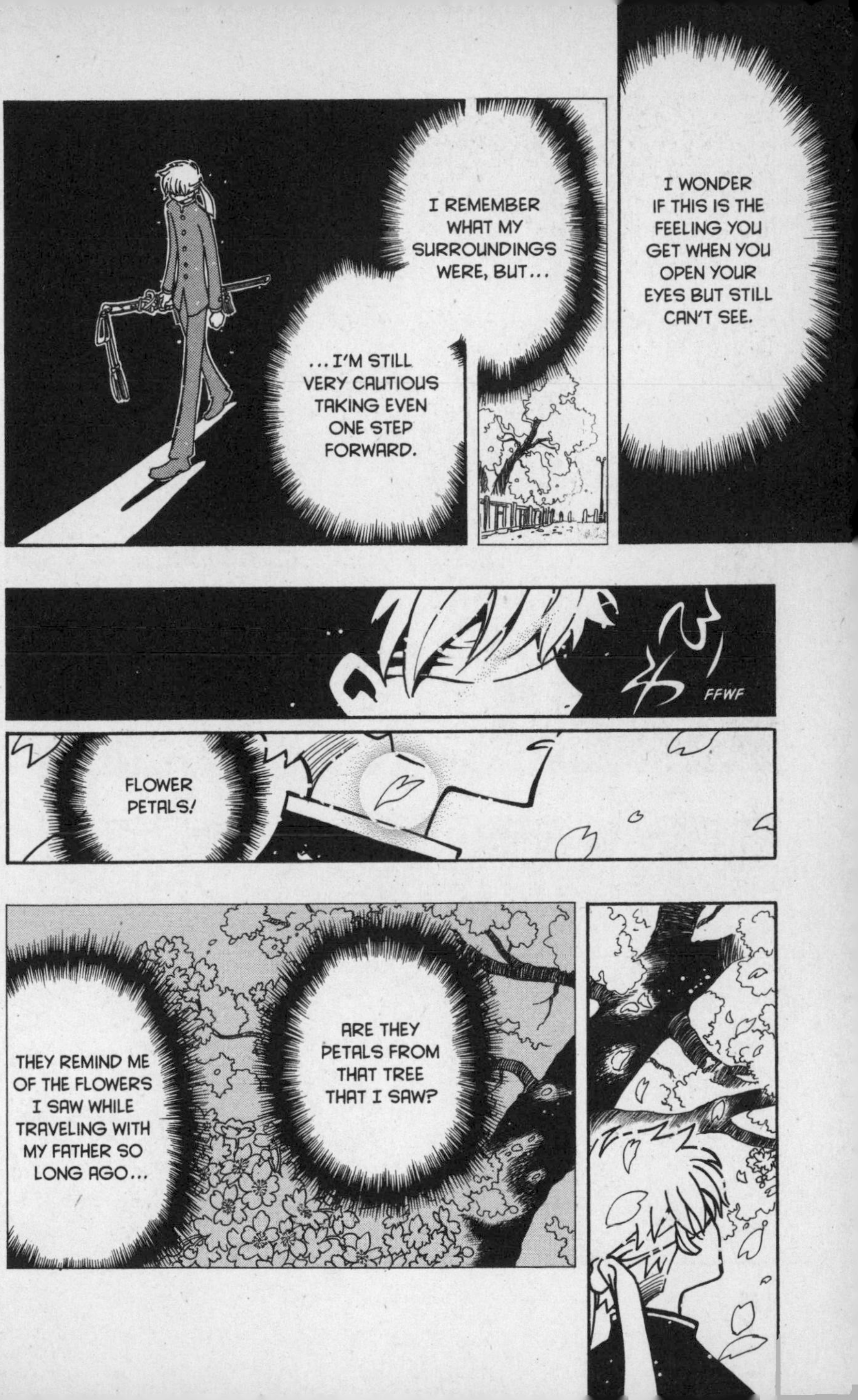
I WONDER IF THIS IS THE FEELING YOU GET WHEN YOU OPEN YOUR EYES BUT STILL CAN'T SEE.
I REMEMBER WHAT MY SURROUNDINGS WERE, BUT...
...I'M STILL VERY CAUTIOUS TAKING EVEN ONE STEP FORWARD.
FFWF
FLOWER PETALS!
ARE THEY PETALS FROM THAT TREE THAT I SAW?
THEY REMIND ME OF THE FLOWERS I SAW WHILE TRAVELING WITH MY FATHER SO LONG AGO...

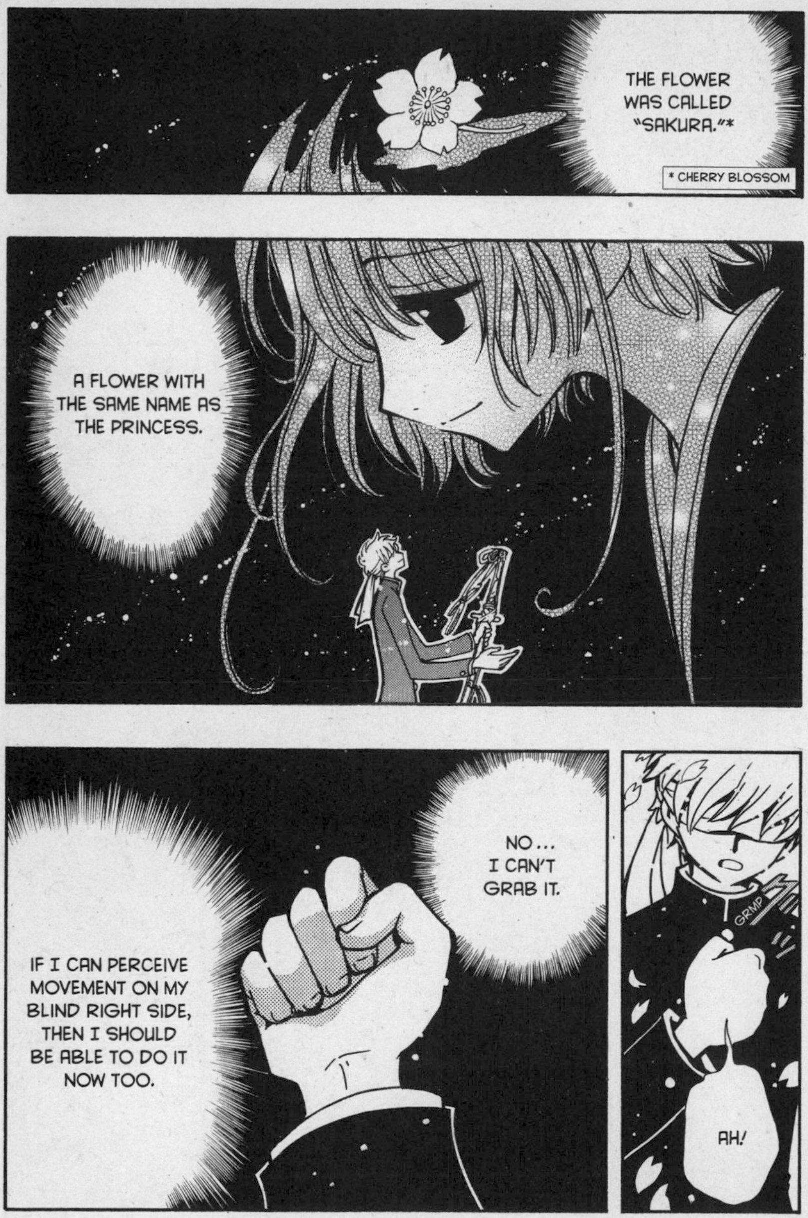
THE FLOWER WAS CALLED "SAKURA."*
* CHERRY BLOSSOM
A FLOWER WITH THE SAME NAME AS THE PRINCESS.
GRMP
AH!
NO... I CAN'T GRAB IT.
IF I CAN PERCEIVE MOVEMENT ON MY BLIND RIGHT SIDE, THEN I SHOULD BE ABLE TO DO IT NOW TOO.

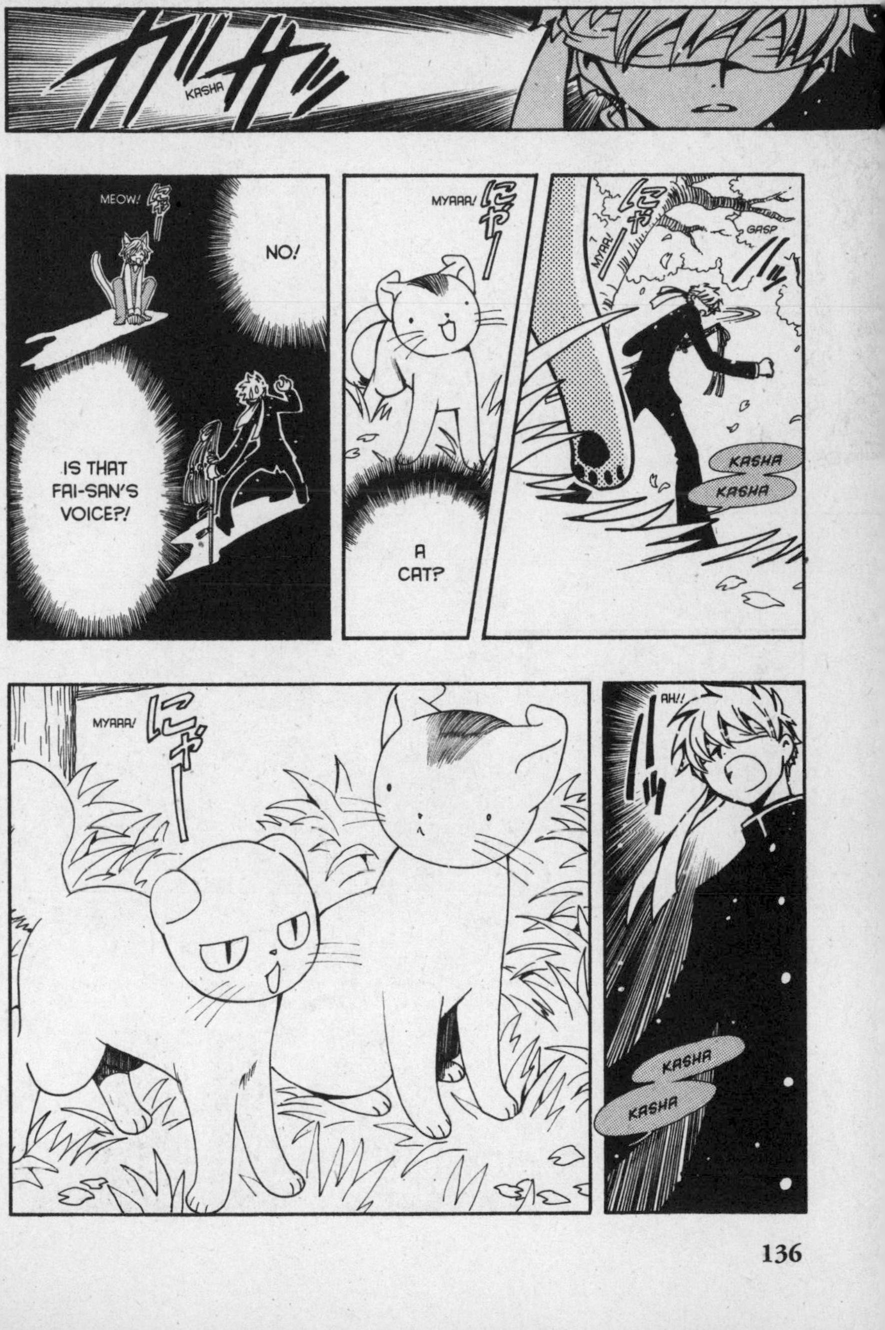

KASHA
GASP
MYAA!
KASHA
KASHA
MYAAA!
A CAT?
MEOW!
NO!
IS THAT FAI-SAN'S VOICE?!
AH!!
KASHA
KASHA
MYAAA!

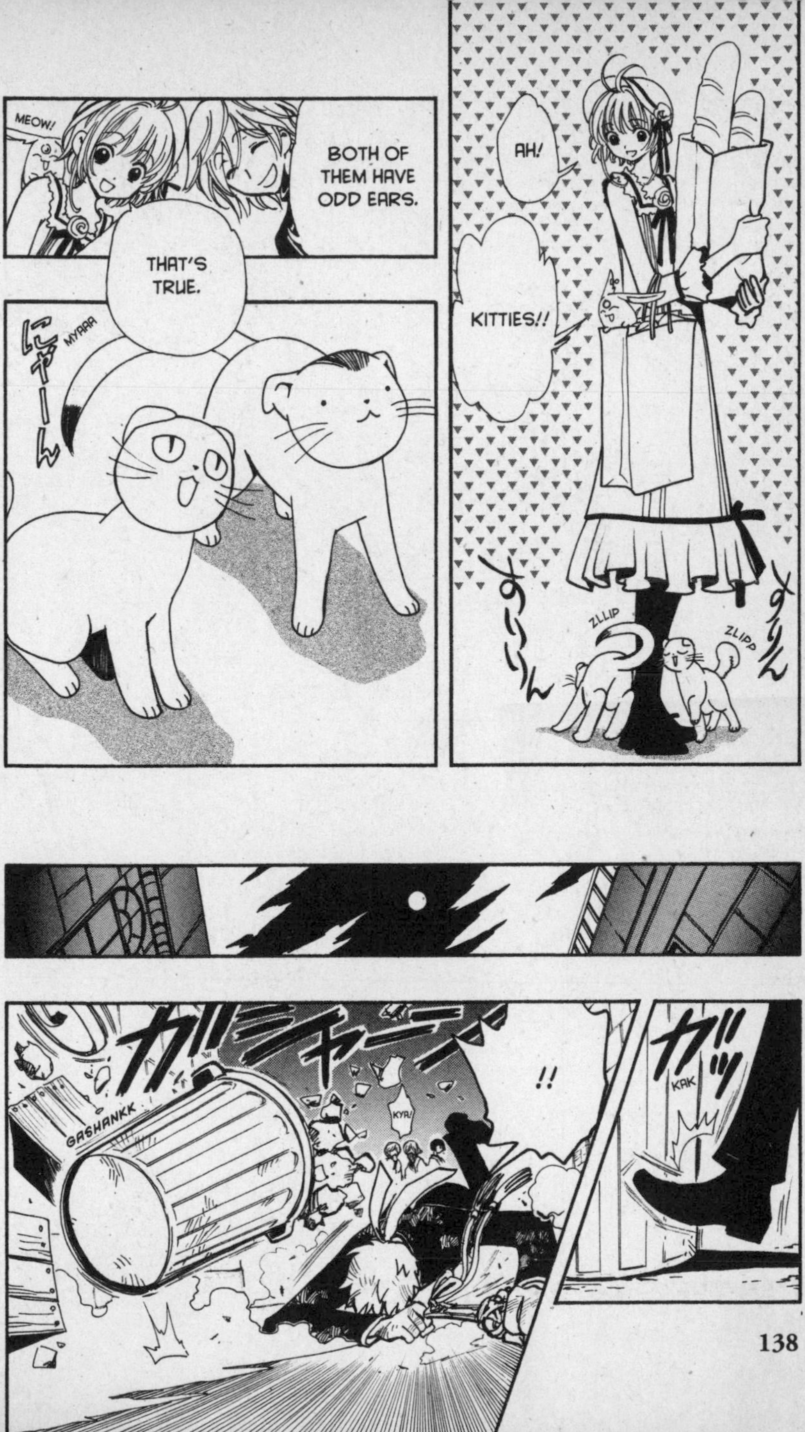
AH!
KITTIES!!
ZLLIP
ZLIPP
MEOW!
BOTH OF THEM HAVE ODD EARS.
THAT'S TRUE.
MYAAA
KAK
!!
KYA!
GASHANKK

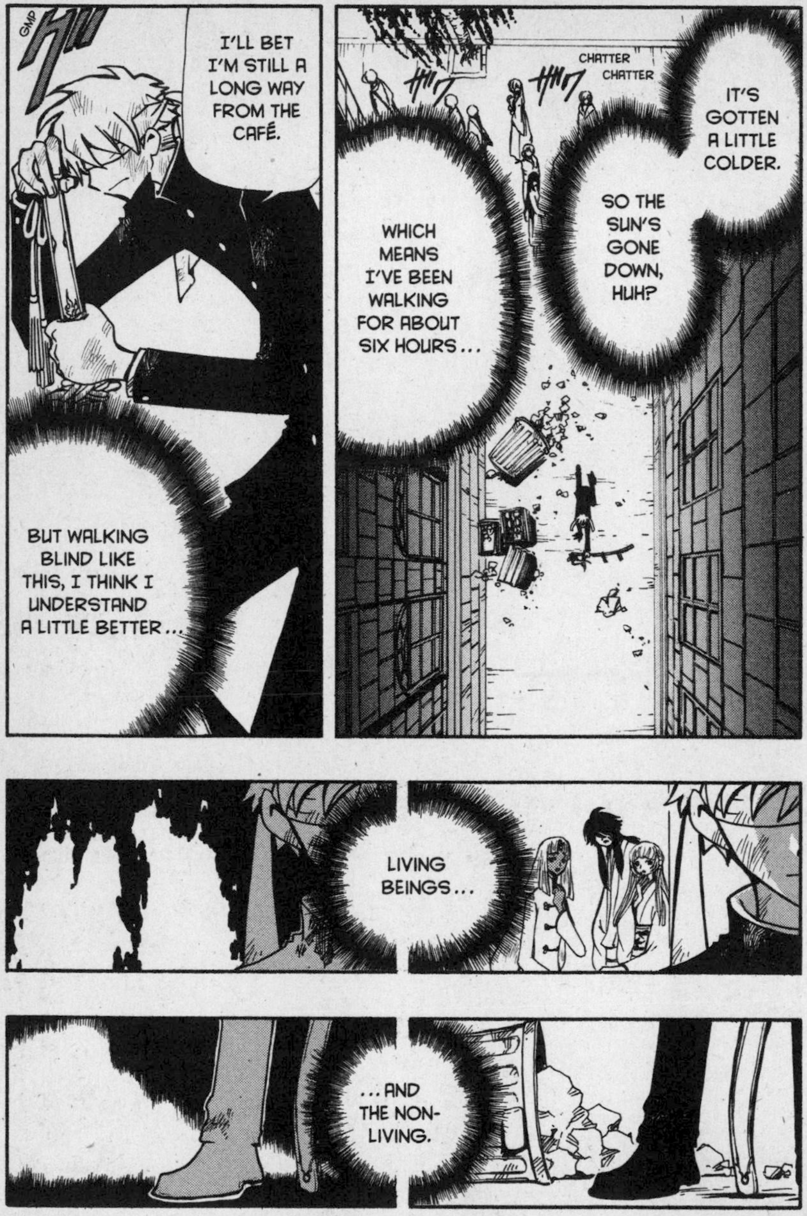
CHATTER
CHATTER
IT'S GOTTEN A LITTLE COLDER.
SO THE SUN'S GONE DOWN, HUH?
WHICH MEANS I'VE BEEN WALKING FOR ABOUT SIX HOURS...
GMP
I'LL BET I'M STILL A LONG WAY FROM THE CAFÉ.
BUT WALKING BLIND LIKE THIS, I THINK I UNDERSTAND A LITTLE BETTER...
LIVING BEINGS...
...AND THE NON-LIVING.

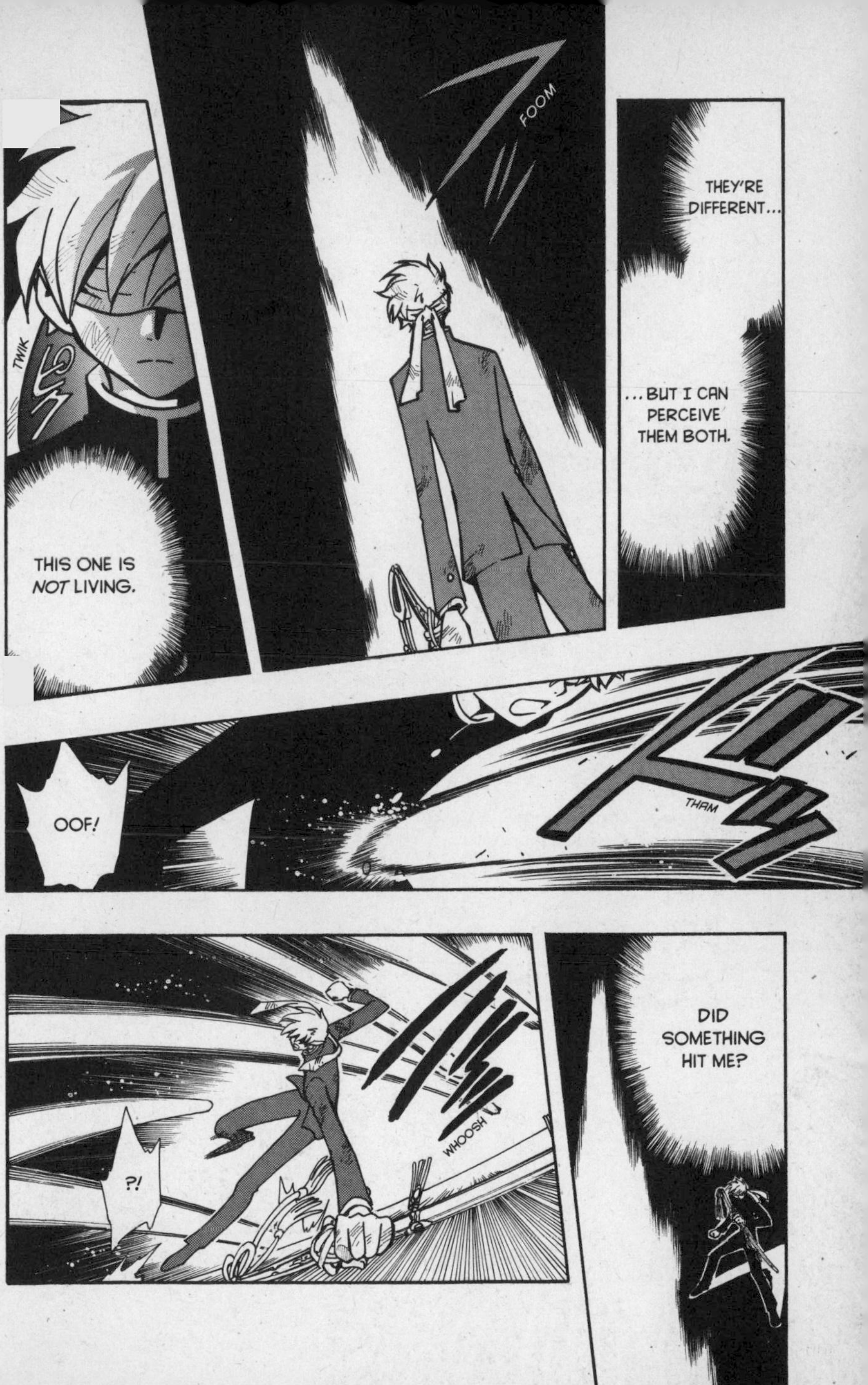
THEY'RE DIFFERENT...
...BUT I CAN PERCEIVE THEM BOTH.
FOOM
TWIK
THIS ONE IS *NOT* LIVING.
THAM
OOF!
DID SOMETHING HIT ME?
WHOOSH
?!

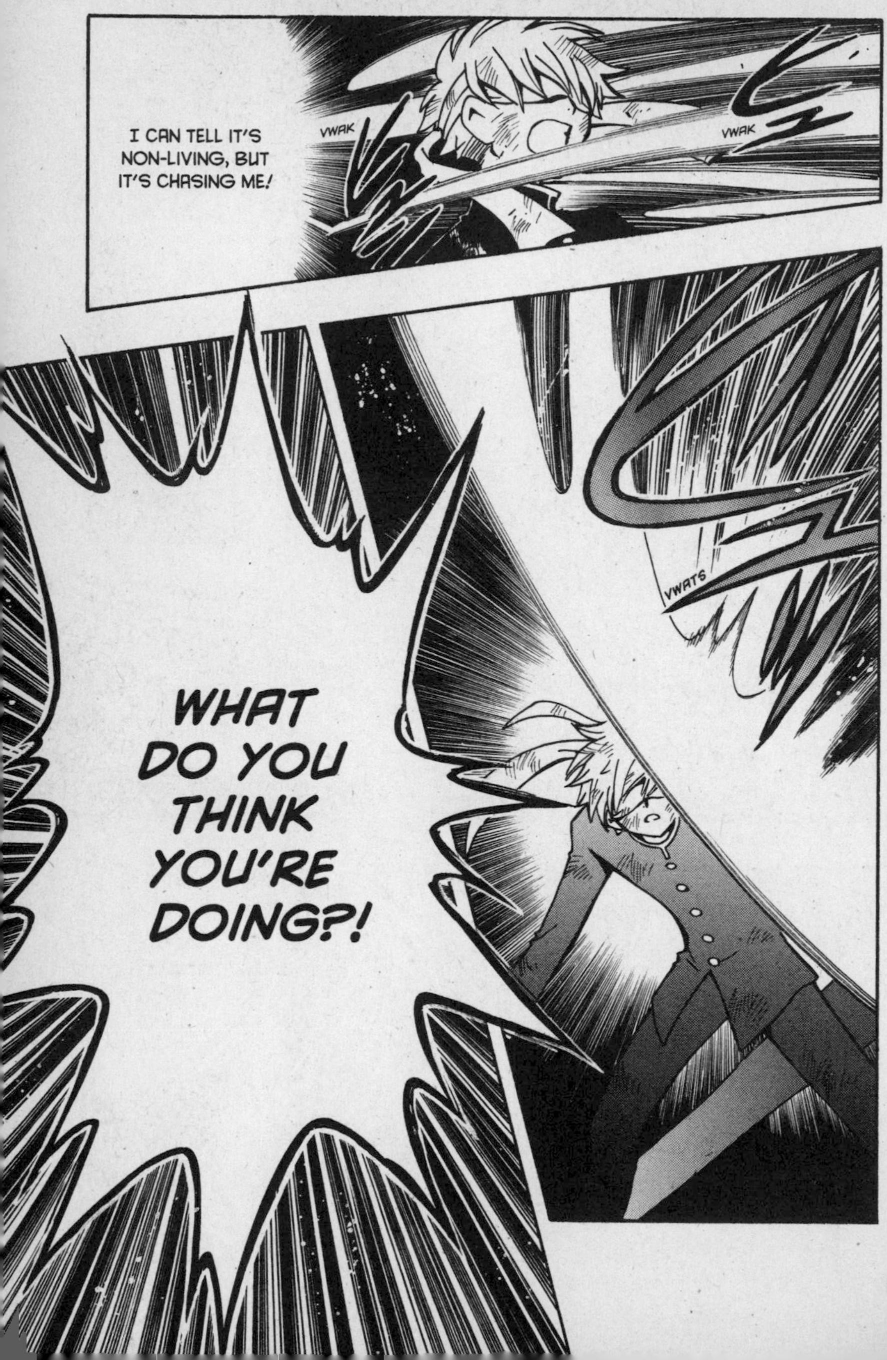
VWAK
VWAK
I CAN TELL IT'S NON-LIVING, BUT IT'S CHASING ME!
VWATS
WHAT DO YOU THINK YOU'RE DOING?!

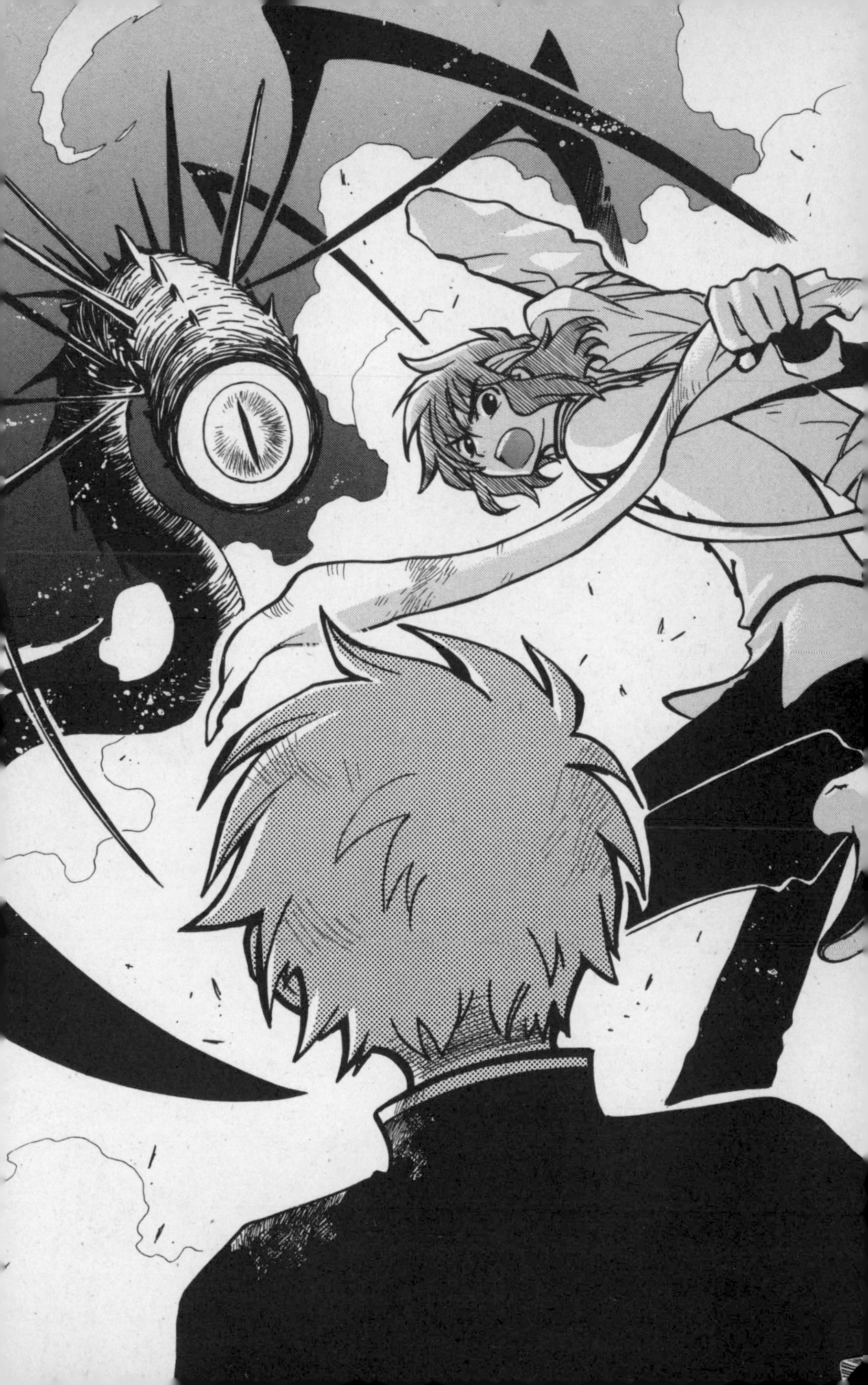

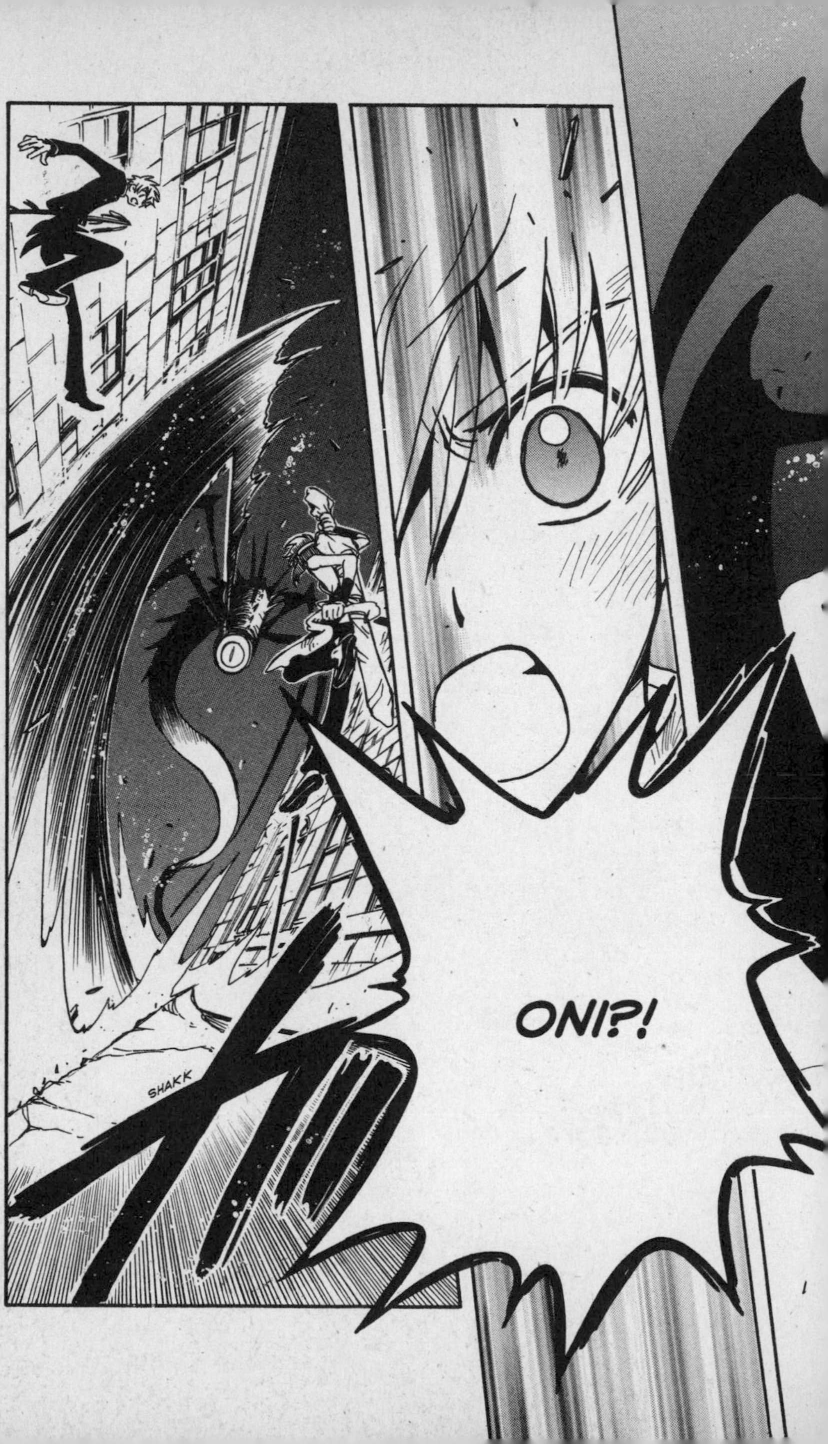
ONI?!
SHAKK

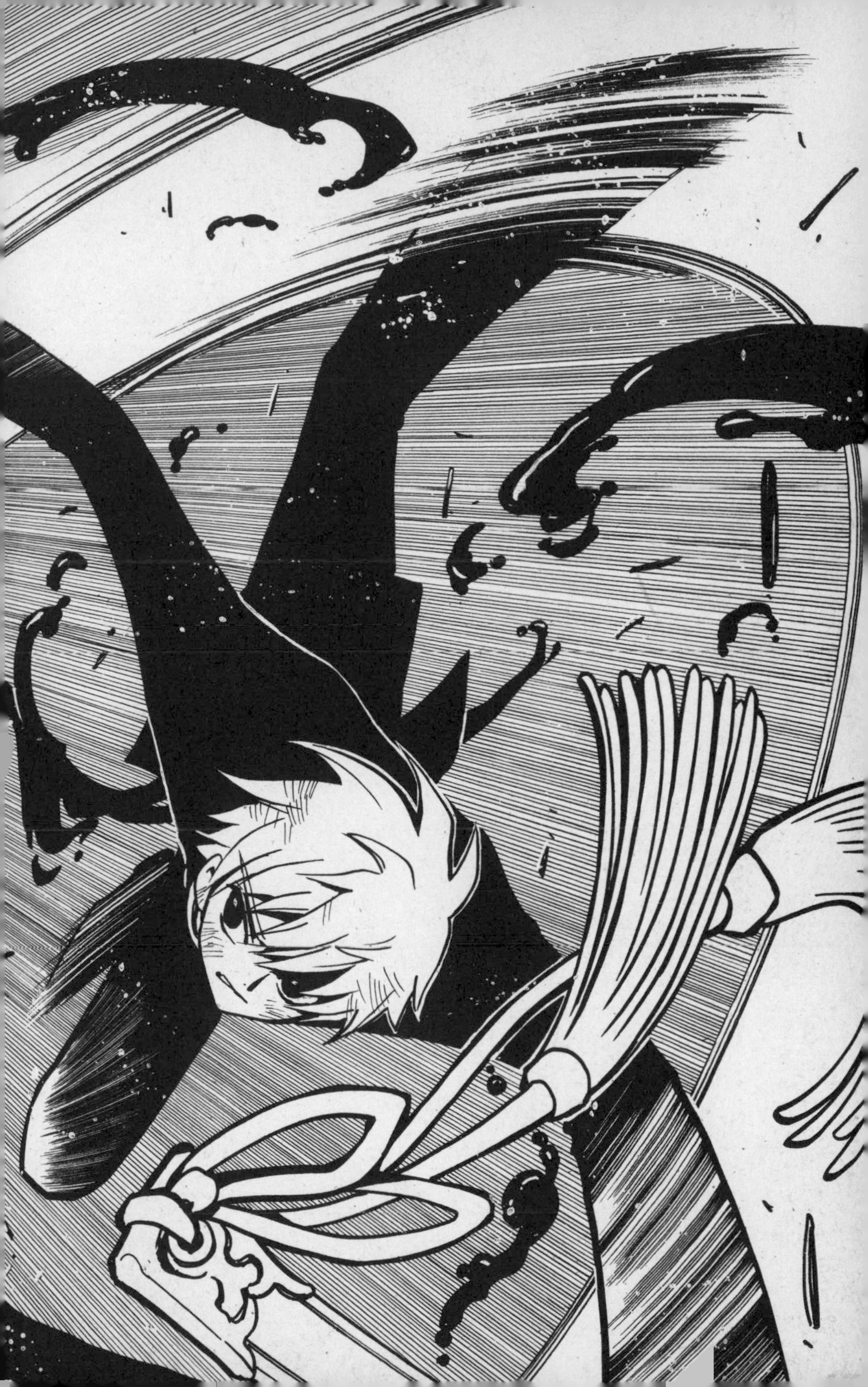

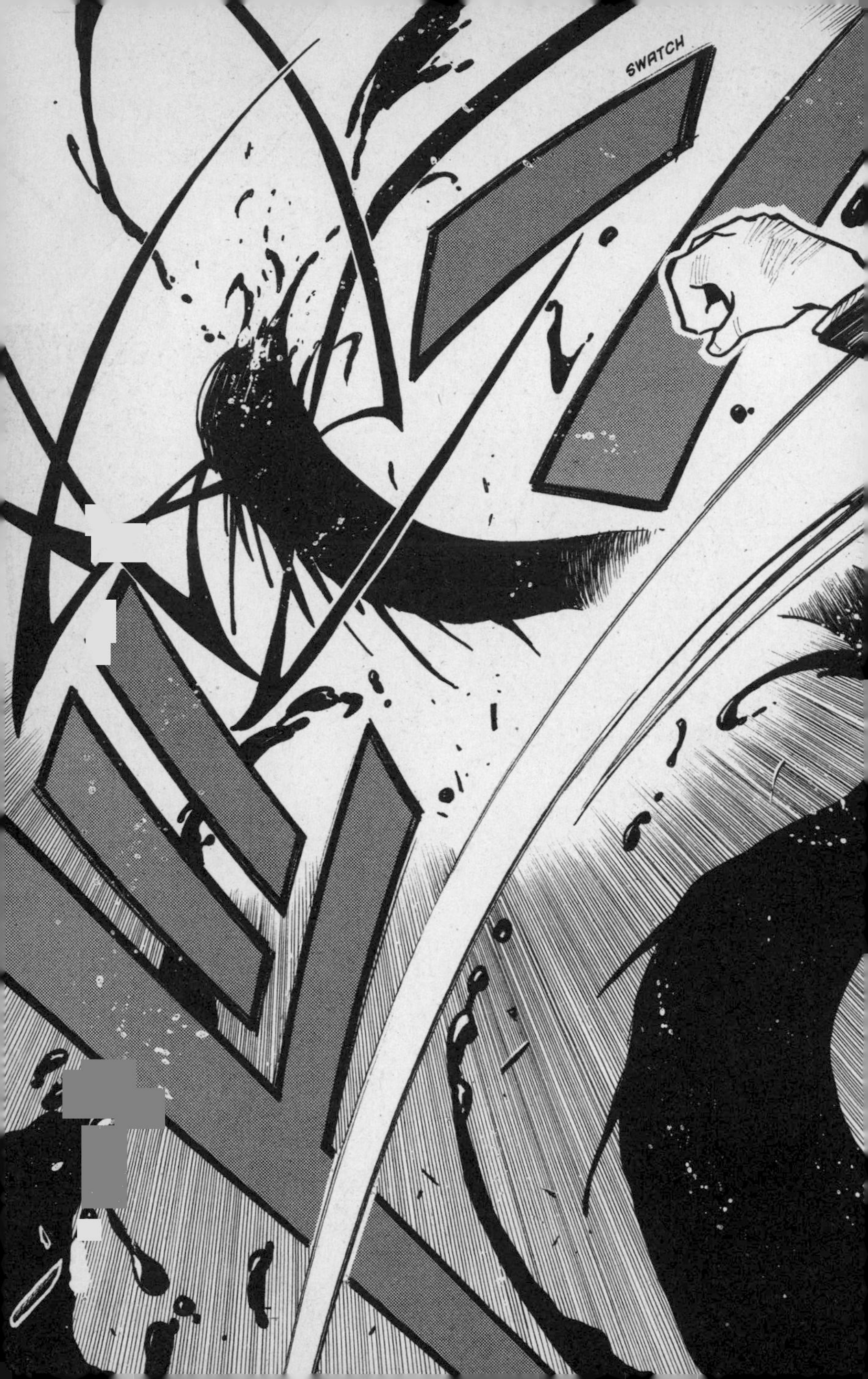
SWATCH

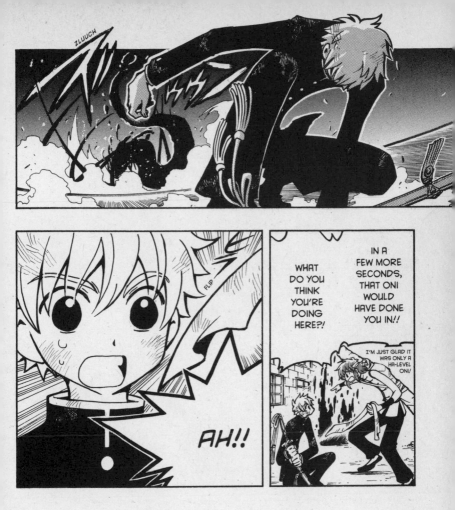

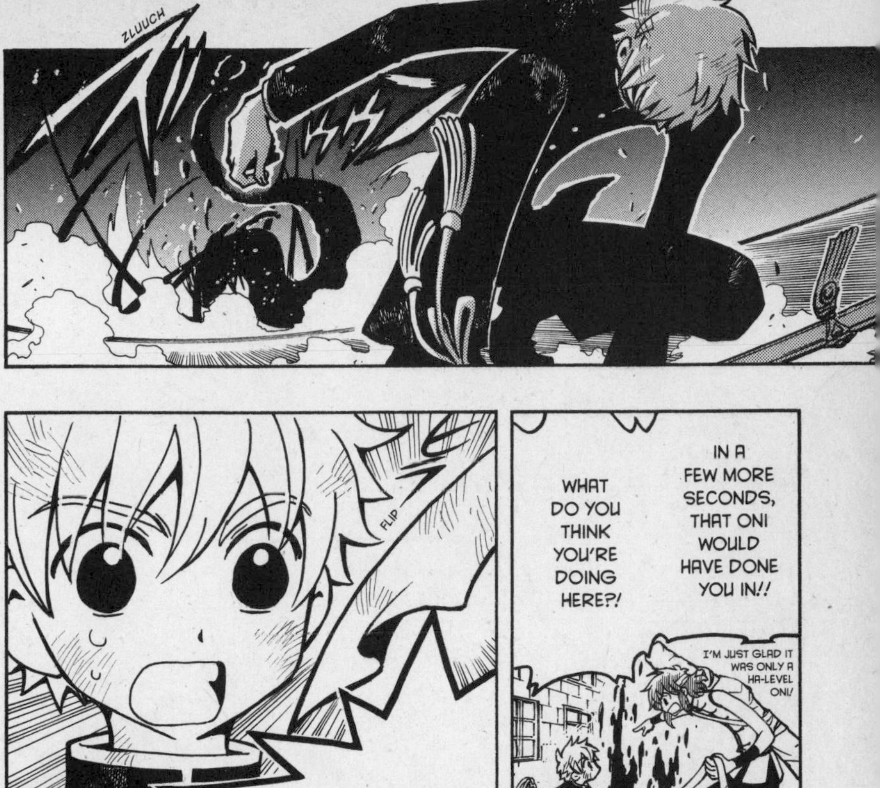
ZLUUCH
IN A FEW MORE SECONDS, THAT ONI WOULD HAVE DONE YOU IN!!
WHAT DO YOU THINK YOU'RE DOING HERE?!
I'M JUST GLAD IT WAS ONLY A HA-LEVEL ONI!
FLIP
AH!!
OH! SWORD TRAINING, HUH?
SORRY. I GUESS I BLEW IT FOR YOU.

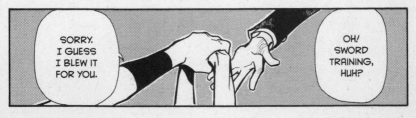

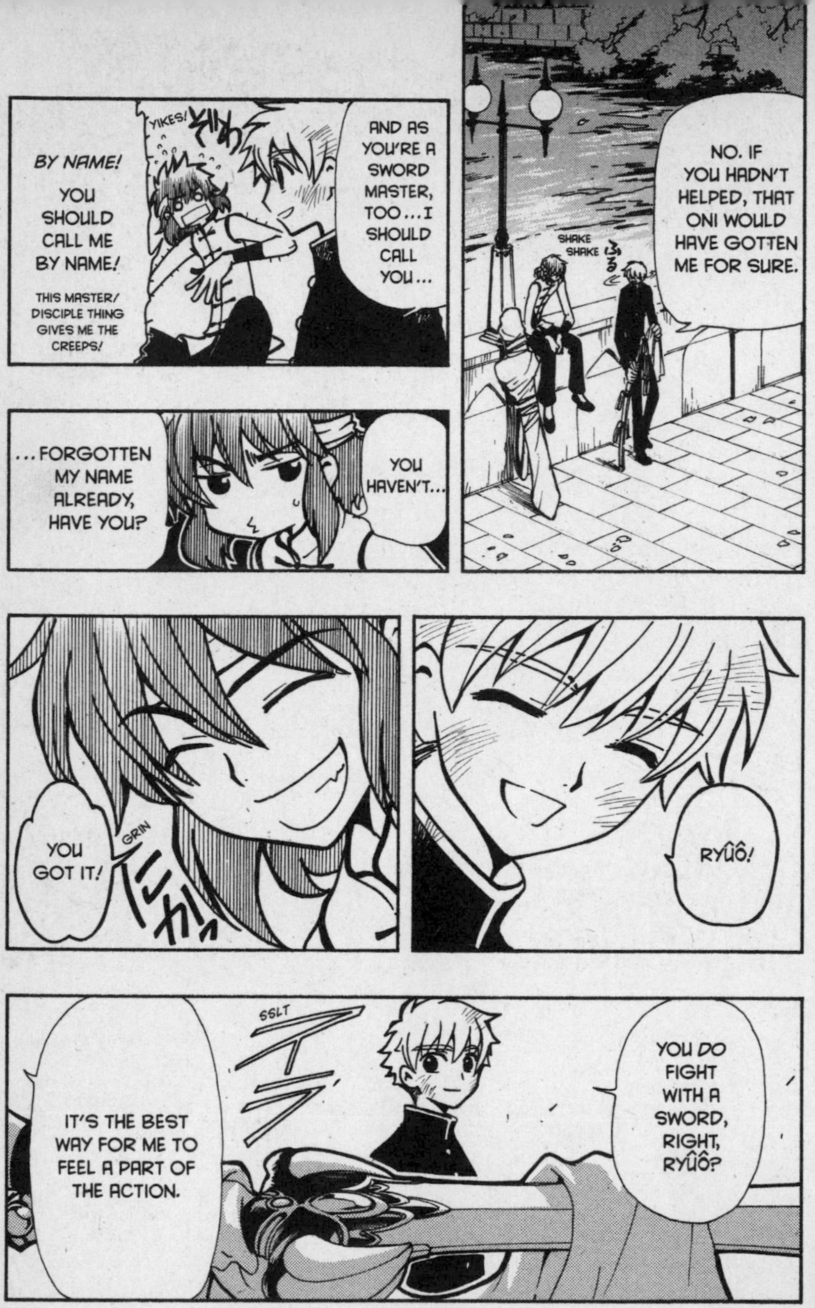
NO. IF YOU HADN'T HELPED, THAT ONI WOULD HAVE GOTTEN ME FOR SURE.
SHAKE SHAKE
AND AS YOU'RE A SWORD MASTER, TOO... I SHOULD CALL YOU...
YIKES!
BY NAME!
YOU SHOULD CALL ME BY NAME!
THIS MASTER/ DISCIPLE THING GIVES ME THE CREEPS!
YOU HAVEN'T...
...FORGOTTEN MY NAME ALREADY, HAVE YOU?
RYÛÔ!
YOU GOT IT!
GRIN
YOU *DO* FIGHT WITH A SWORD, RIGHT, RYÛÔ?
SSLT
IT'S THE BEST WAY FOR ME TO FEEL A PART OF THE ACTION.

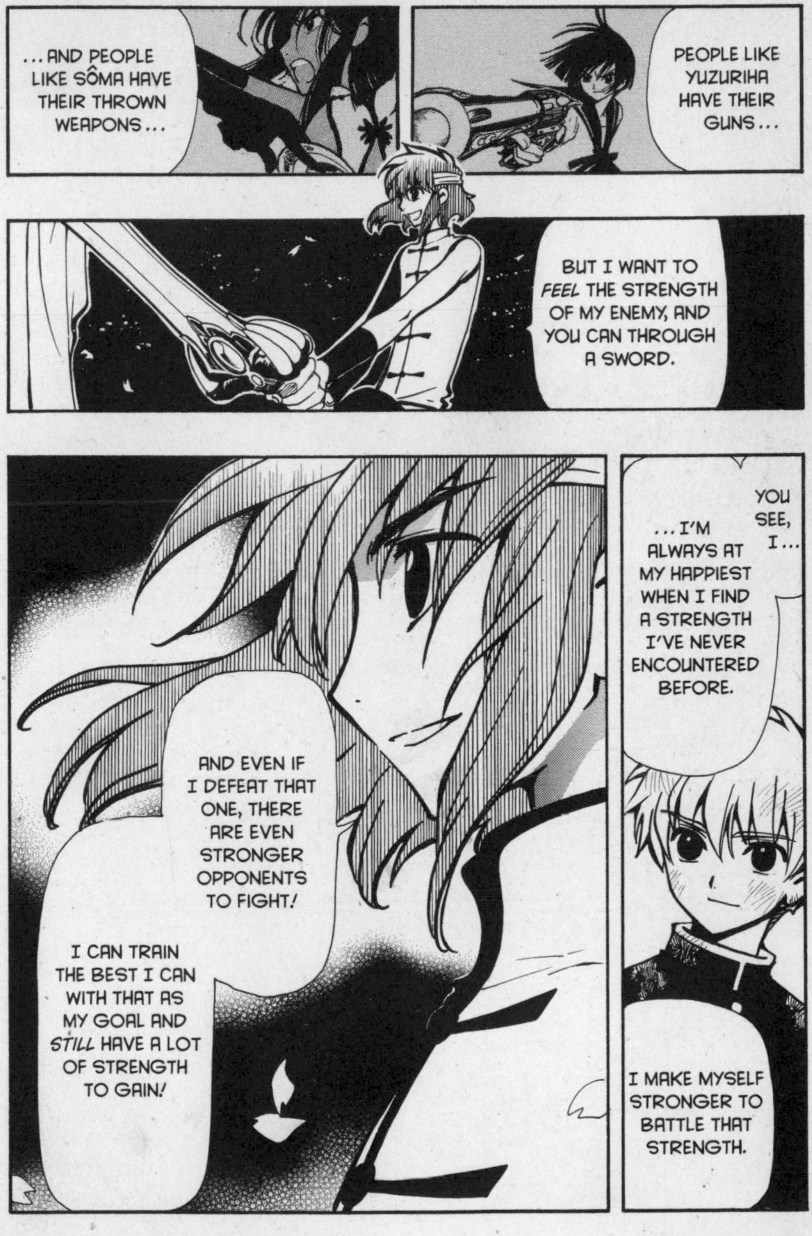
PEOPLE LIKE YUZURIHA HAVE THEIR GUNS...
...AND PEOPLE LIKE SÔMA HAVE THEIR THROWN WEAPONS...
BUT I WANT TO *FEEL* THE STRENGTH OF MY ENEMY, AND YOU CAN THROUGH A SWORD.
YOU SEE, I...
...I'M ALWAYS AT MY HAPPIEST WHEN I FIND A STRENGTH I'VE NEVER ENCOUNTERED BEFORE.
I MAKE MYSELF STRONGER TO BATTLE THAT STRENGTH.
AND EVEN IF I DEFEAT THAT ONE, THERE ARE EVEN STRONGER OPPONENTS TO FIGHT!
I CAN TRAIN THE BEST I CAN WITH THAT AS MY GOAL AND *STILL* HAVE A LOT OF STRENGTH TO GAIN!

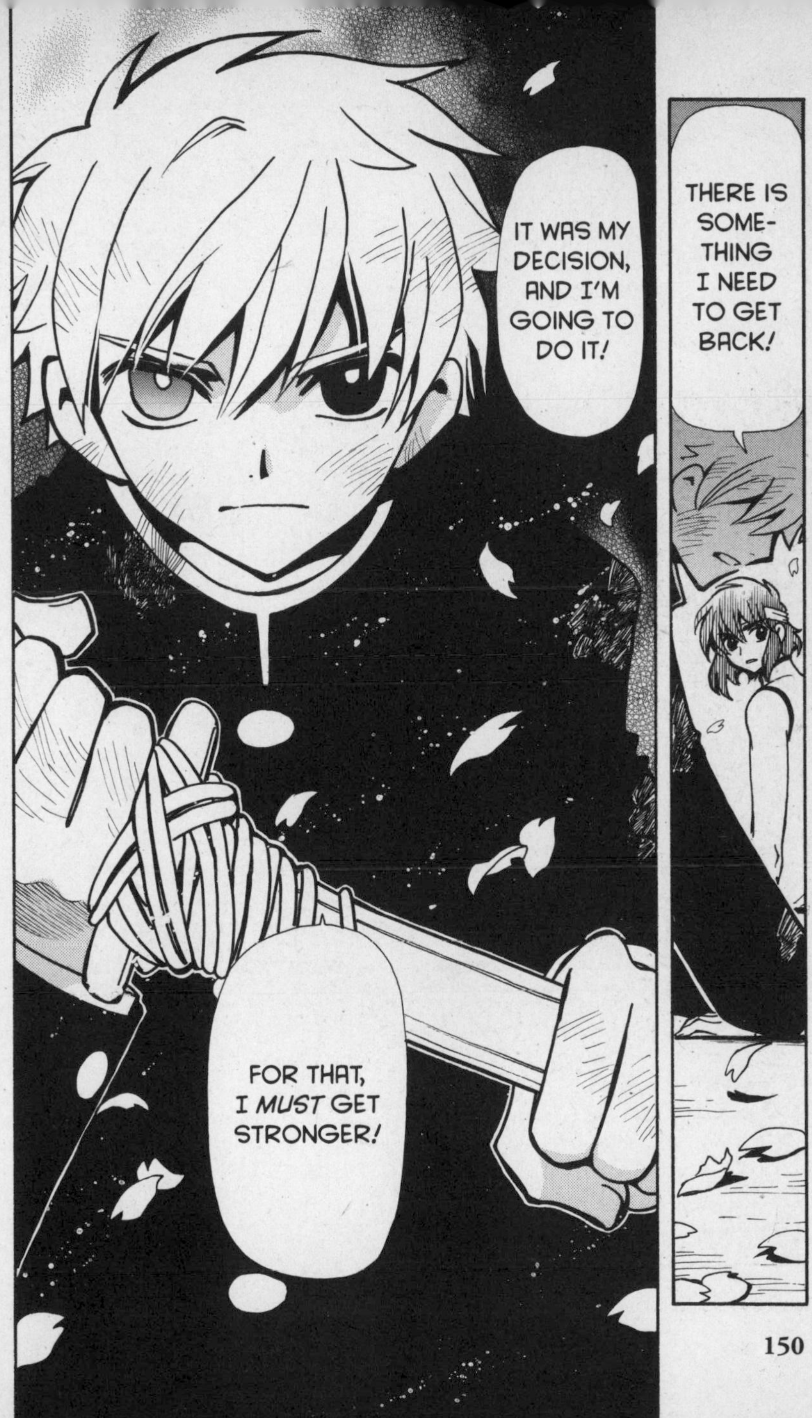
THERE IS SOME-THING I NEED TO GET BACK!
IT WAS MY DECISION, AND I'M GOING TO DO IT!
FOR THAT, I *MUST* GET STRONGER!

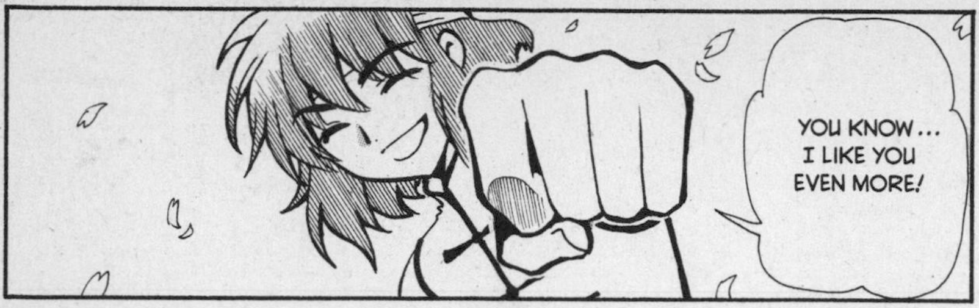
YOU KNOW... I LIKE YOU EVEN MORE!

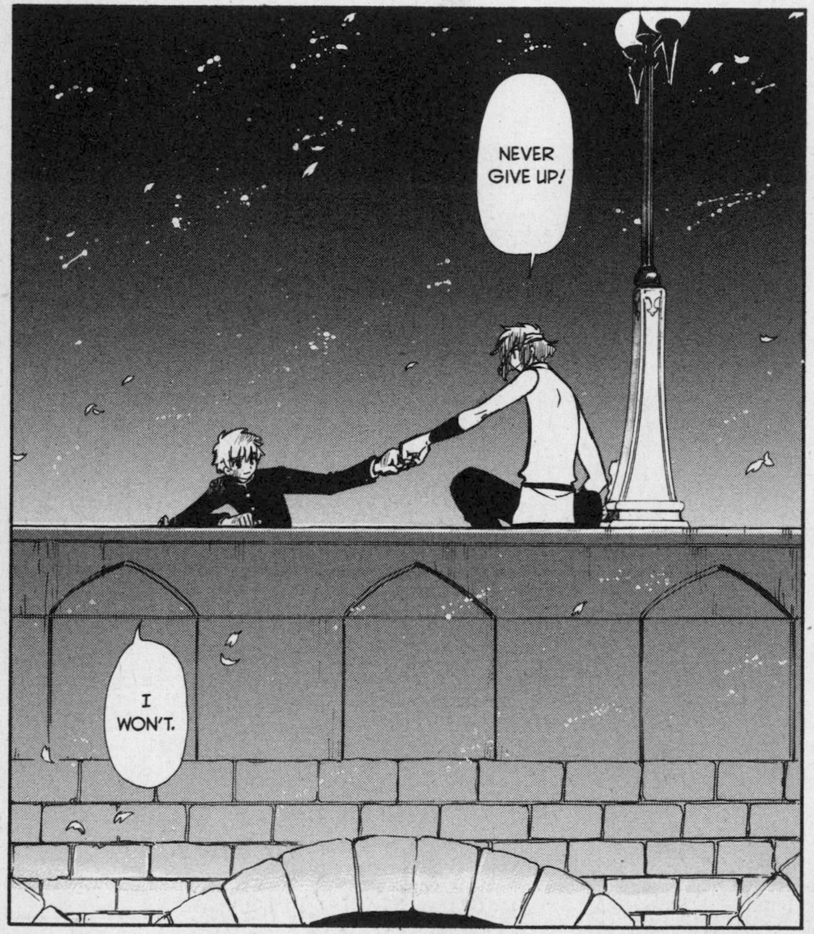
NEVER GIVE UP!
I WON'T.

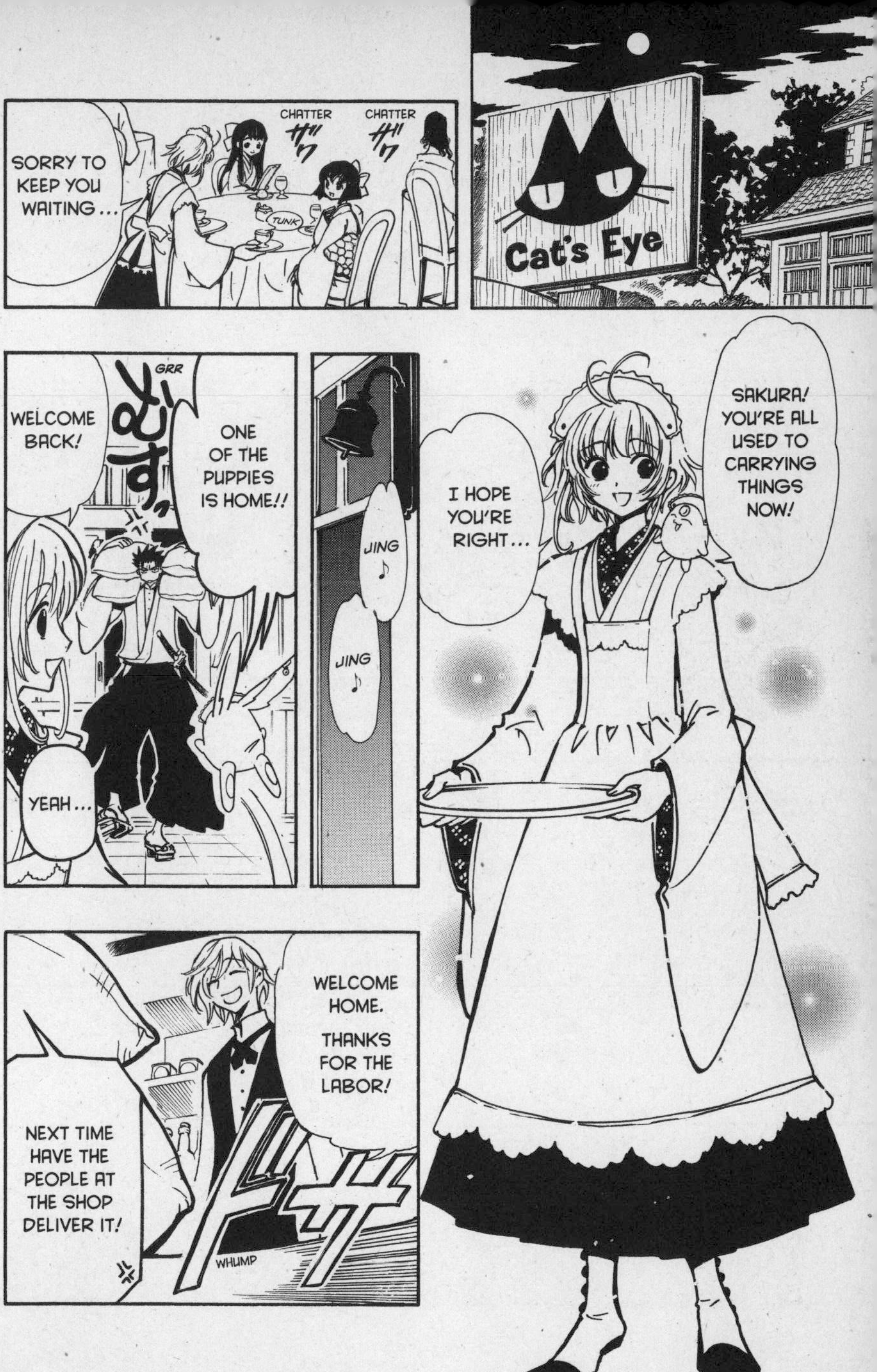
Cat's Eye
CHATTER
ザワ
CHATTER
ザワ
SORRY TO KEEP YOU WAITING...
TUNK
SAKURA! YOU'RE ALL USED TO CARRYING THINGS NOW!
I HOPE YOU'RE RIGHT...
JING ♪
JING ♪
ONE OF THE PUPPIES IS HOME!!
GRR
むすっ
WELCOME BACK!
YEAH...
WELCOME HOME.
THANKS FOR THE LABOR!
NEXT TIME HAVE THE PEOPLE AT THE SHOP DELIVER IT!
WHUMP

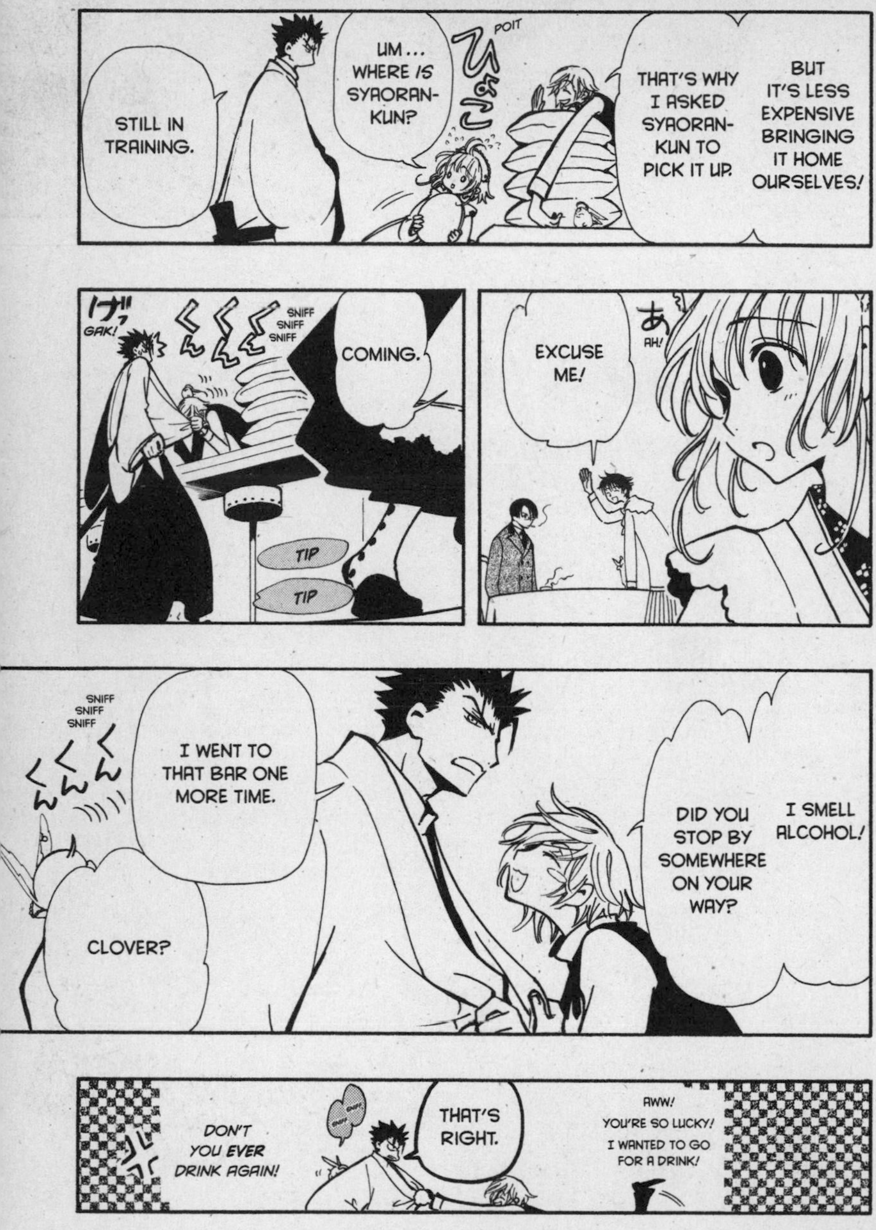
BUT IT'S LESS EXPENSIVE BRINGING IT HOME OURSELVES!
THAT'S WHY I ASKED SYAORAN-KUN TO PICK IT UP.
ひょこ
POIT
UM... WHERE IS SYAORAN-KUN?
STILL IN TRAINING.
あ
AH!
EXCUSE ME!
COMING.
SNIFF SNIFF SNIFF
くんくんくん
げっ
GAK!
TIP
TIP
I SMELL ALCOHOL!
DID YOU STOP BY SOMEWHERE ON YOUR WAY?
I WENT TO THAT BAR ONE MORE TIME.
SNIFF SNIFF SNIFF
くんくんくん
CLOVER?
AWW! YOU'RE SO LUCKY! I WANTED TO GO FOR A DRINK!
THAT'S RIGHT.
SNIFF SNIFF
DON'T YOU EVER DRINK AGAIN!

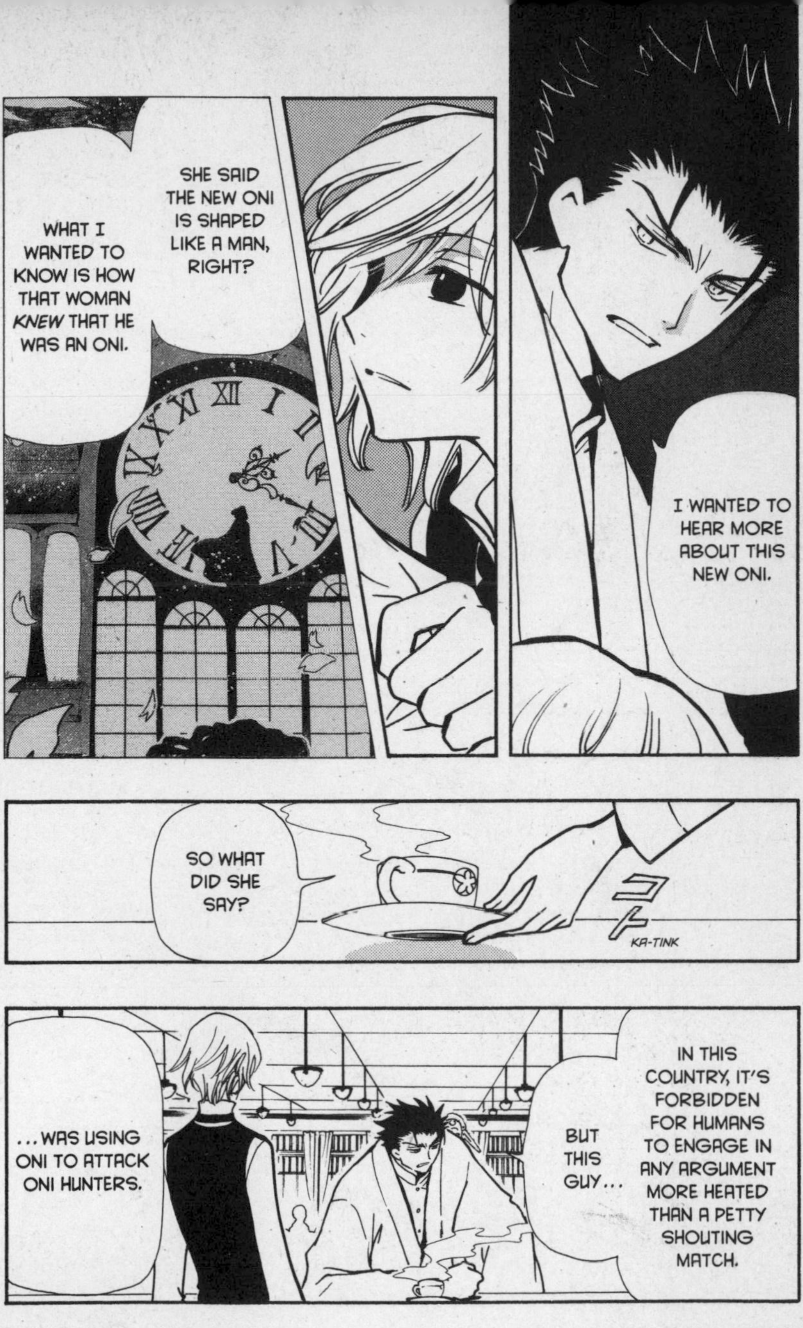
I WANTED TO HEAR MORE ABOUT THIS NEW ONI.
SHE SAID THE NEW ONI IS SHAPED LIKE A MAN, RIGHT?
WHAT I WANTED TO KNOW IS HOW THAT WOMAN *KNEW* THAT HE WAS AN ONI.
SO WHAT DID SHE SAY?
KA-TINK
IN THIS COUNTRY, IT'S FORBIDDEN FOR HUMANS TO ENGAGE IN ANY ARGUMENT MORE HEATED THAN A PETTY SHOUTING MATCH.
BUT THIS GUY...
...WAS USING ONI TO ATTACK ONI HUNTERS.

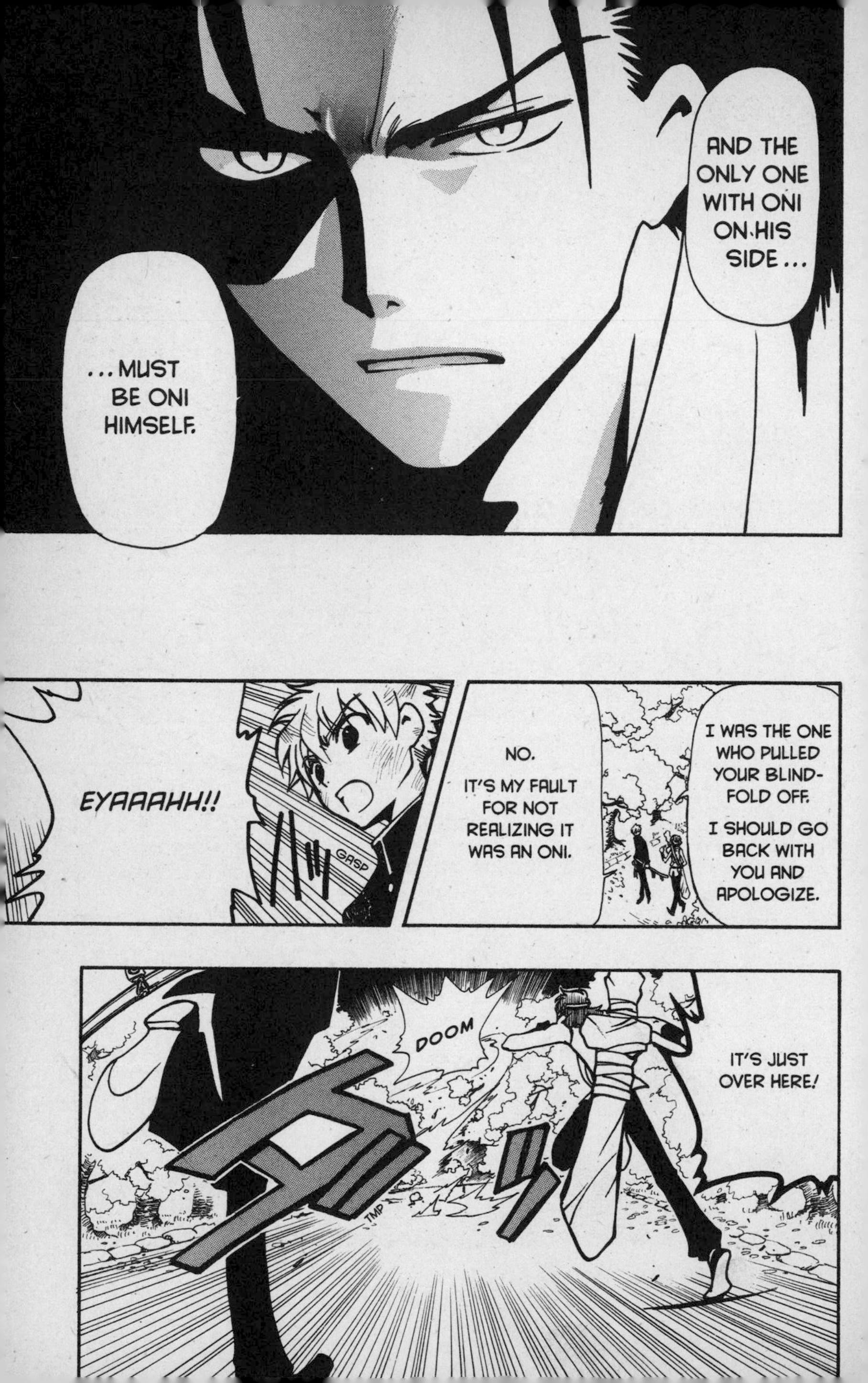
AND THE ONLY ONE WITH ONI ON HIS SIDE...
...MUST BE ONI HIMSELF.
I WAS THE ONE WHO PULLED YOUR BLIND-FOLD OFF.
I SHOULD GO BACK WITH YOU AND APOLOGIZE.
NO.
IT'S MY FAULT FOR NOT REALIZING IT WAS AN ONI.
GASP
EYAAAHH!!
IT'S JUST OVER HERE!
DOOM
TMP

'IT'S ONLY A HA-LEVEL ONI!'

WHY IS IT SO STRONG?!

WE CUT IT AND SLICE IT, BUT IT WON'T DISAPPEAR!

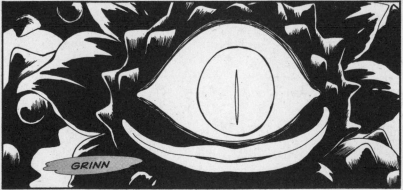

GRINN

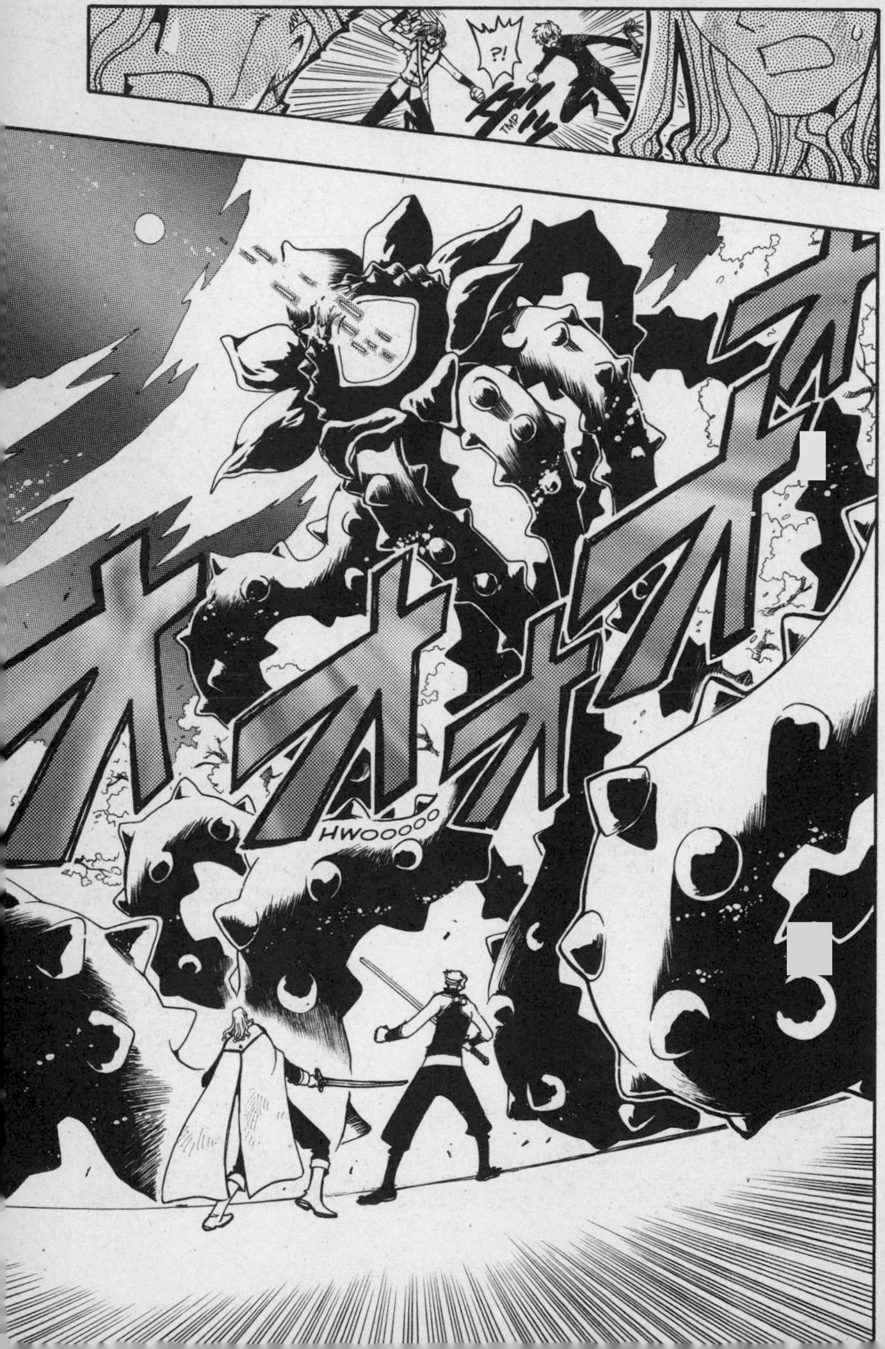
?!
TMP
HWOOOOO

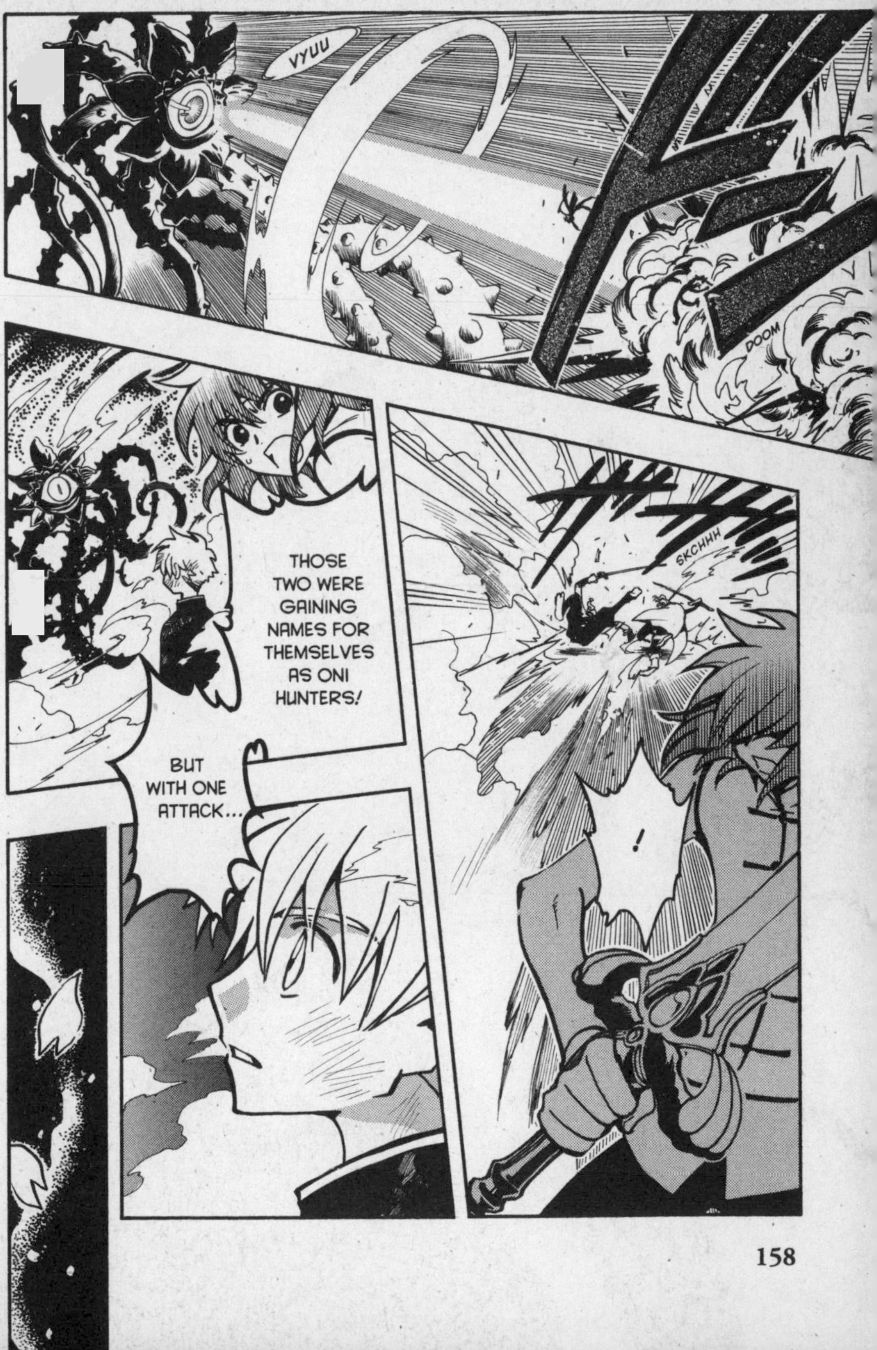
VYUU
DOOM
SKCHHH
!
THOSE TWO WERE GAINING NAMES FOR THEMSELVES AS ONI HUNTERS!
BUT WITH ONE ATTACK...

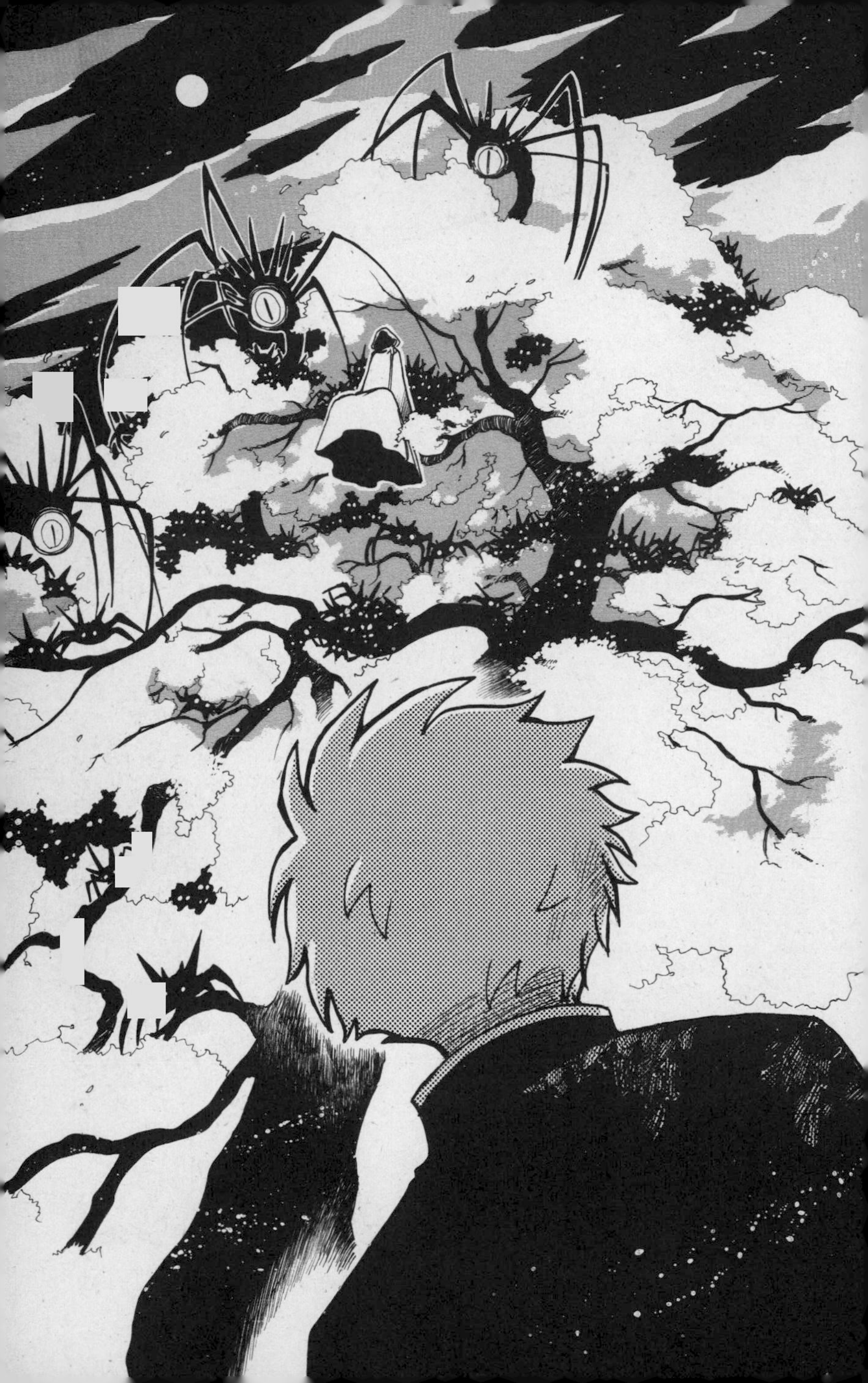

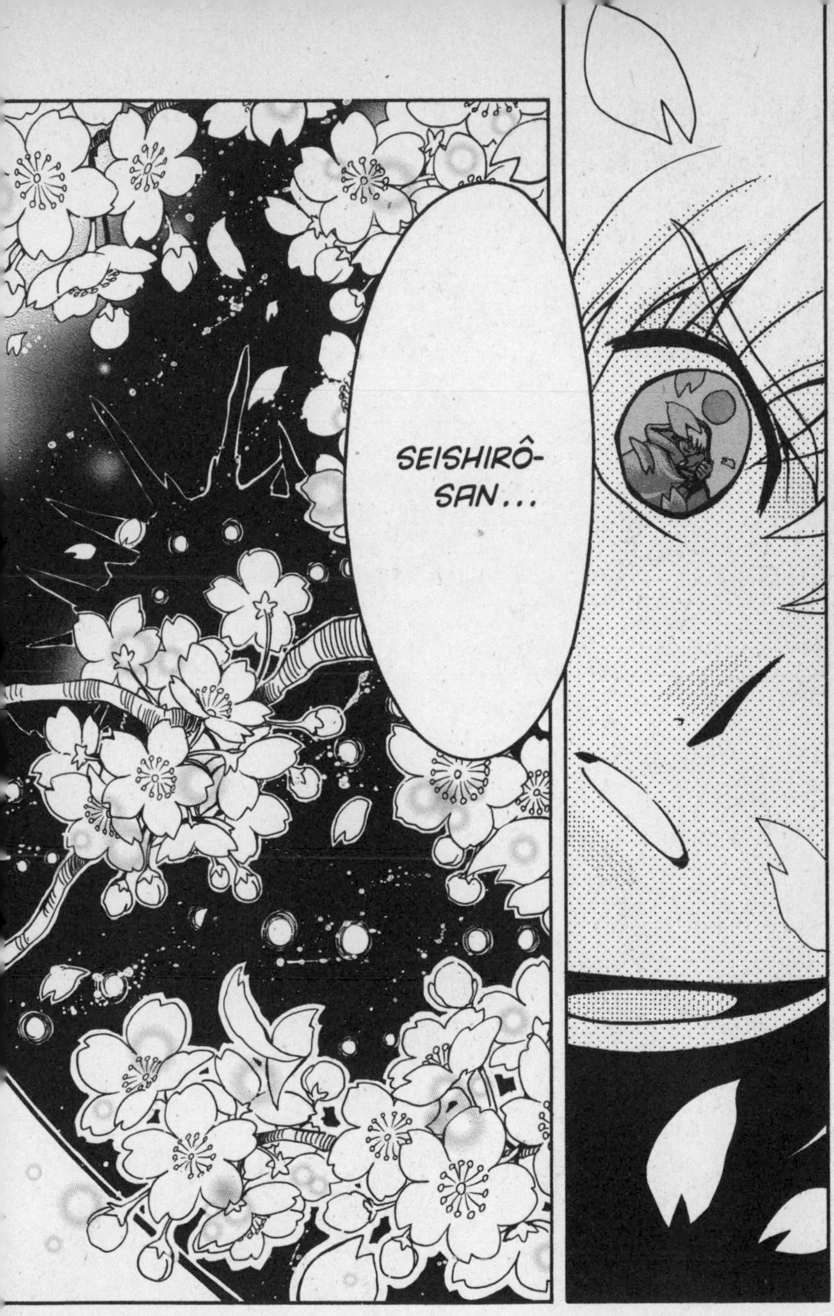
SEISHIRÔ-SAN...

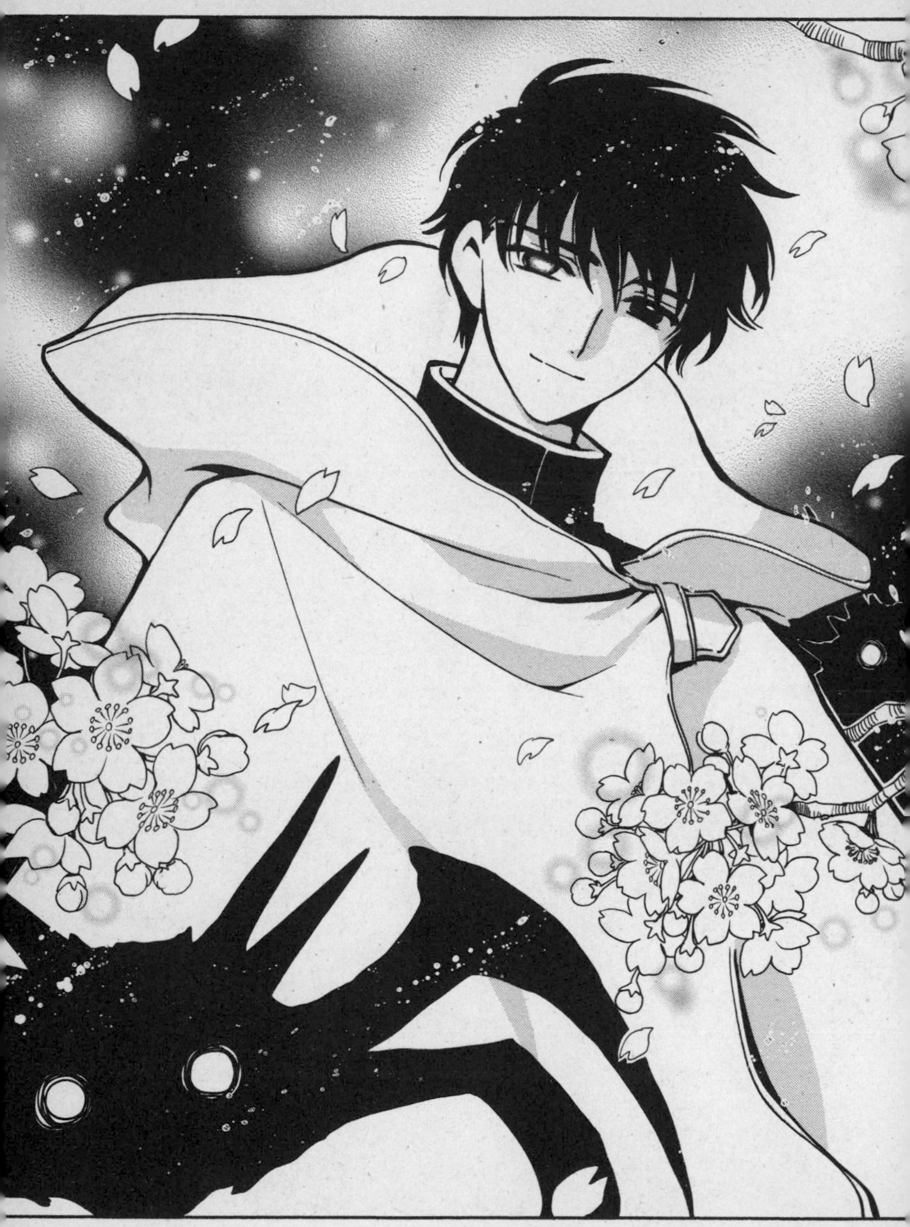

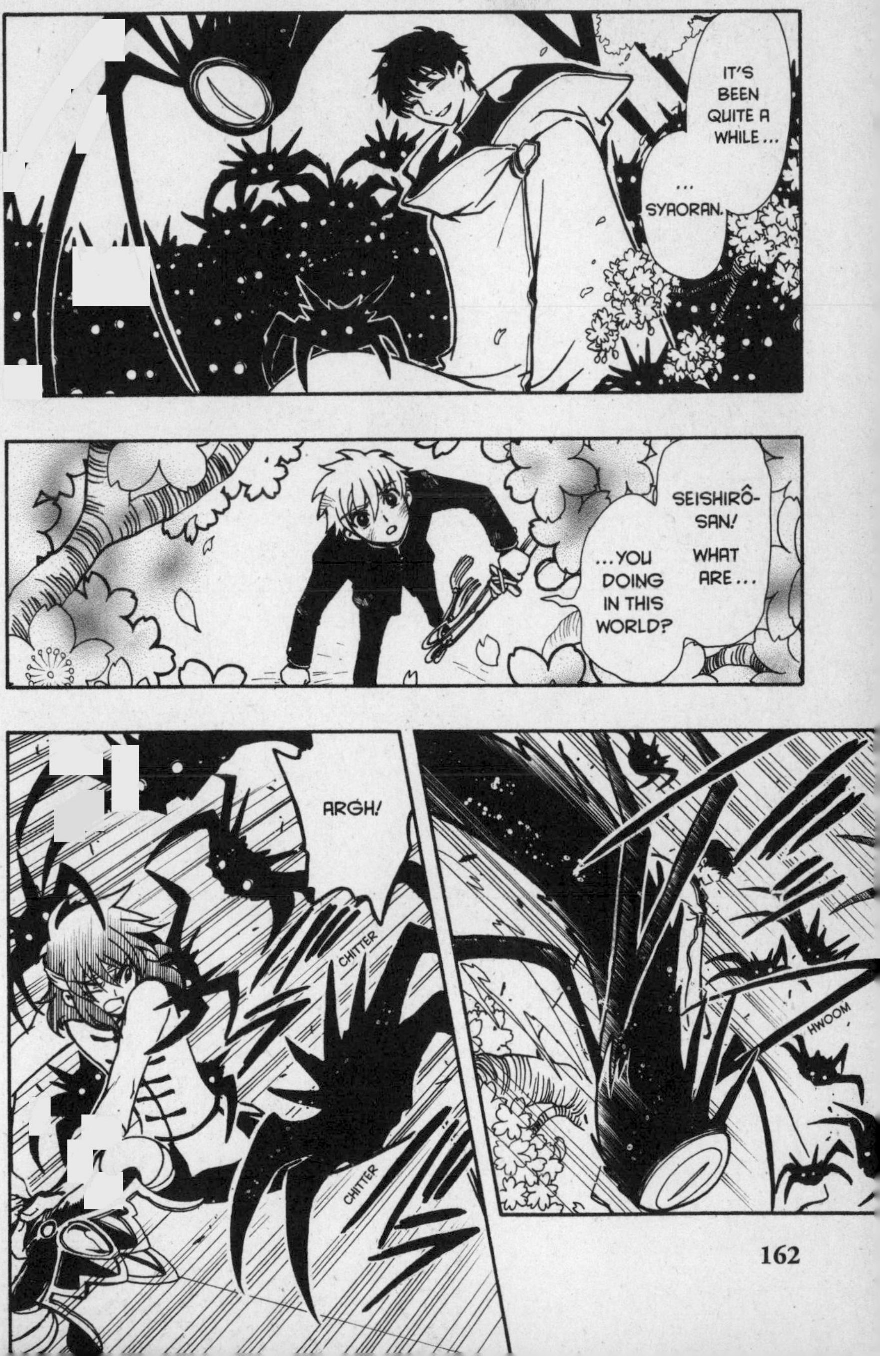
IT'S BEEN QUITE A WHILE...
...SYAORAN.
SEISHIRÔ-SAN!
WHAT ARE...
...YOU DOING IN THIS WORLD?
HWOOM
ARGH!
CHITTER
CHITTER

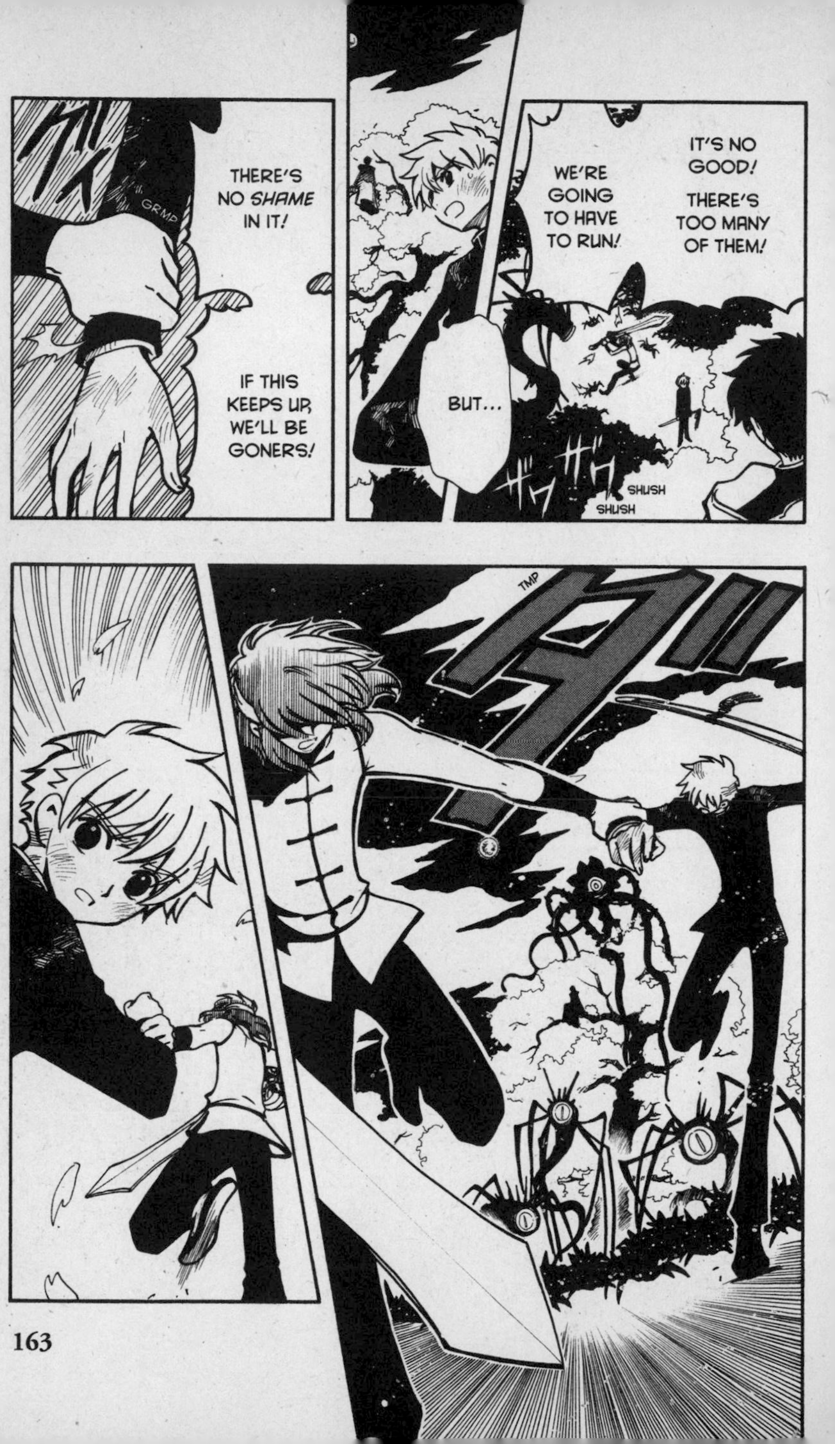
IT'S NO GOOD!
THERE'S TOO MANY OF THEM!
WE'RE GOING TO HAVE TO RUN!
SHUSH
SHUSH
BUT...
THERE'S NO *SHAME* IN IT!
GRMP
IF THIS KEEPS UP, WE'LL BE GONERS!
TMP

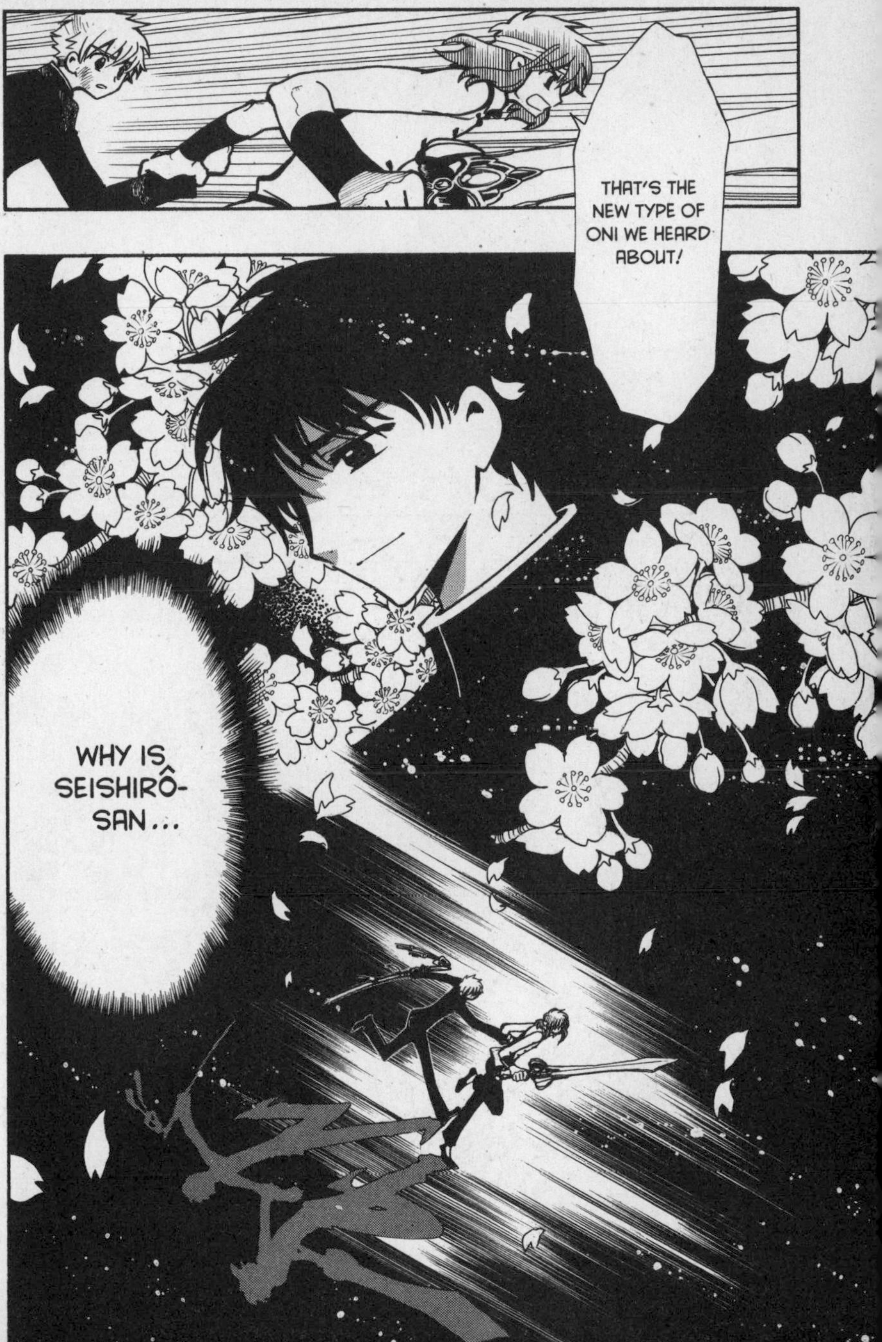
THAT'S THE NEW TYPE OF ONI WE HEARD ABOUT!
WHY IS SEISHIRÔ-SAN...

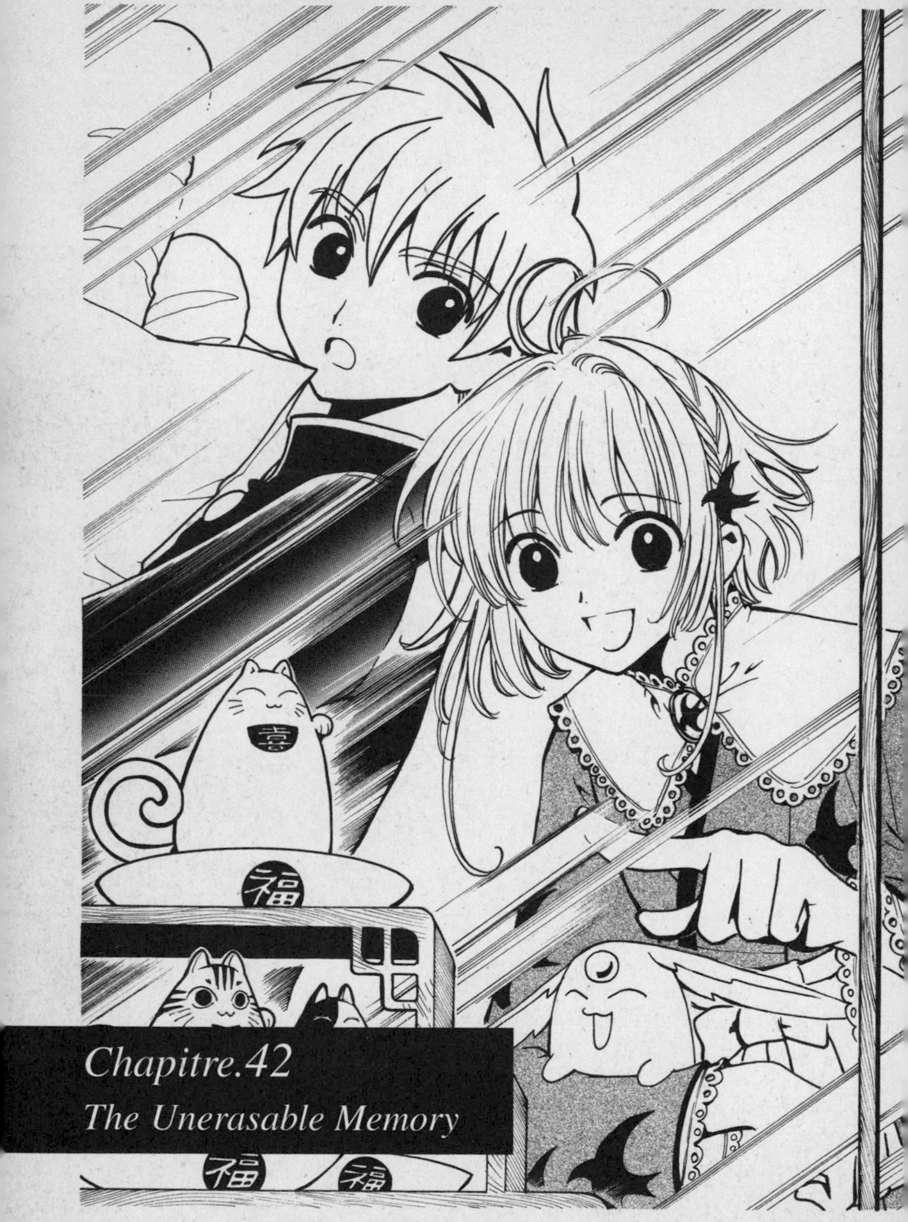

Chapitre.42

The Unerasable Memory

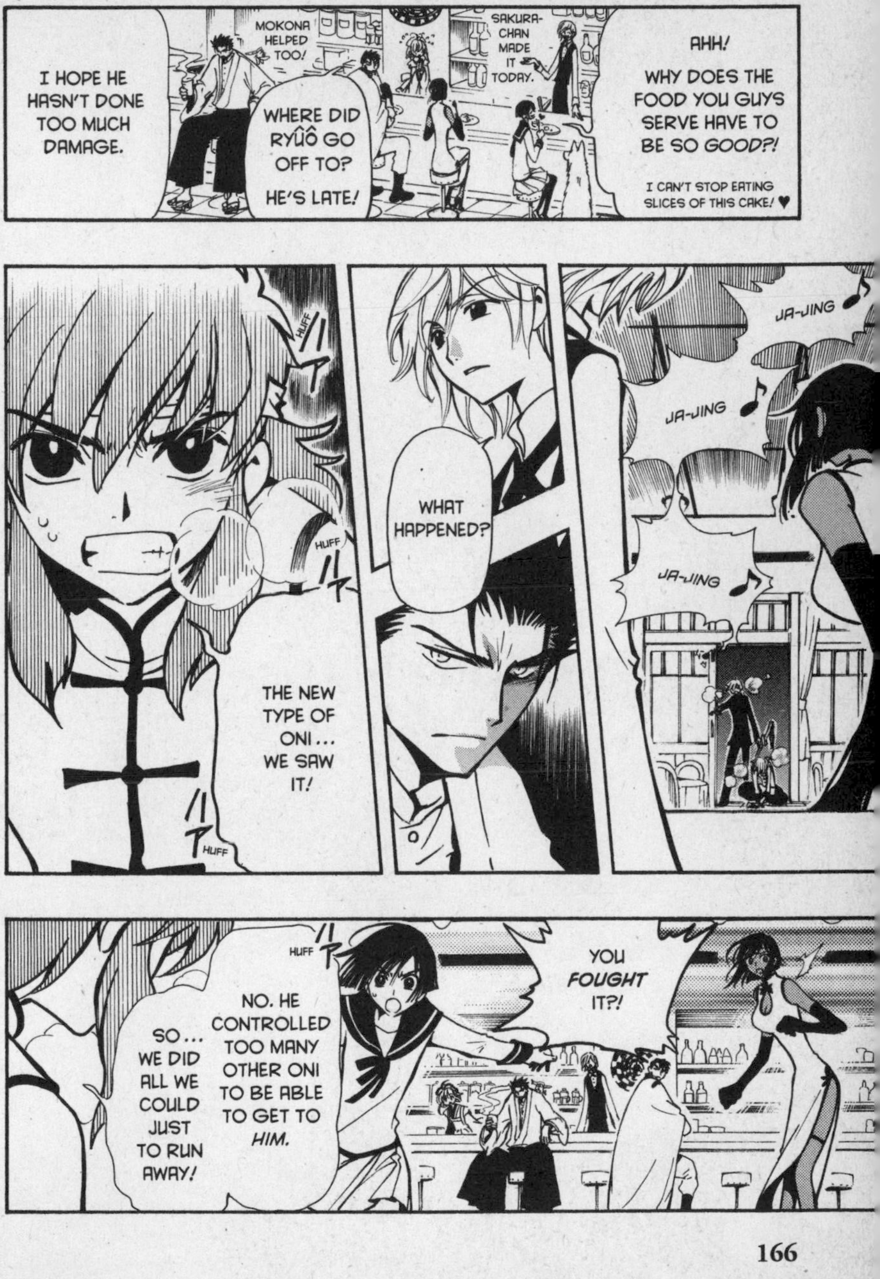
AHH!
WHY DOES THE FOOD YOU GUYS SERVE HAVE TO BE SO *GOOD?!*
I CAN'T STOP EATING SLICES OF THIS CAKE! ♥
SAKURA-CHAN MADE IT TODAY.
MOKONA HELPED TOO!
WHERE DID RYÛÔ GO OFF TO?
HE'S LATE!
I HOPE HE HASN'T DONE TOO MUCH DAMAGE.
JA-JING
JA-JING
JA-JING
WHAT HAPPENED?
HUFF
HUFF
THE NEW TYPE OF ONI... WE SAW IT!
HUFF
YOU *FOUGHT* IT?!
HUFF
NO. HE CONTROLLED TOO MANY OTHER ONI TO BE ABLE TO GET TO *HIM.*
SO... WE DID ALL WE COULD JUST TO RUN AWAY!

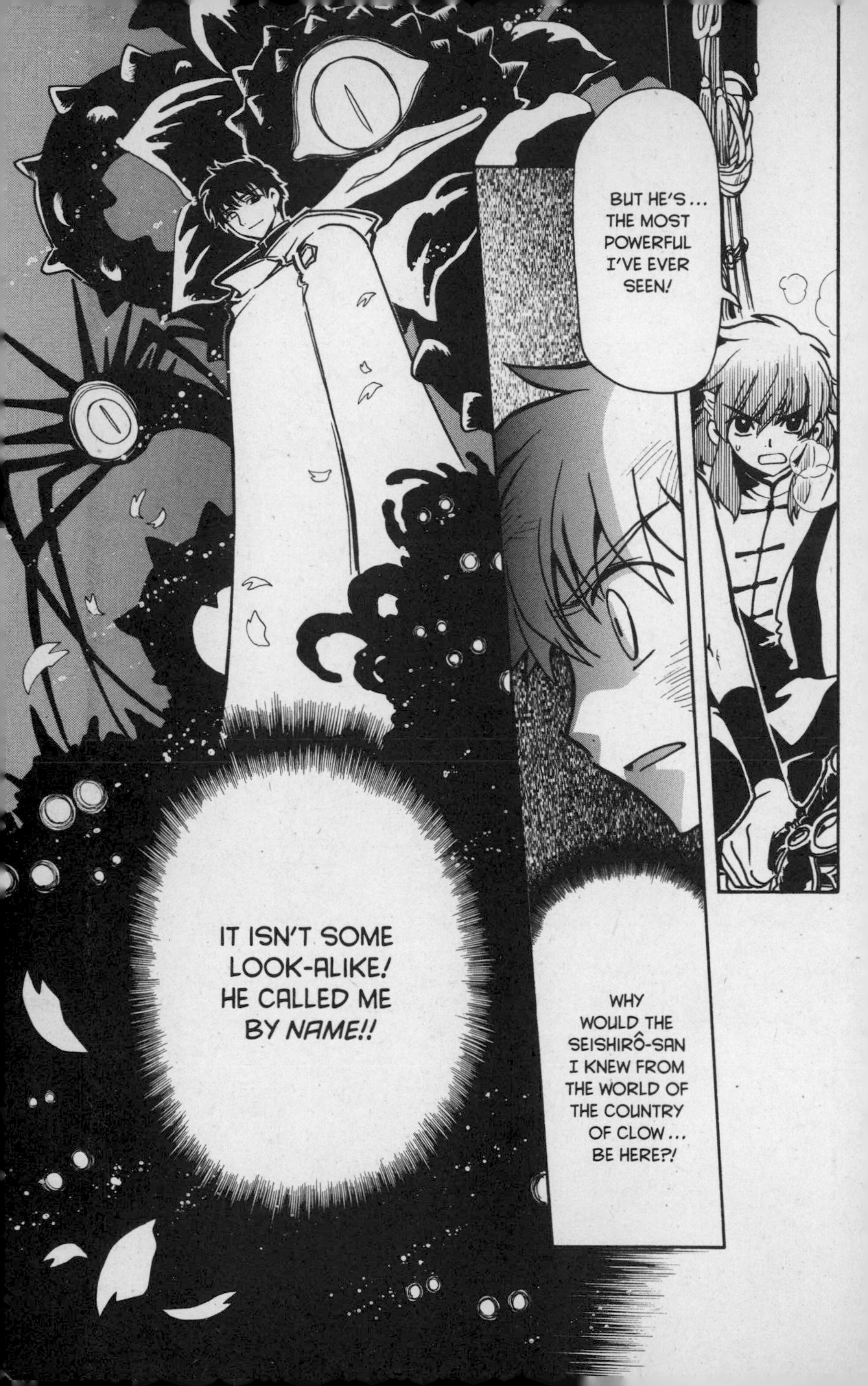
BUT HE'S... THE MOST POWERFUL I'VE EVER SEEN!
WHY WOULD THE SEISHIRÔ-SAN I KNEW FROM THE WORLD OF THE COUNTRY OF CLOW... BE HERE?!
IT ISN'T SOME LOOK-ALIKE! HE CALLED ME BY *NAME!!*

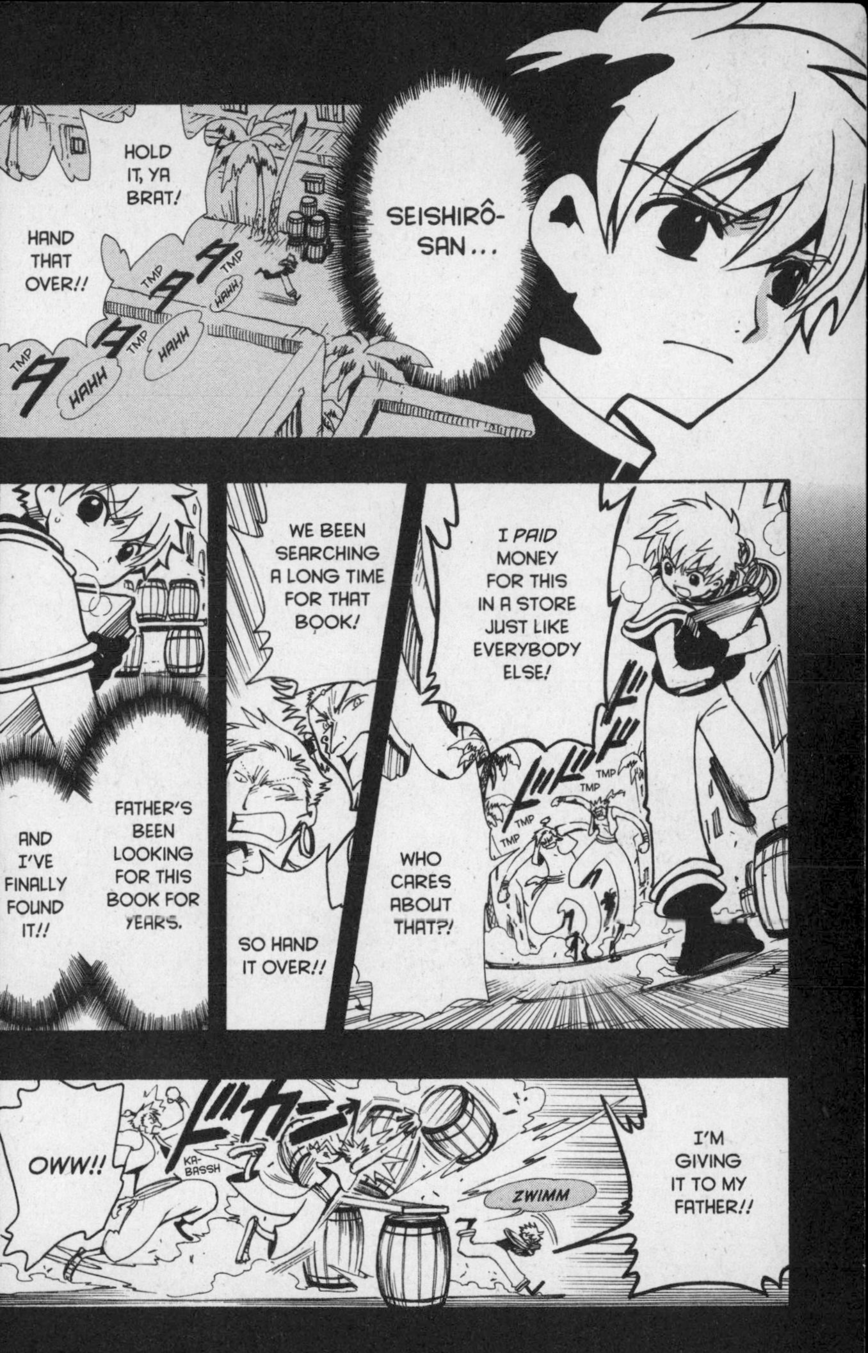
SEISHIRÔ-SAN...
HOLD IT, YA BRAT!
HAND THAT OVER!!
TMP TMP TMP TMP
HAHH HAHH HAHH
I PAID MONEY FOR THIS IN A STORE JUST LIKE EVERYBODY ELSE!
TMP TMP TMP TMP
WHO CARES ABOUT THAT?!
WE BEEN SEARCHING A LONG TIME FOR THAT BOOK!
SO HAND IT OVER!!
FATHER'S BEEN LOOKING FOR THIS BOOK FOR YEARS.
AND I'VE FINALLY FOUND IT!!
I'M GIVING IT TO MY FATHER!!
ZWIMM
KA-BASSH
OWW!!

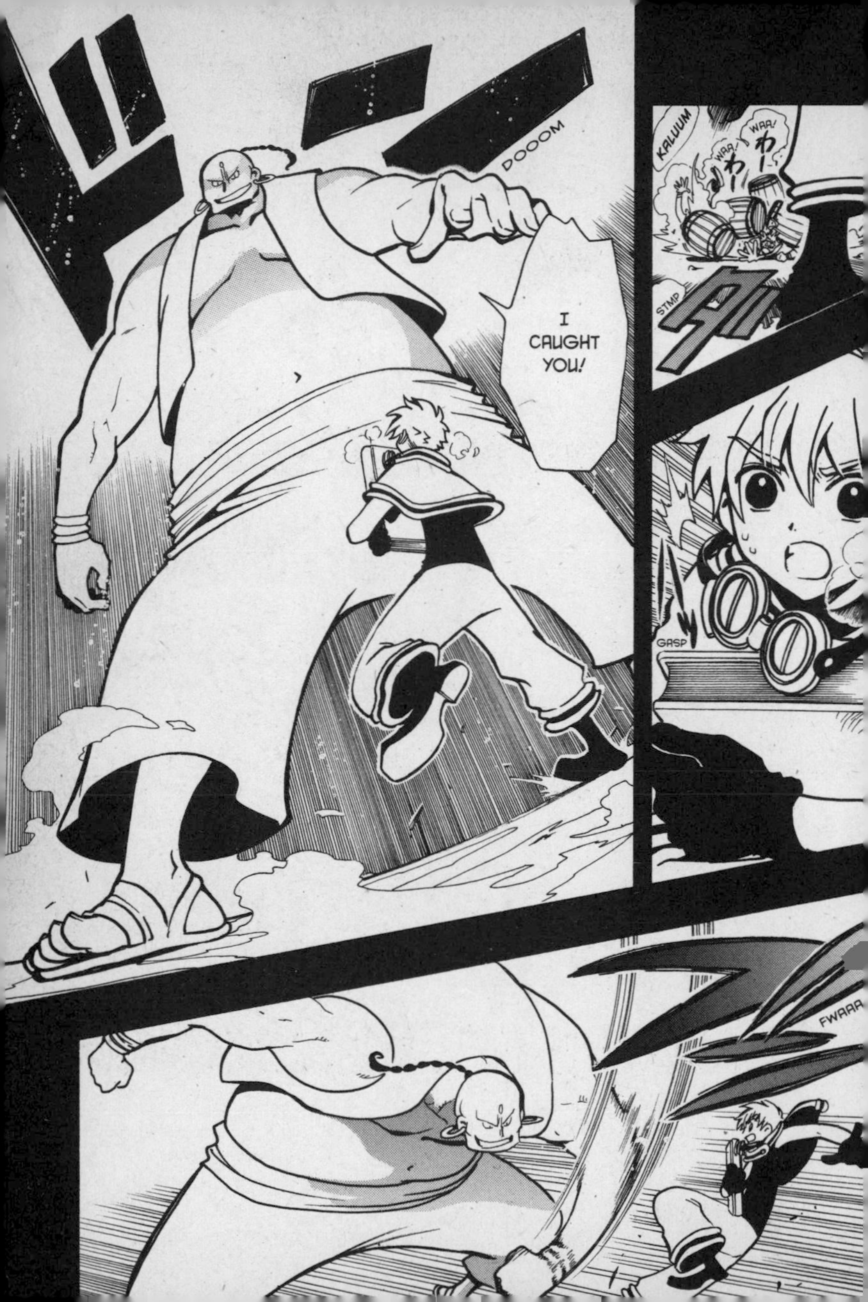
WAA!
わー
WAA!
わー
KALUUM
STMP
GASP
DOOOM
I CAUGHT YOU!
FWAAA

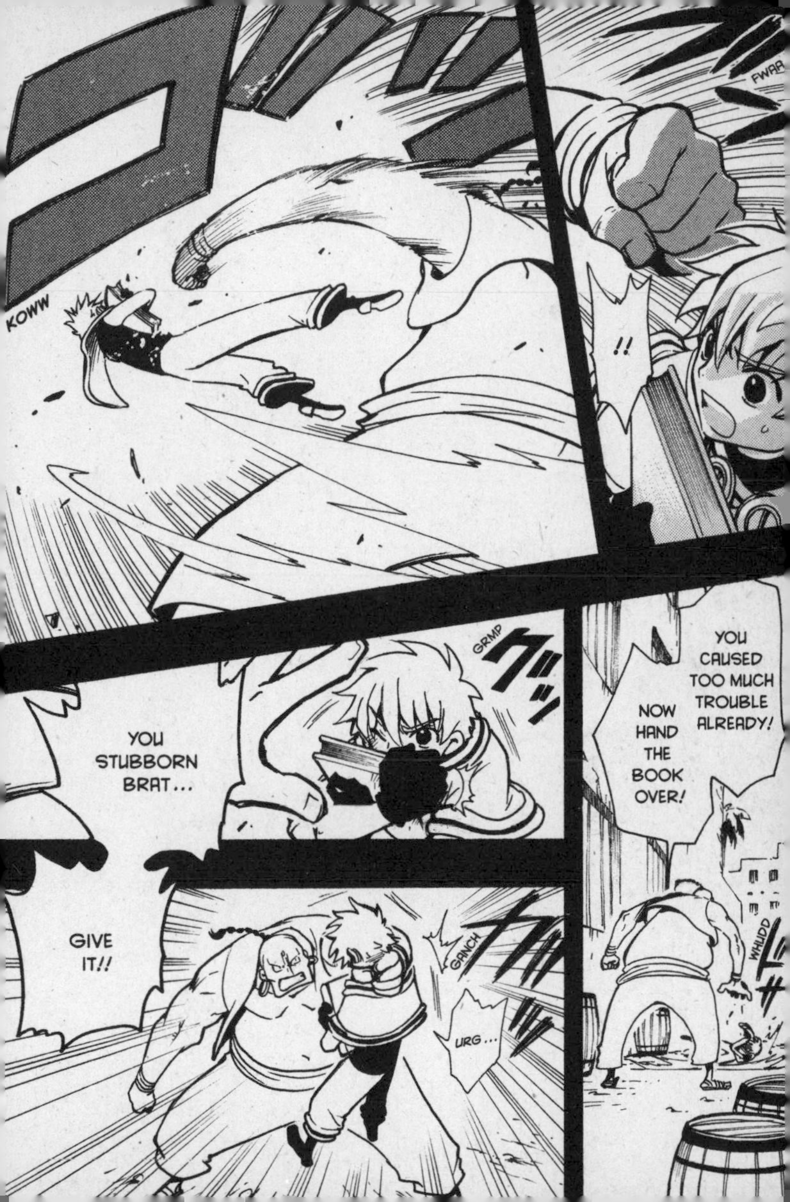
FWAR
!!
KOWW
YOU CAUSED TOO MUCH TROUBLE ALREADY!
NOW HAND THE BOOK OVER!
WHUDD
GRMP
YOU STUBBORN BRAT...
GANCH
URG...
GIVE IT!!

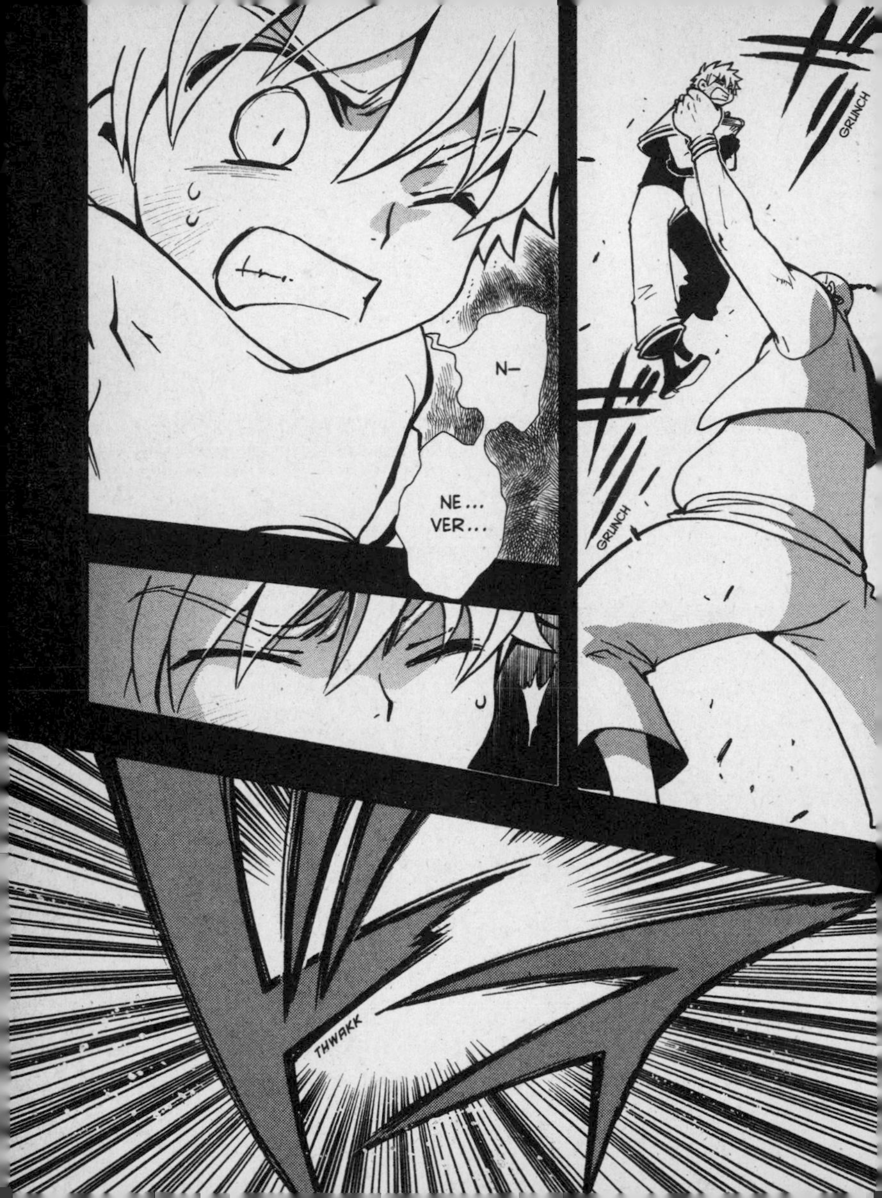
GRUNCH
GRUNCH
N–
NE... VER...
THWAKK

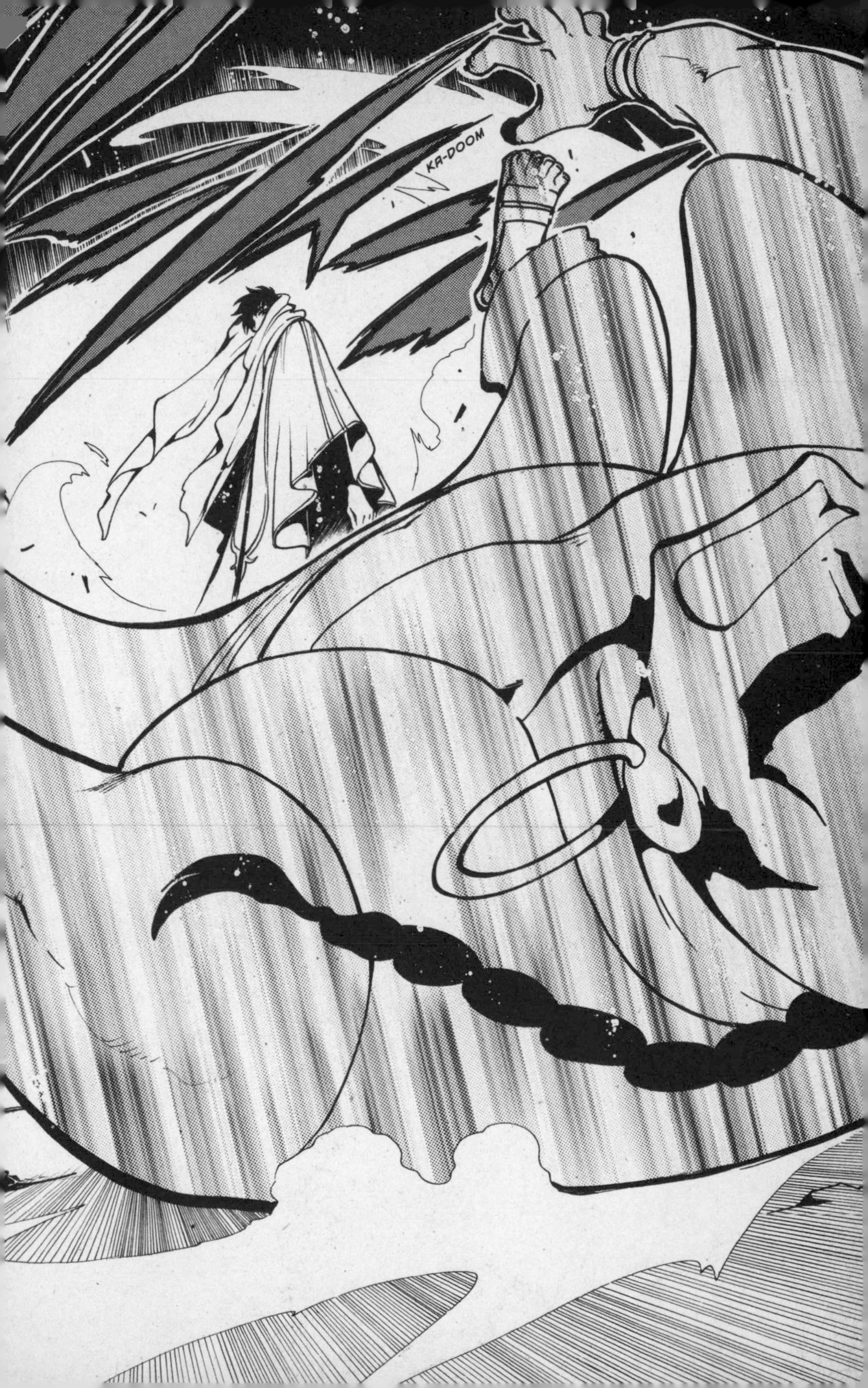
KA-DOOM

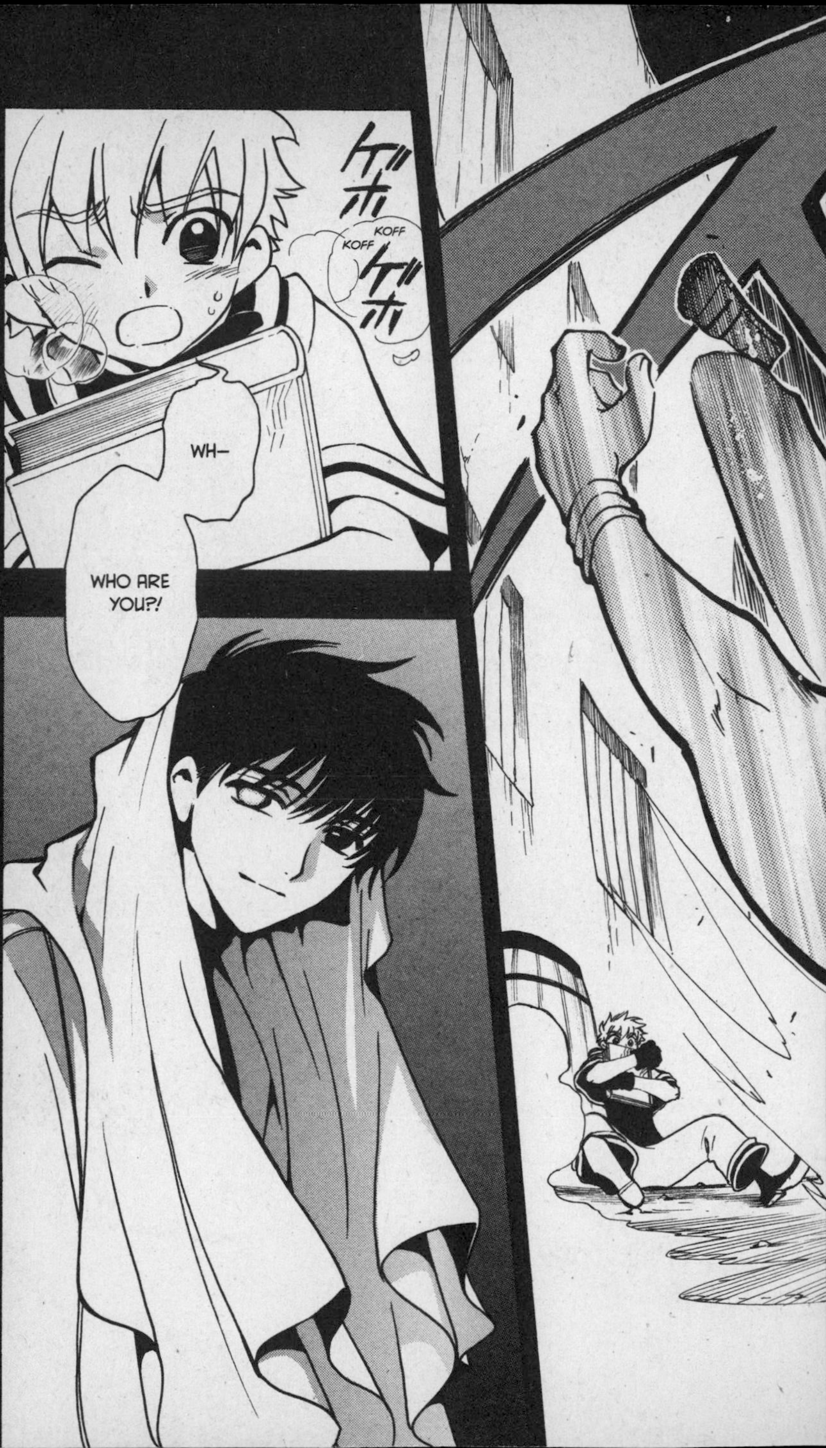
ケホ ケホ
KOFF KOFF
WH–
WHO ARE YOU?!

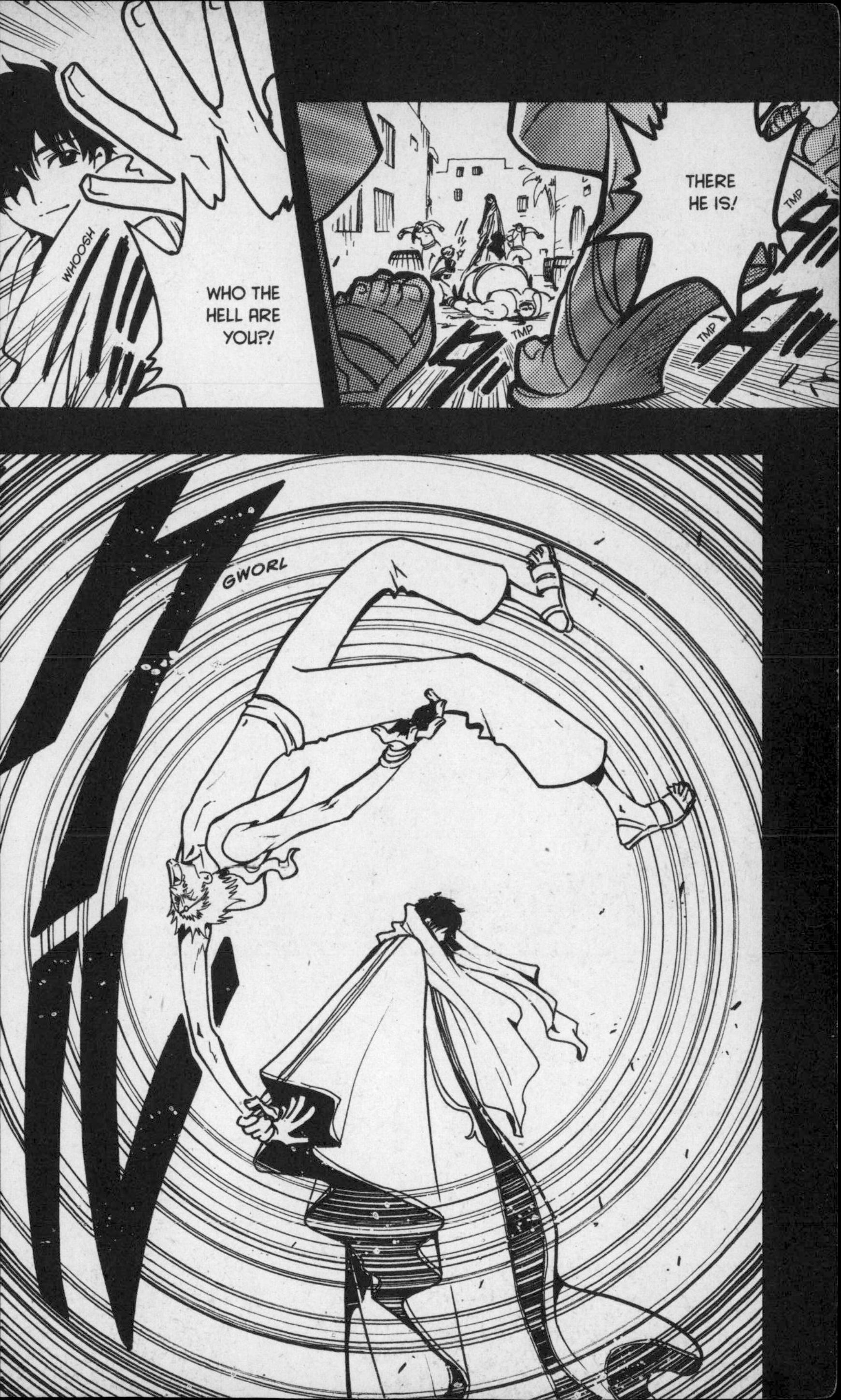
THERE HE IS!
TMP
TMP
TMP
WHOOSH
WHO THE HELL ARE YOU?!
GWORL

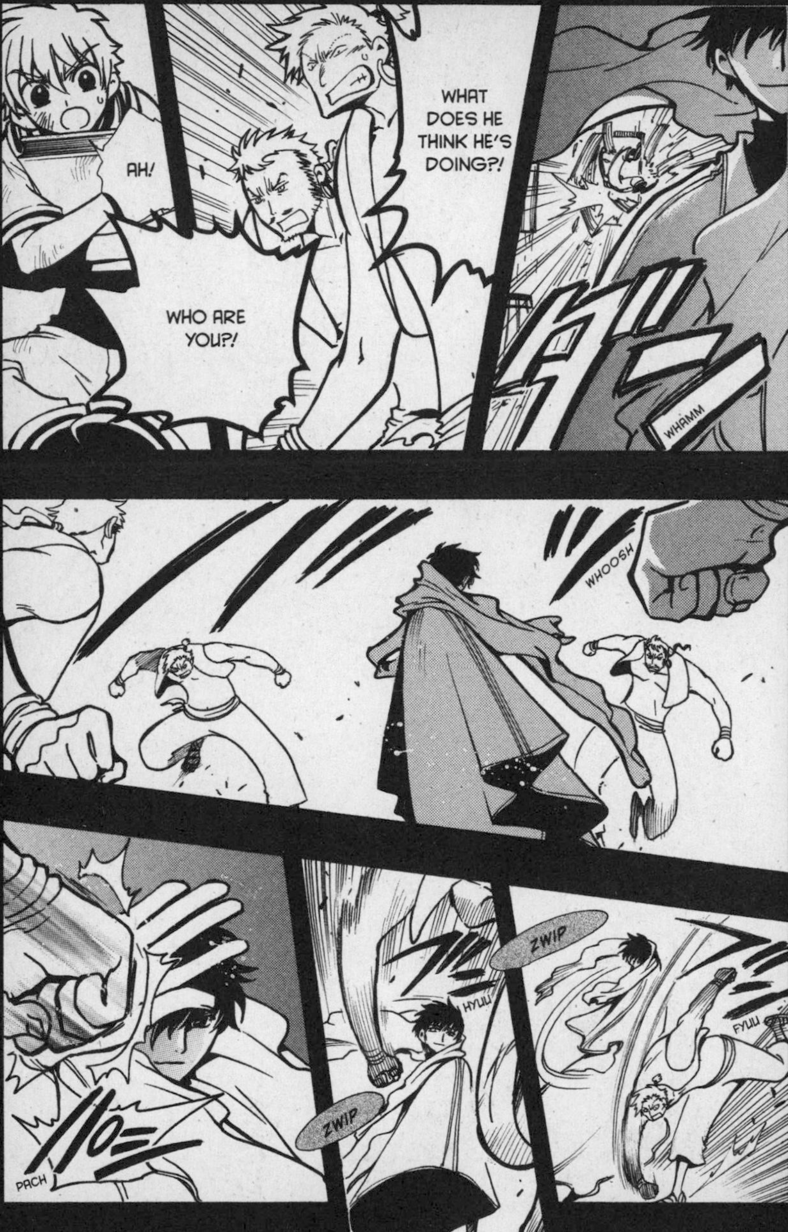
WHAMM
WHAT DOES HE THINK HE'S DOING?!
WHO ARE YOU?!
AH!
WHOOSH
FYUU
ZWIP
HYUU
ZWIP
PACH

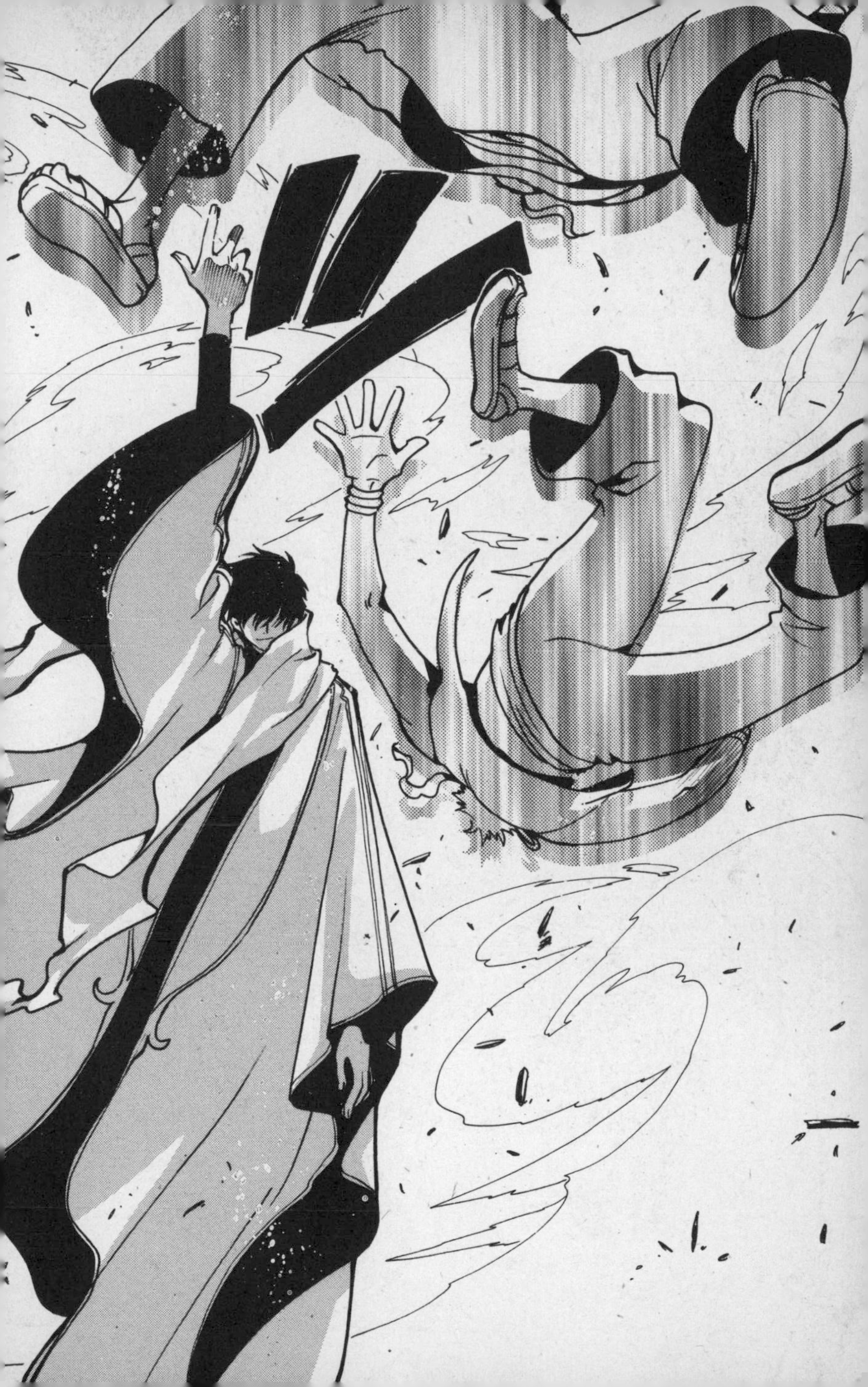

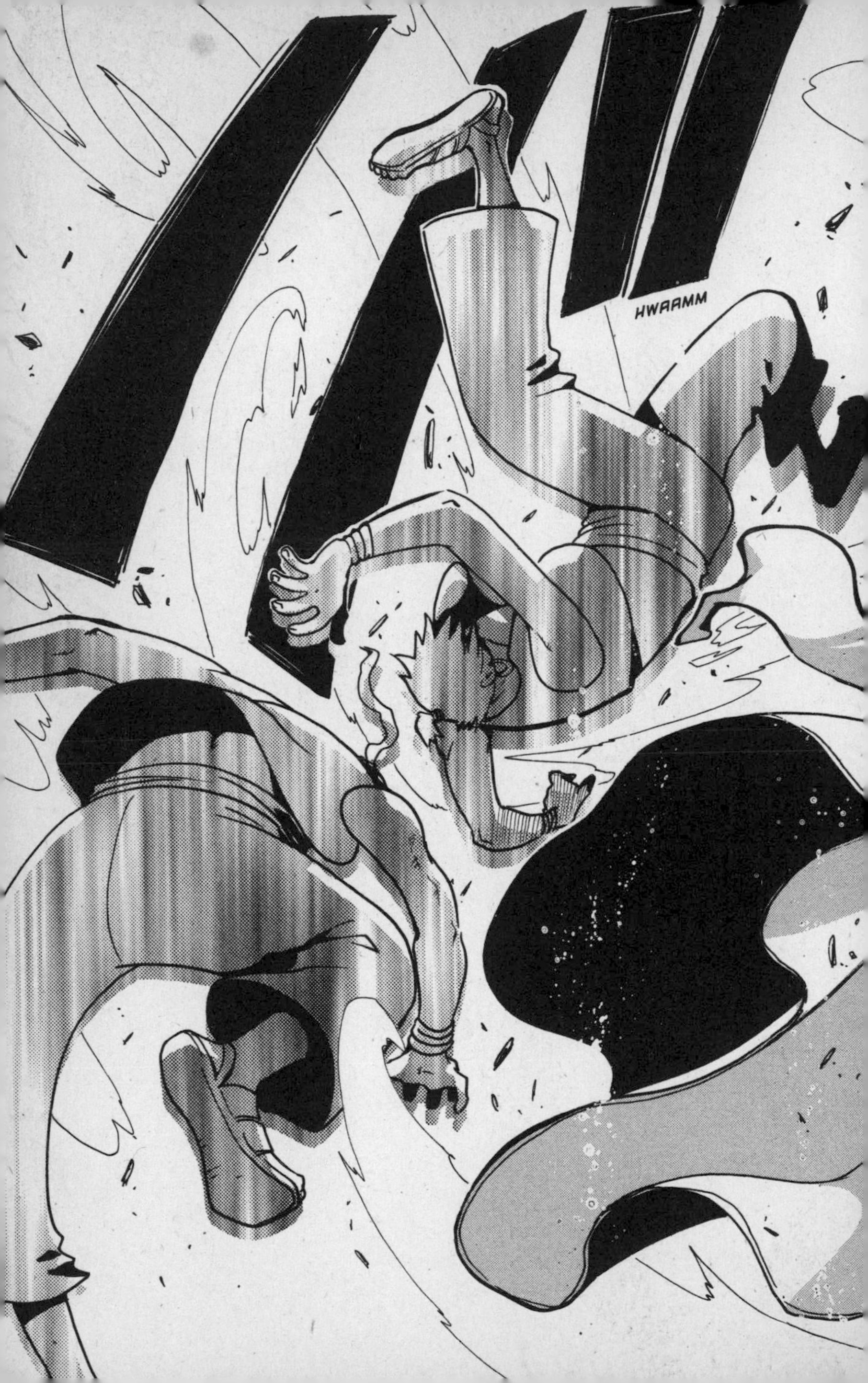
HWAAMM

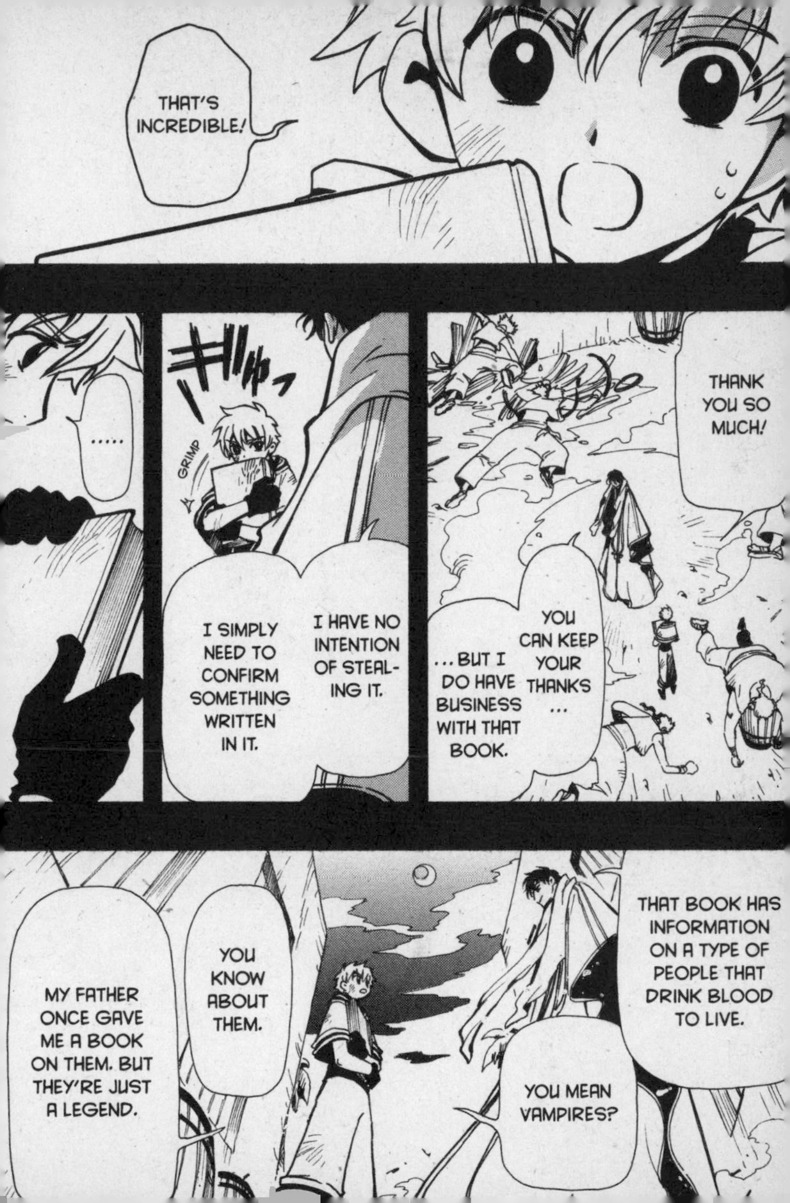
THAT'S INCREDIBLE!
THANK YOU SO MUCH!
YOU CAN KEEP YOUR THANKS ...
... BUT I DO HAVE BUSINESS WITH THAT BOOK.
GRIMP
I HAVE NO INTENTION OF STEAL-ING IT.
I SIMPLY NEED TO CONFIRM SOMETHING WRITTEN IN IT.
......
THAT BOOK HAS INFORMATION ON A TYPE OF PEOPLE THAT DRINK BLOOD TO LIVE.
YOU MEAN VAMPIRES?
YOU KNOW ABOUT THEM.
MY FATHER ONCE GAVE ME A BOOK ON THEM. BUT THEY'RE JUST A LEGEND.

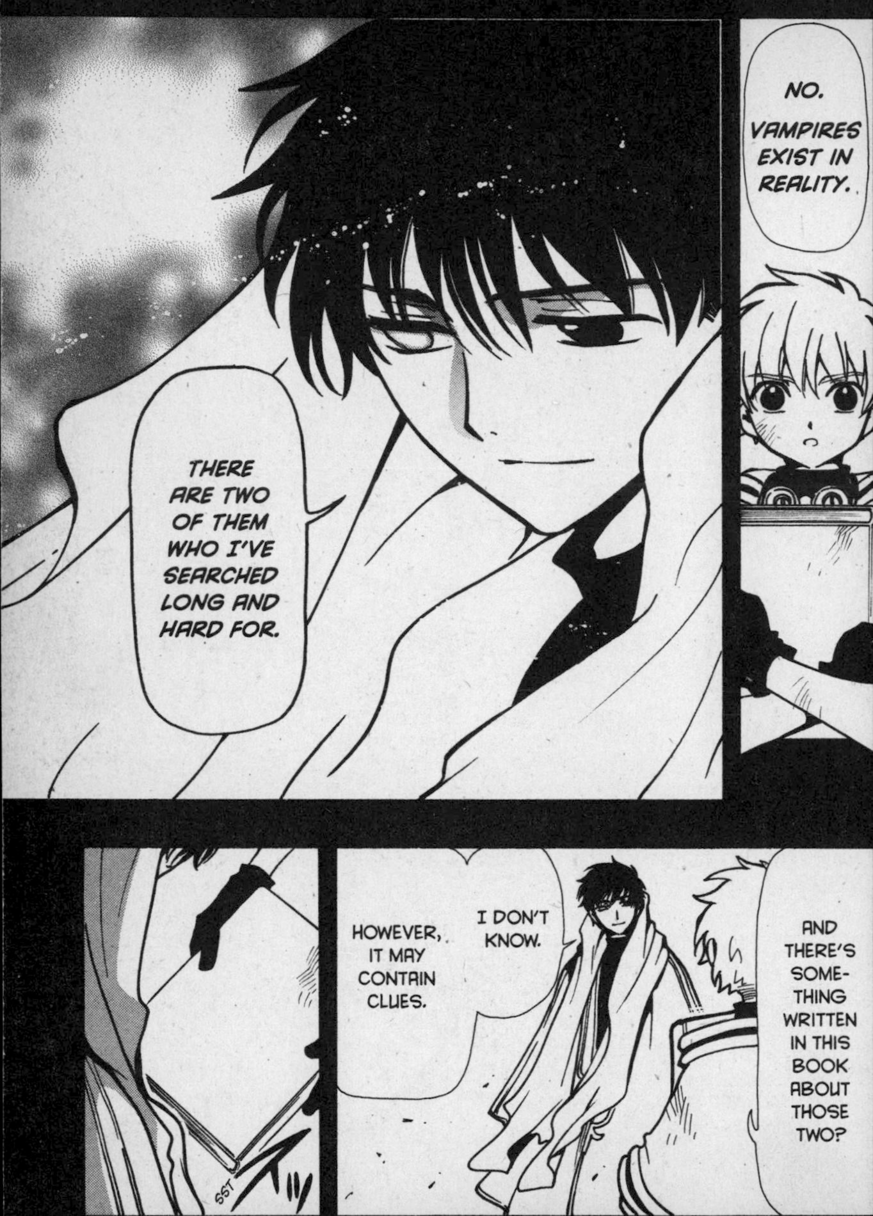
NO.
VAMPIRES EXIST IN REALITY.
THERE ARE TWO OF THEM WHO I'VE SEARCHED LONG AND HARD FOR.
AND THERE'S SOME-THING WRITTEN IN THIS BOOK ABOUT THOSE TWO?
I DON'T KNOW.
HOWEVER, IT MAY CONTAIN CLUES.
SST

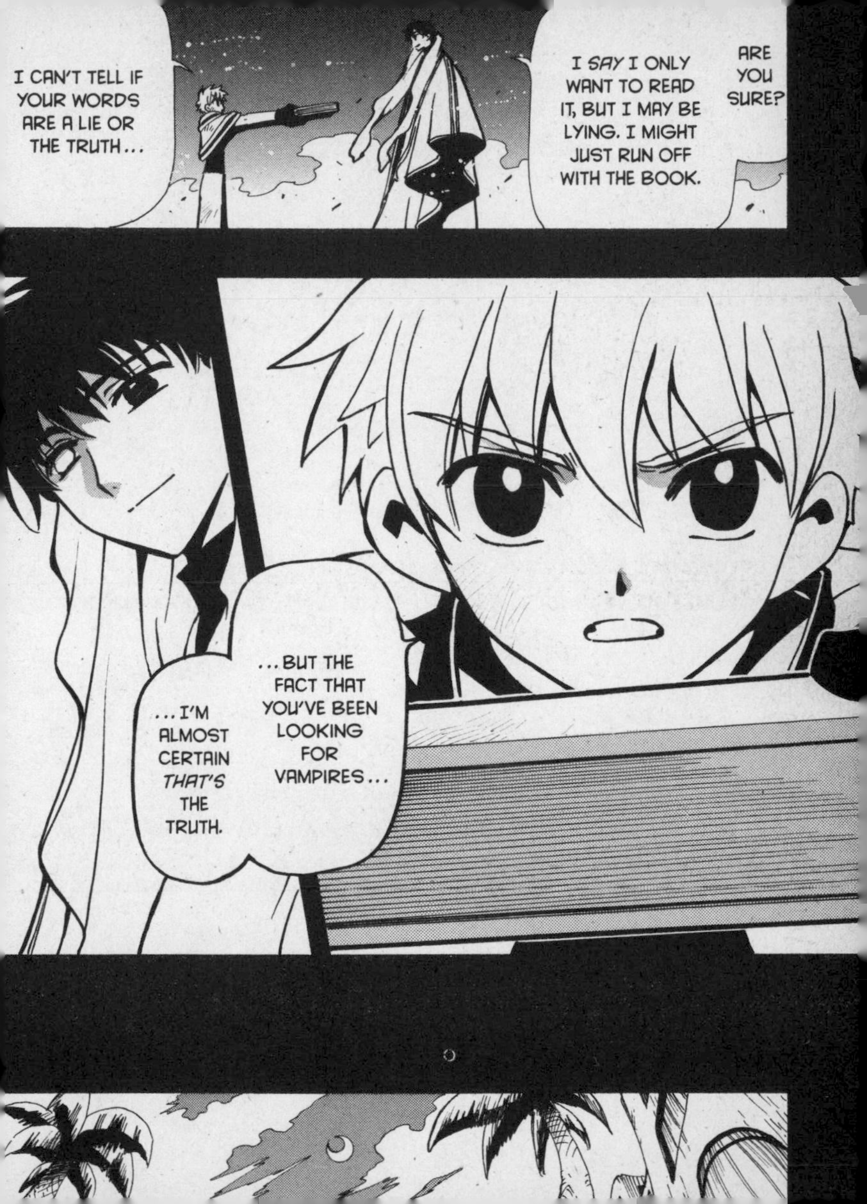
ARE YOU SURE?
I *SAY* I ONLY WANT TO READ IT, BUT I MAY BE LYING. I MIGHT JUST RUN OFF WITH THE BOOK.
I CAN'T TELL IF YOUR WORDS ARE A LIE OR THE TRUTH...
...BUT THE FACT THAT YOU'VE BEEN LOOKING FOR VAMPIRES...
...I'M ALMOST CERTAIN *THAT'S* THE TRUTH.

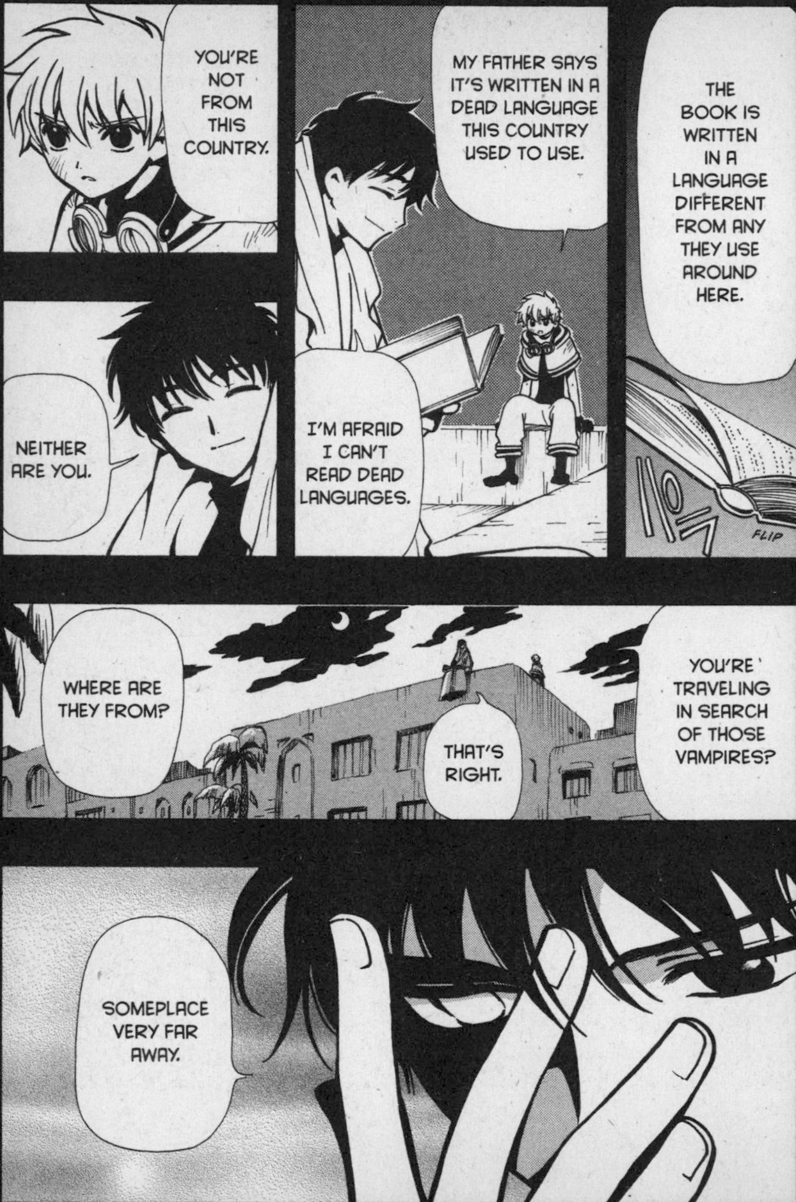
THE BOOK IS WRITTEN IN A LANGUAGE DIFFERENT FROM ANY THEY USE AROUND HERE.
FLIP
MY FATHER SAYS IT'S WRITTEN IN A DEAD LANGUAGE THIS COUNTRY USED TO USE.
I'M AFRAID I CAN'T READ DEAD LANGUAGES.
YOU'RE NOT FROM THIS COUNTRY.
NEITHER ARE YOU.
YOU'RE TRAVELING IN SEARCH OF THOSE VAMPIRES?
THAT'S RIGHT.
WHERE ARE THEY FROM?
SOMEPLACE VERY FAR AWAY.

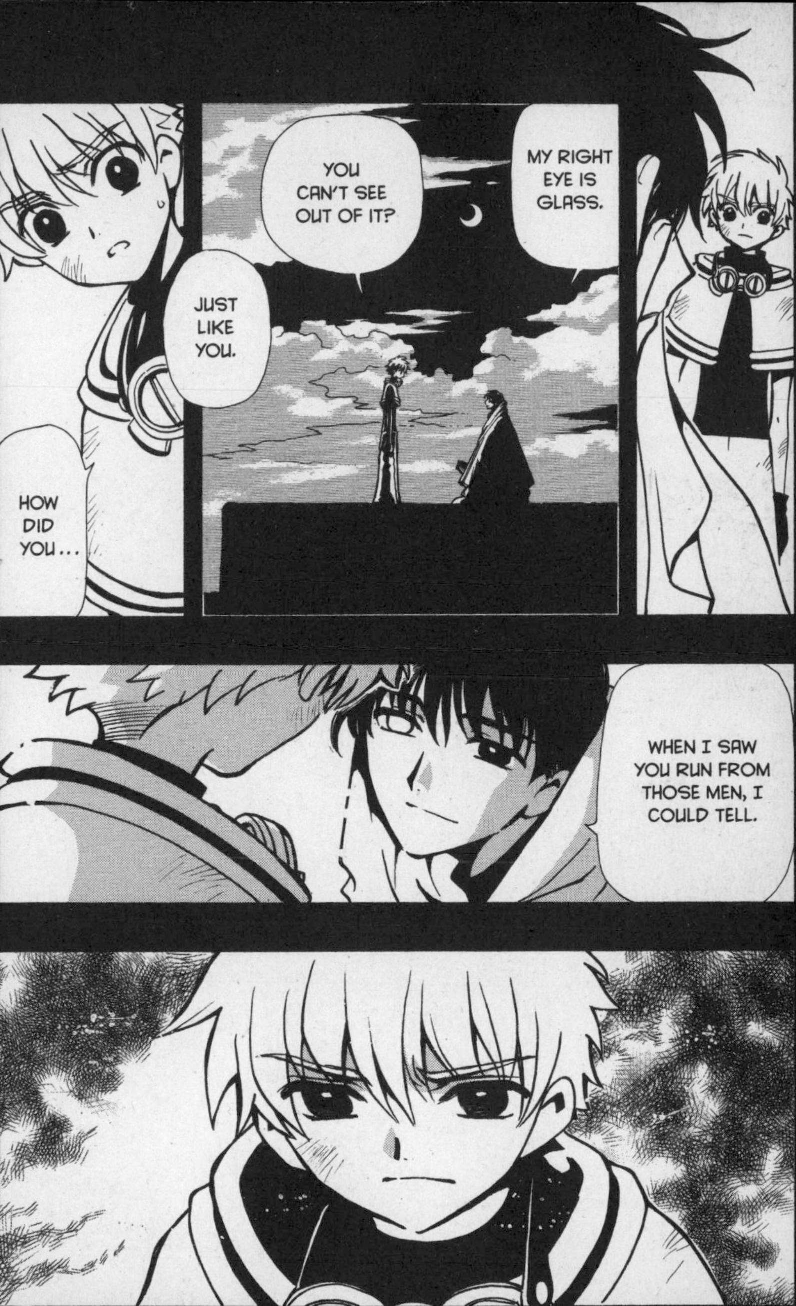
MY RIGHT EYE IS GLASS.
YOU CAN'T SEE OUT OF IT?
JUST LIKE YOU.
HOW DID YOU...
WHEN I SAW YOU RUN FROM THOSE MEN, I COULD TELL.

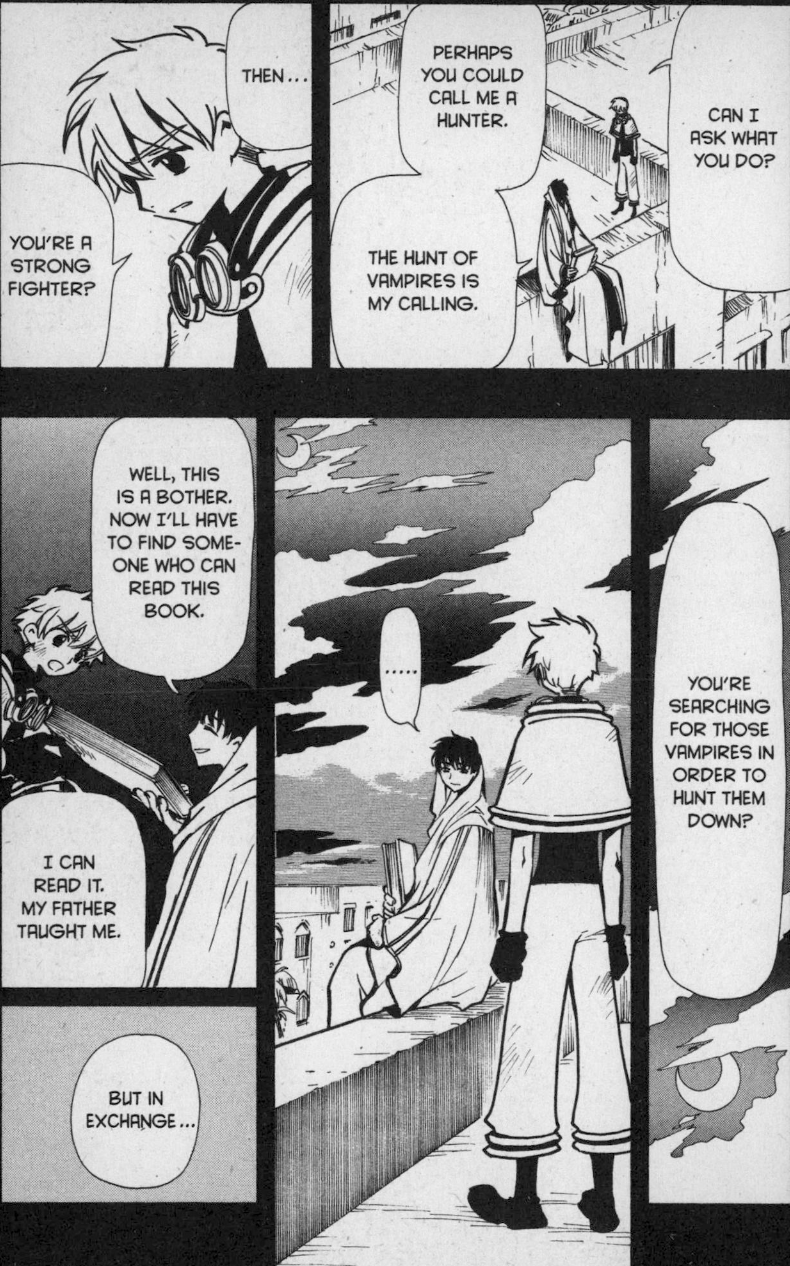

CAN I ASK WHAT YOU DO?
PERHAPS YOU COULD CALL ME A HUNTER.
THE HUNT OF VAMPIRES IS MY CALLING.
THEN...
YOU'RE A STRONG FIGHTER?
YOU'RE SEARCHING FOR THOSE VAMPIRES IN ORDER TO HUNT THEM DOWN?
......
WELL, THIS IS A BOTHER. NOW I'LL HAVE TO FIND SOME-ONE WHO CAN READ THIS BOOK.
I CAN READ IT. MY FATHER TAUGHT ME.
BUT IN EXCHANGE...

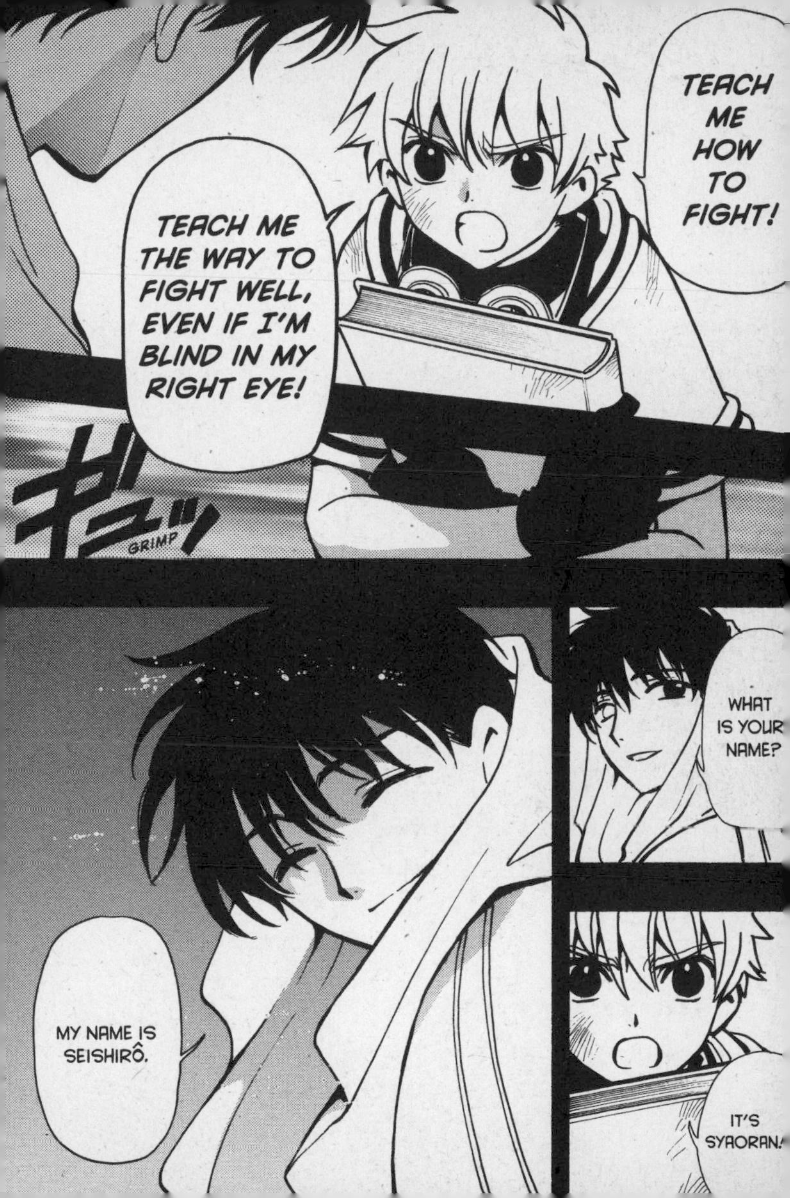
TEACH ME HOW TO FIGHT!
TEACH ME THE WAY TO FIGHT WELL, EVEN IF I'M BLIND IN MY RIGHT EYE!
ギュッ
GRIMP
WHAT IS YOUR NAME?
IT'S SYAORAN!
MY NAME IS SEISHIRÔ.

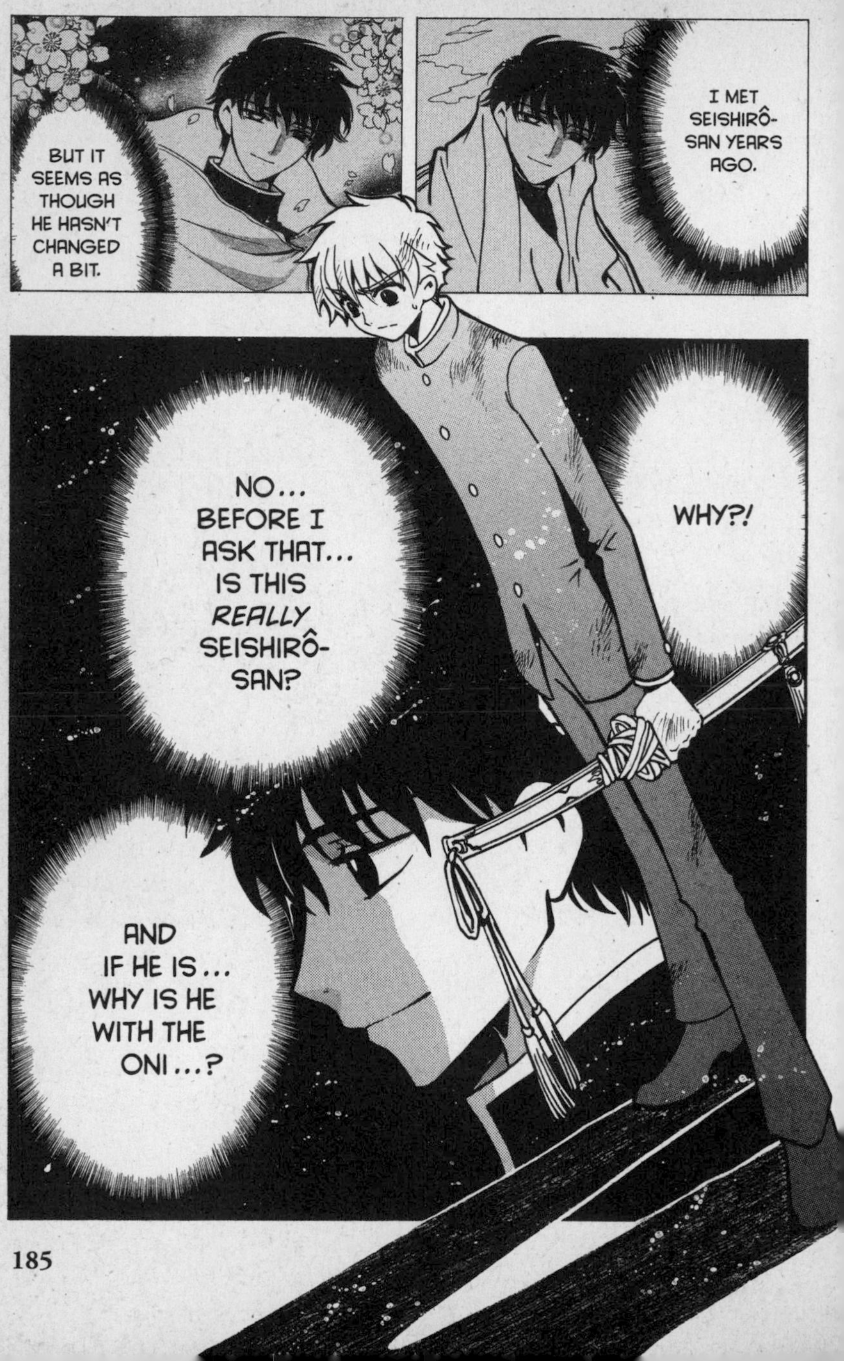
I MET SEISHIRÔ-SAN YEARS AGO.
BUT IT SEEMS AS THOUGH HE HASN'T CHANGED A BIT.
WHY?!
NO... BEFORE I ASK THAT... IS THIS *REALLY* SEISHIRÔ-SAN?
AND IF HE IS... WHY IS HE WITH THE ONI...?

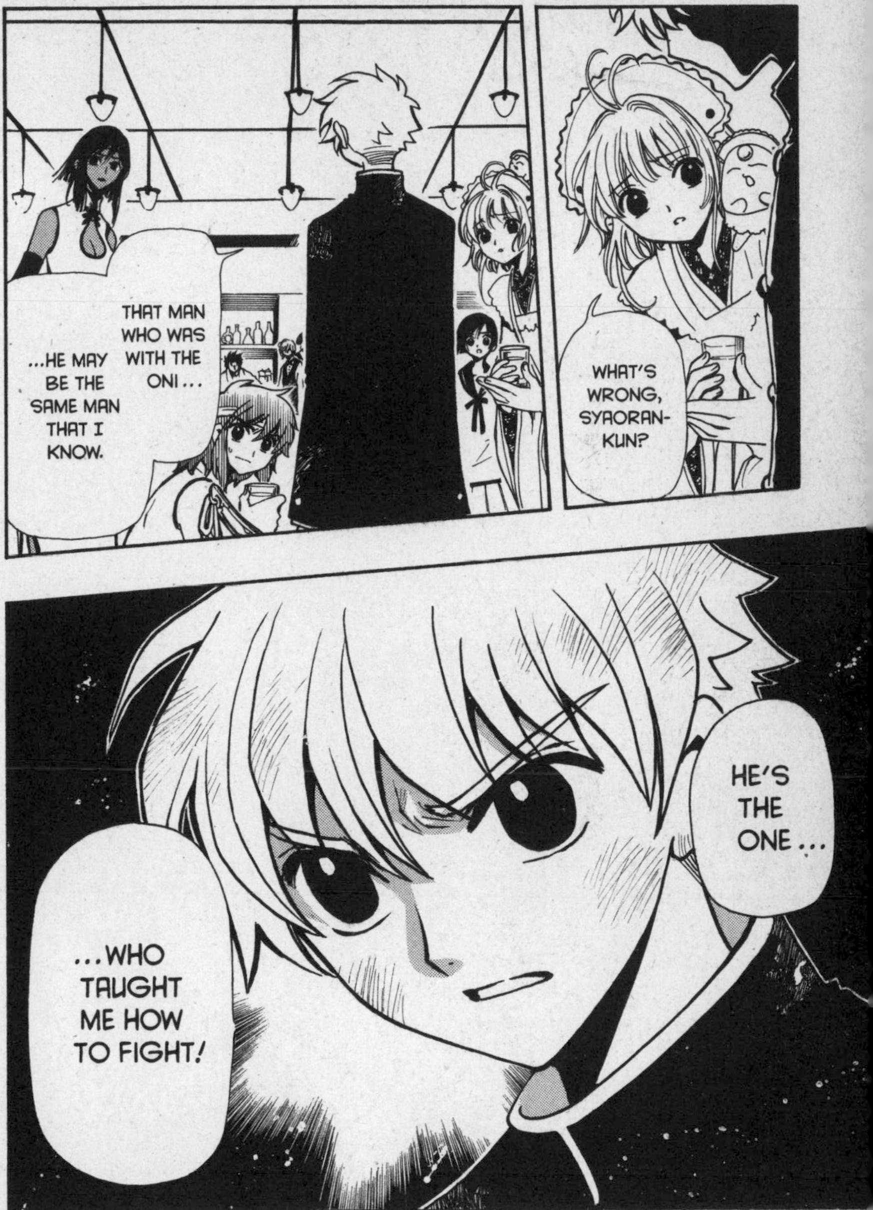
WHAT'S WRONG, SYAORAN-KUN?
THAT MAN WHO WAS WITH THE ONI...
...HE MAY BE THE SAME MAN THAT I KNOW.
HE'S THE ONE...
...WHO TAUGHT ME HOW TO FIGHT!

To Be Continued

About the Creators

CLAMP is a group of four women who have become the most popular manga artists in America—Ageha Ohkawa, Mokona, Satsuki Igarashi, and Tsubaki Nekoi. They started out as doujinshi (fan comics) creators, but their skill and craft brought them to the attention of publishers very quickly. Their first work from a major publisher was *RG Veda*, but their first mass success was with *Magic Knight Rayearth*. From there, they went on to write many series, including *Cardcaptor Sakura* and *Chobits*, two of the most popular manga in the United States. Like many Japanese manga artists, they prefer to avoid the spotlight, and little is known about them personally.

CLAMP is currently publishing three series in Japan: *Tsubasa* and *xxxHOLiC* with Kodansha and *Gohou Drug* with Kadokawa.

Translation Notes

Japanese is a tricky language for most Westerners, and translation is often more art than science. For your edification and reading pleasure, here are notes on some of the places where we could have gone in a different direction in our translation of the work, or where a Japanese cultural reference is used.

Just to catch you up . . .

The country of Ôto is based on the romantic notion of early twentieth-century Japan, where the traditional feudal Japanese lifestyle still mixed with strong Western influences. The enemies, oni, are ranked in a system known to the Japanese as Iroha, a way of counting that might be compared to counting in English using "Eenie meanie minie moe," but with more historical and poetic relevance (see more on Iroha in the notes from Volume 5). The ranking of oni start with I, which is the highest, down to To, which is the lowest. Each rank has a level with 1 being the highest and 5 being the lowest. Thus we have:

Rank	
I	levels 5 to 1
Ro	levels 5 to 1
Ha	levels 5 to 1
Ni	levels 5 to 1
Ho	levels 5 to 1
He	levels 5 to 1
To	levels 5 to 1

Breakfast food, page 7

Traditional Japanese breakfast food is fish with soy sauce and rice. It wasn't until Western influences swept the country in the late 1800s and early 1900s that tastes began to change toward sweet things like jams and frosted buns in the morning.

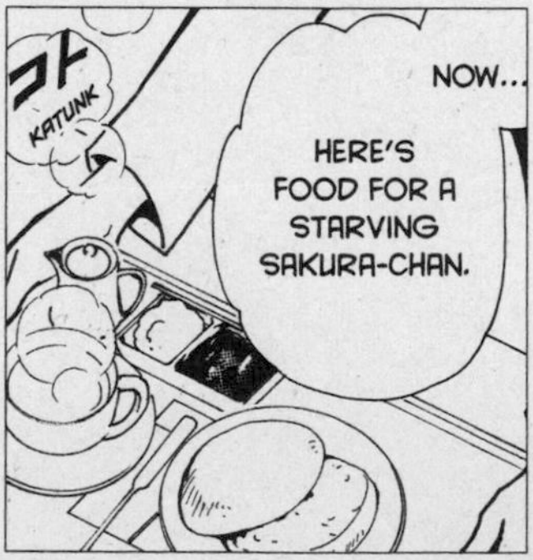
KATUNK
NOW...
HERE'S FOOD FOR A STARVING SAKURA-CHAN.

Sneezing, page 8

The old wives' tale goes that when you sneeze, someone is talking about you. It isn't easy to find anyone who actually believes in the saying, but the idea sure comes up in anime and manga quite a lot!

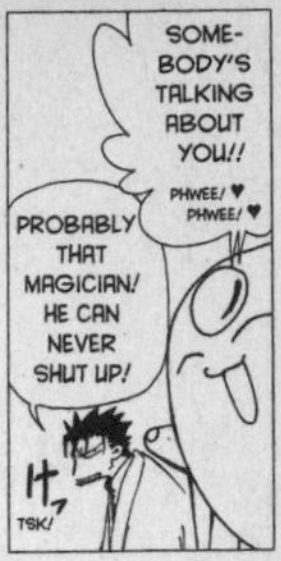
SOME-BODY'S TALKING ABOUT YOU!!
PHWEE! ♥ PHWEE! ♥
PROBABLY THAT MAGICIAN! HE CAN NEVER SHUT UP!
TSK!

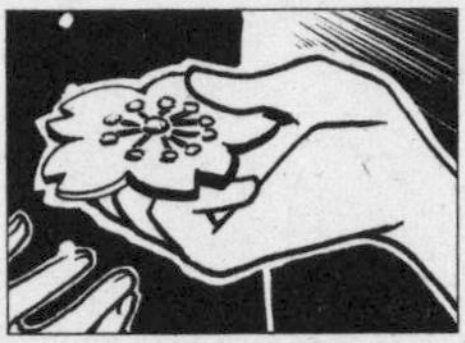

The Sakura shape, page 21

The first kanji in the spelling of the country of Ôto is the same kanji for Sakura, cherry blossom (see more on the cultural significance of the cherry blossom in the notes from Volume 5). So it is only natural that the "debit card" of Syaoran and friends would be in the shape of a cherry blossom.

Ryûô & Sôma, page 28

Anyone who has ever seen the anime or manga for RG Veda will have no problem recognizing the rambunctious attitude and ridiculously large sword of Ryûô (also spelled Ryuoh in the animated version). Sôma (also from Kurogane's world in the first volume) is the ninja servant of Kendappa, also from RG Veda.

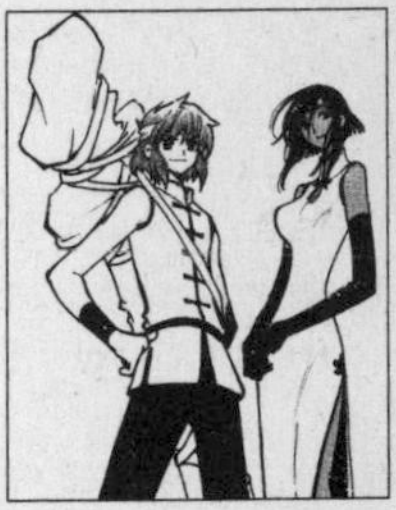

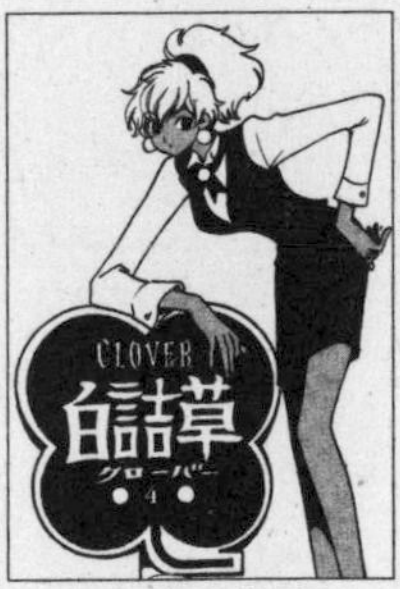
CLOVER
白詰草
クローバー
4

Caldina and the bar, page 55

The bar is obviously a reference to CLAMP's series Clover, and Caldina is borrowed from Magic Knight Rayearth.

Mokona coming downstairs, page 58

Sharp-eyed readers of *xxxHOLiC* will remember a scene in *xxxHOLiC* Volume 4 when Mokona ends a conversation with Yûko to check on a noise. You've just found out what noise Mokona was checking on.

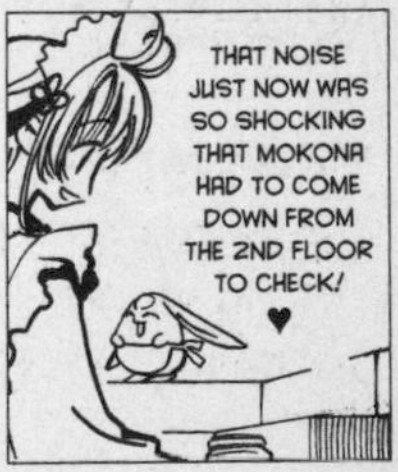
THAT NOISE JUST NOW WAS SO SHOCKING THAT MOKONA HAD TO COME DOWN FROM THE 2ND FLOOR TO CHECK! ♥

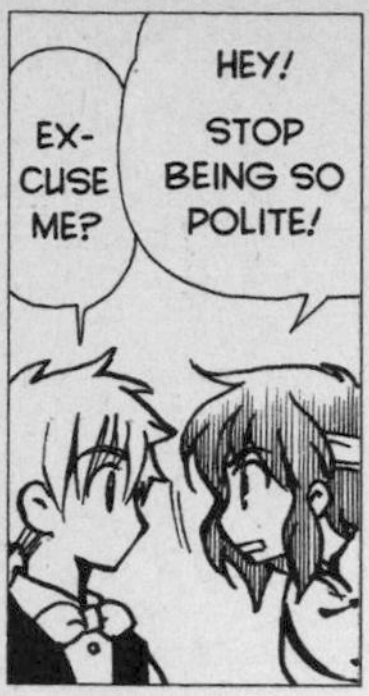
HEY!
STOP BEING SO POLITE!
EX-CUSE ME?

Polite language, page 60

There is a movement toward less formalized language among the young people of Japan, and Ryûô personifies it with his insistence that Syaoran stop using polite speech with him. Similarly in North America, we use the titles Mr., Mrs., and Ms. less now than earlier generations have, and we use first names more.

Talking like the Hanshin Republic, page 64

Caldina speaks with a "Kansai" accent (Kansai being the region encompassing the big cities of Osaka, Kyoto, Nara, and Kobe as well as the surrounding region), and since the Hanshin Republic was based on Osaka, Caldina's Kansai accent would sound like what Fai remembers from that country. The Kansai accent tends to be thought of as warm and folksy, much as the western drawl might be thought of in the United States.

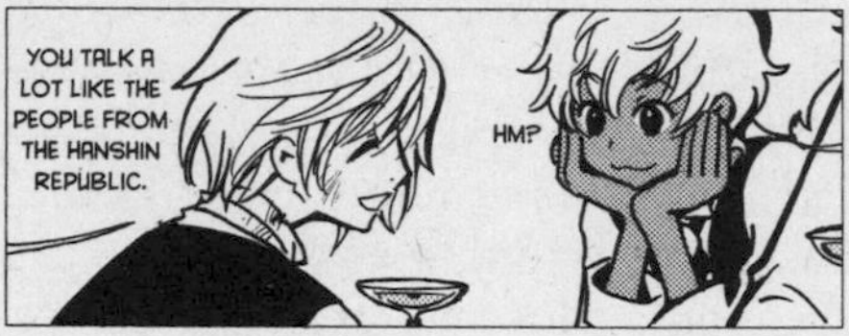
HM?
YOU TALK A LOT LIKE THE PEOPLE FROM THE HANSHIN REPUBLIC.

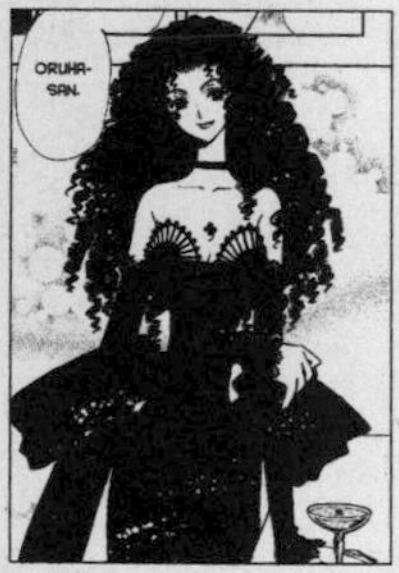
ORUHA-SAN.

Oruha, page 68

The character Ora from the manga series Clover has a crossover character in the country of Ôto by the name of Oruha. Since Ôto is based on Japan in a more traditional time, and since her name is given kanji that mean "weaved leaves"—another reference to clovers—we've decided to leave the pronunciation of her name with the more Japanese-sounding Oruha.

Polite with customers, page 72

Even though there is a move toward less formality in Japan, treatment of one's customers remains very polite and formal.

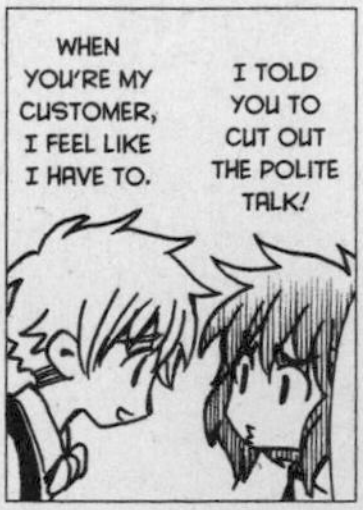
I TOLD YOU TO CUT OUT THE POLITE TALK!
WHEN YOU'RE MY CUSTOMER, I FEEL LIKE I HAVE TO.

Cat's Eye, page 96

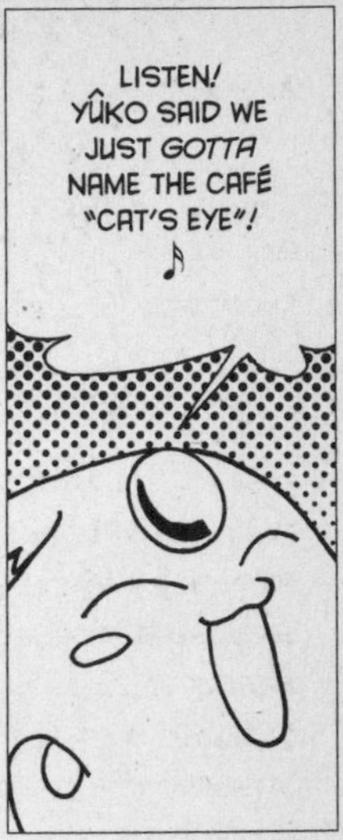
LISTEN! YÛKO SAID WE JUST GOTTA NAME THE CAFÉ "CAT'S EYE"! ♪

This is a reference to the witch Yûko Ishihara's (*xxxHOLiC*) love of the first hit manga series by artist Tsukasa Hojo (*City Hunter, Angel Heart*) named *Cat's Eye*. Three beautiful sisters become a group of thieves in order to steal back their father's priceless art collection stolen from them years ago—while at the same time trying to find clues to their father's disappearance. The sisters are being hunted by a young police officer who also happens to be in love with the middle sister, Hitomi. With the cat burglars "Cat's Eye" as their secret identities, their public identities are that of three sisters who run a small Tokyo café also named "Cat's Eye." The manga for *Cat's Eye* became a long-running animated TV series, and it has also spawned several popular live-action movies.

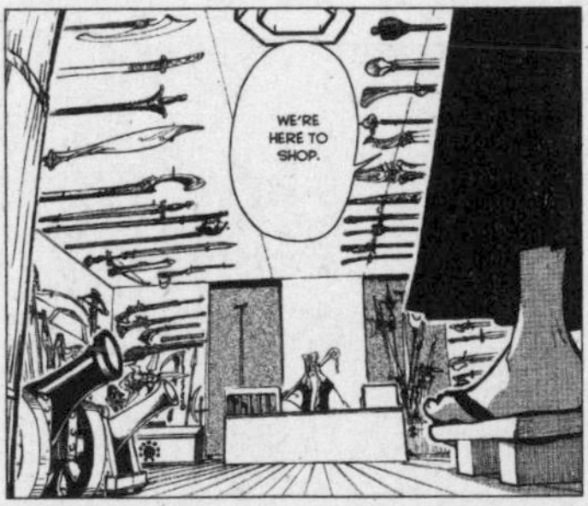
WE'RE HERE TO SHOP.

Chanan and Sanyun, page 106

Clamp fans may remember Chanan's shop from Magic Knight Rayearth.

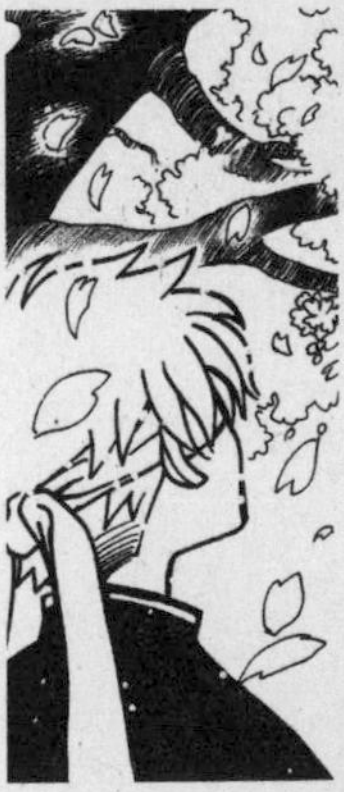

The blossoming and falling of Sakura petals, page 134

Anyone who has been to one of the many cherry-tree filled parks of Japan in early spring will need no more explanation as to why the Japanese consider the cherry blossom as one of the symbols of their nation. There are few views inside or out of Japan that are quite as stunning as seeing the pale-pink petals falling like a snow flurry on the newly budding Japanese landscape.

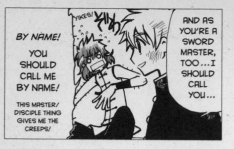

AND AS YOU'RE A SWORD MASTER, TOO...I SHOULD CALL YOU...
YIKES!
BY NAME!
YOU SHOULD CALL ME BY NAME!
THIS MASTER/DISCIPLE THING GIVES ME THE CREEPS!

Kimi, page 147

Here's a passage that didn't quite translate. In it, Syaoran refers to Ryûô as "kimi," which translates out to "you." First of all, the Japanese very rarely use their words for "you" in conversation since all of them have strange overtones. ("Anata" is almost exclusively used these days as a name a woman calls her husband, much like "darling" or "honey" is used in North America.) Kimi has been used for addressing the emperor, and also used to address people beneath the speaker in station. Ryûô just seems to find being called "kimi" raises his hackles, so he asks Syaoran to refer to him by name rather than by pronoun. However, if Syaoran never said the word "you" to Ryûô in the English edition, the dialogue would have come out sounding unnatural. Besides, there are no bad nuances to the word "you" in English. So the translator had to borrow a different prejudice that Ryûô would certainly have—the aversion of a student to be treated as a master, especially by a friend, to make the scene work in the English version.

Seishirô, page 161

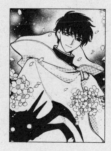

Seishirô is one of CLAMP's classic characters. He first appeared in Tokyo Babylon, then, along with his lifetime friend and enemy Subaru, moved to X (X/1999).

Preview of Volume 7

We're pleased to present you a preview from Volume 7, available in English now.

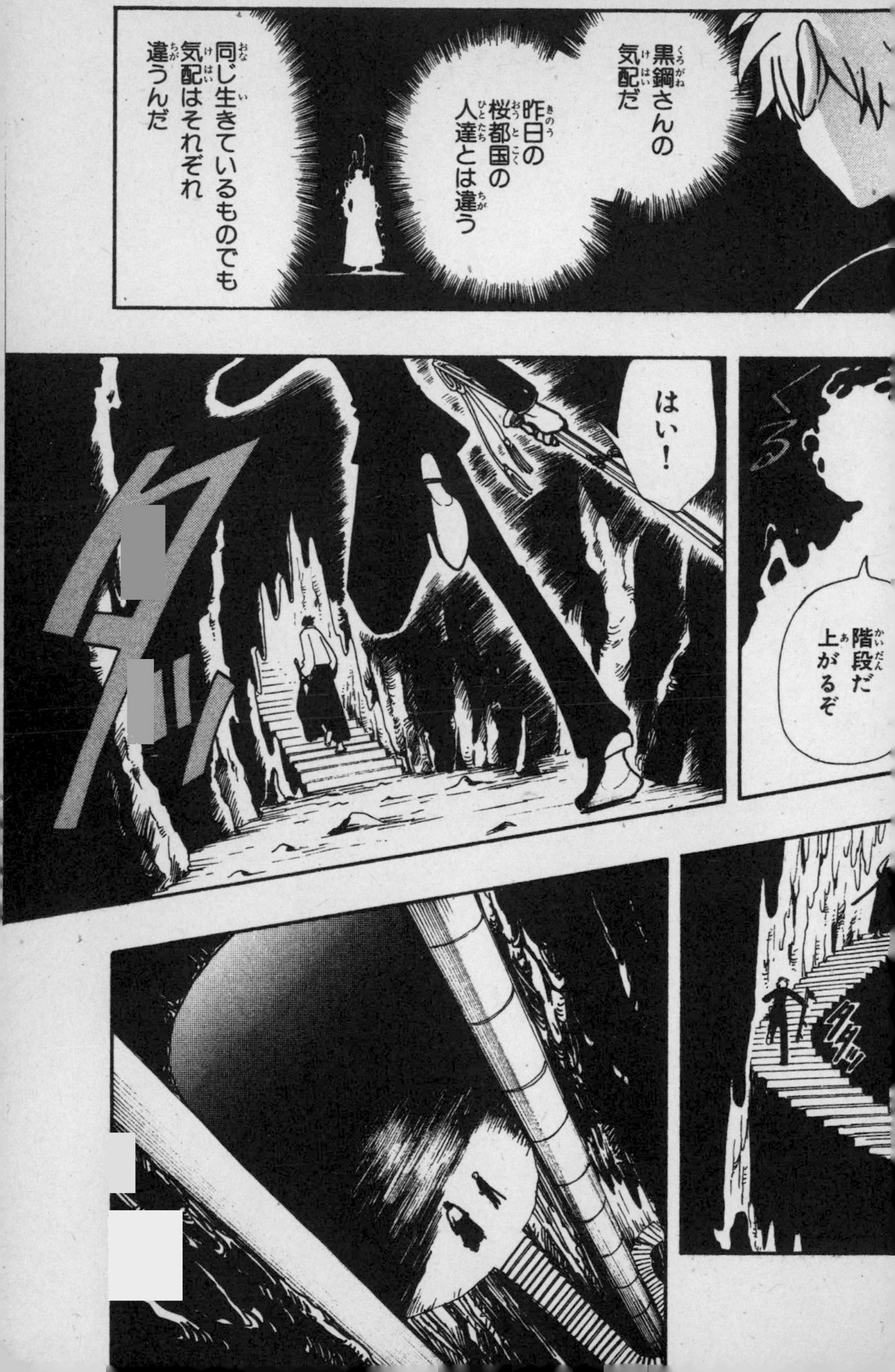
黒鋼さんの気配だ
昨日の桜都国の人達とは違う
同じ生きているものでも気配はそれぞれ違うんだ
くる
階段だ上がるぞ
はい！
タタッ
タタッ

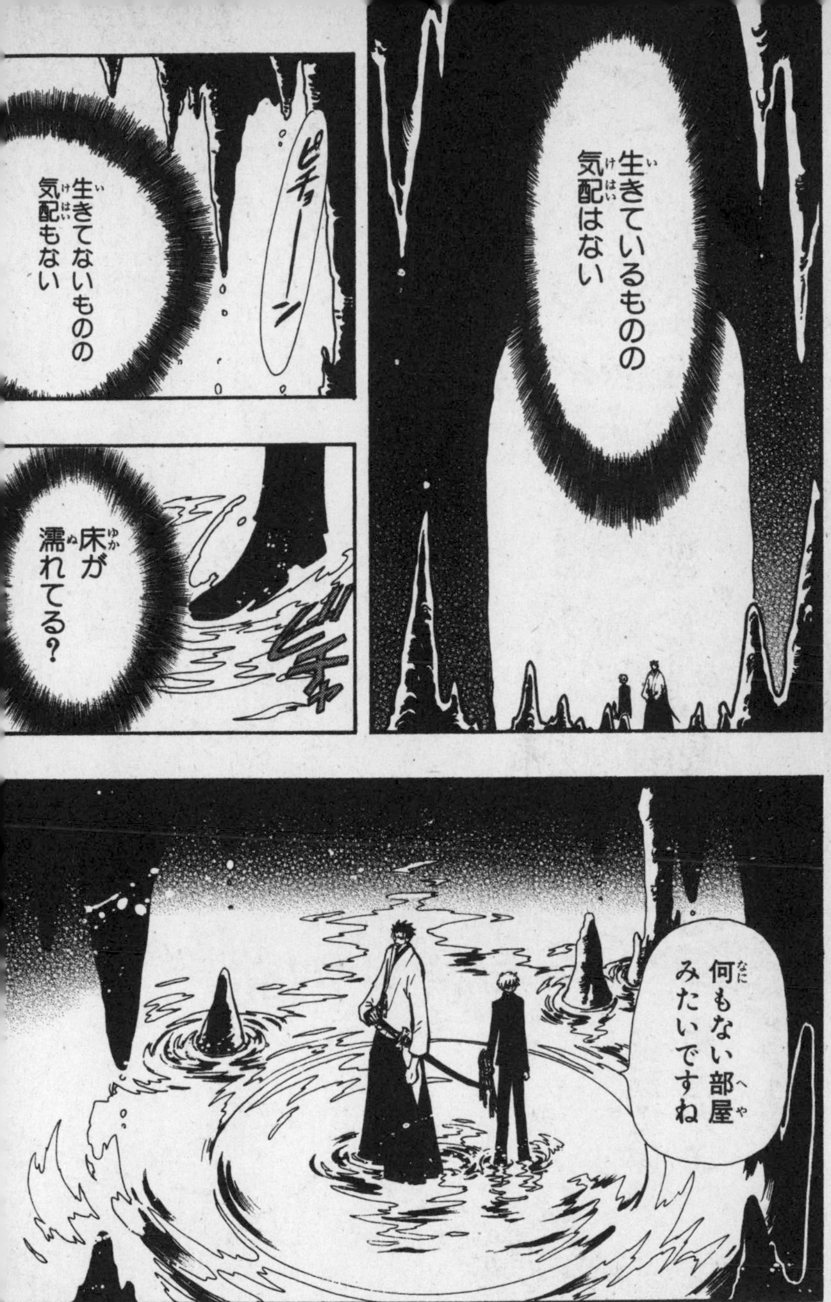

生きているものの気配はない
ピチョーン
生きてないものの気配もない
床が濡れてる?
ピチャ
何もない部屋みたいですね

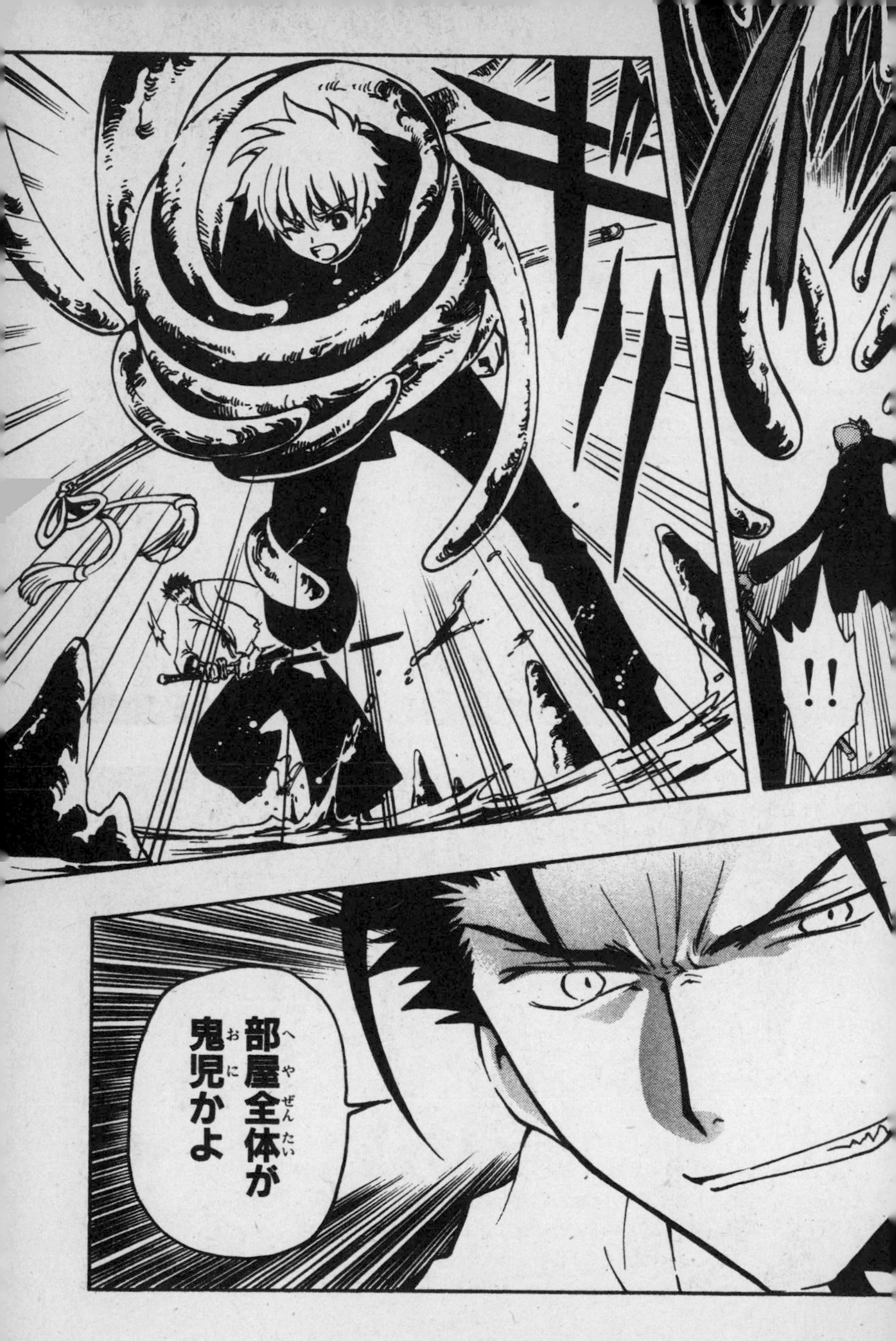
!!
部屋全体が鬼児かよ

BY CLAMP

Watanuki Kimihiro is haunted by visions. When he finds himself irresistibly drawn into a shop owned by Yûko, a mysterious witch, he is offered the chance to rid himself of the spirits that plague him. He accepts, but soon realizes that he's just been tricked into working for the shop to pay off the cost of Yûko's services! But this isn't any ordinary kind of shop . . . In this shop, Yûko grants wishes to those in need. But they must have the strength of will not only to truly understand their need, but to give up something incredibly precious in return.

Ages: 13+

Special extras in each volume! Read them all!

VISIT WWW.DELREYMANGA.COM TO:
• View release date calendars for upcoming volumes
• Sign up for Del Rey's free manga e-newsletter
• Find out the latest about new Del Rey Manga series

NEGIMA!™

BY KEN AKAMATSU

Negi Springfield is a ten-year-old wizard teaching English at an all-girls Japanese school. He dreams of becoming a master wizard like his legendary father, the Thousand Master. At first his biggest concern was concealing his magic powers, because if he's ever caught using them publicly, he thinks he'll be turned into an ermine! But in a world that gets stranger every day, it turns out that the strangest people of all are Negi's students! From a librarian with a magic book to a centuries-old vampire, from a robot to a ninja, Negi will risk his own life to protect the girls in his care!

Ages: 16+

Special extras in each volume! Read them all!

BY SATOMI IKEZAWA

Yaya Higuchi has a rough life. Constantly teased and tormented by her classmates, she takes her solace in dressing up as a member of her favorite rock band, Juliet, on the weekends. Things begin to look up for Yaya when a cute classmate befriends her. Her devotion to Juliet, however, eventually just brings her more of the teasing and harassment she gets at school. Unable to cope, Yaya . . . changes. Suddenly, Yaya is gone—and in the blink of an eye, a new personality emerges. She is now Nana and she is tough, confident, and in charge. Nana can do things that Yaya could never do—like beating up the boys and taking care of all of Yaya's problems. How will Yaya live with this new, super-confident alternate personality? Who will be the dominant one, and who is the REAL Yaya?

Ages: 16+

Special extras in each volume! Read them all!

TOMARE!

[STOP!]

You're going the wrong way!

Manga is a completely
different type of reading
experience.

To start at the *beginning*,
go to the *end*!

That's right! Authentic manga is read the traditional Japanese way—from right to left. Exactly the *opposite* of how American books are read. It's easy to follow: Just go to the other end of the book, and read each page—and each panel—from right side to left side, starting at the top right. Now you're experiencing manga as it was meant to be.